Y0-BSE-873

RENEWALS 691-4574

DATE DUE			
GAYLORD			PRINTED IN U.S.A.

A CRITICAL INTRODUCTION TO LAW AND LITERATURE

Despite their apparent separation, law and literature have been closely linked fields throughout history. Linguistic creativity is central to the law, with literary modes such as narrative and metaphor infiltrating legal texts. Equally, legal norms of good and bad conduct, of identity and human responsibility, are reflected or subverted in literature's engagement with questions of law and justice. Law seeks to regulate creative expression, while literary texts critique and sometimes openly resist the law. Kieran Dolin introduces this interdisciplinary field, focusing on the many ways that law and literature have addressed and engaged with each other. He charts the history of the shifting relations between the two disciplines, from the open affiliation between literature and law in the sixteenth-century Inns of Court to the less visible links of contemporary culture. Each chapter is organized around close analysis of a famous trial or literary-legal encounter. The wide resonance of such trials illuminates the cultural centrality of law, and the social responsiveness of literature. This book provides an accessible guide to one of the most exciting areas of interdisciplinary scholarship today.

KIERAN DOLIN is Senior Lecturer in English and Cultural Studies at the University of Western Australia. He is the author of *Fiction and the Law: Legal Discourse in Victorian and Modernist Literature* (Cambridge, 1999).

A CRITICAL INTRODUCTION
TO LAW AND LITERATURE

KIERAN DOLIN

CAMBRIDGE
UNIVERSITY PRESS

CAMBRIDGE UNIVERSITY PRESS
Cambridge, New York, Melbourne, Madrid, Cape Town, Singapore, São Paulo

Cambridge University Press
The Edinburgh Building, Cambridge CB2 8RU, UK

Published in the United States of America by Cambridge University Press, New York

www.cambridge.org
Information on this title: www.cambridge.org/9780521807432

© Kieran Dolin 2007

This publication is in copyright. Subject to statutory exception
and to the provisions of relevant collective licensing agreements,
no reproduction of any part may take place without
the written permission of Cambridge University Press.

First published 2007

Printed in the United Kingdom at the University Press, Cambridge

A catalogue record for this publication is available from the British Library

ISBN 978-0-521-80743-2 hardback

Cambridge University Press has no responsibility for
the persistence or accuracy of URLs for external or
third-party internet websites referred to in this publication,
and does not guarantee that any content on such
websites is, or will remain, accurate or appropriate.

Library
University of Texas
at San Antonio

Contents

WITHDRAWN
UTSA Libraries

Preface

'Poetry, like the law, is a fiction', wrote William Hazlitt in a critical essay of 1816. Hazlitt the critic took as his subject all aspects of his society's culture, including the connections between law, literature and power. He analysed the rhetoric of the lawyers and the legislative acts of politicians as products of a legal imagination comparable with the literary imagination of the poets. He examined the effects of those imaginings on the people, who were subjects of the law as well as readers of literary fictions. With characteristic forthrightness, he appended an aesthetic judgment to the comparison: 'Poetry, like the law, is a fiction; only a more agreeable one.'

This book shares the conviction that law and literature have common properties of language and vision. In it I try to show how this connection matters, how it works to shape a culture's notions of justice and legal entitlement. The first three chapters explore the bases for linking law and literature; the next six present a historical account of shifts in their relationship in Anglophone culture from the Renaissance to the present.

In undertaking this study I have had the benefit of advice and support from many colleagues at the University of Western Australia. I would particularly like to thank Daniel Brown, Victoria Burrows, Tanya Dalziell, Gareth Griffiths, Tony Hughes-d'Aeth, Judith Johnston, Gail Jones, Andrew Lynch, Ian Saunders, Bob White and Chris Wortham. For administrative support I am grateful to Sue Lewis and Linda Cresswell. I would also like to acknowledge the pleasure and profit I have derived from conversations with Michael Meehan, Penelope Pether, Simon Petch, Peter Rush, Richard Weisberg and other Law and Literature scholars. Over many years Hilary Fraser and Richard Freadman have provided inspiration as well as guidance. My brother Tim Dolin has generously shared his great critical acuity. However, the author accepts liability for any mistakes herein.

It is a pleasure to acknowledge the financial support of an Australian Research Council Discovery Grant, which funded time to write, research assistance and travel to archives. My research assistants, Victoria Bladen, Duc Dau and Catherine Johns, found an abundance of material and offered accurate summaries and fruitful suggestions. I would also like to thank my own university for the award of UWA Research Grants enabling me to concentrate on this study through teaching relief. I have drawn heavily on the resources of the Scholars' Centre in the UWA Library and would like to express my appreciation to Dr Toby Burrows, the Director, and the staff there, for their efficiency and expert help. I wish to thank the staff of the Bodleian Library, Oxford, for assisting me to make use of their unrivalled collection.

I am deeply grateful to Cambridge University Press: to my editor, Ray Ryan, for supporting this project from its inception, and for his encouragement and advice. I would also like to thank the assistant editor Maartje Scheltens, and the readers of both the original proposal and the manuscript, whose suggestions were extremely helpful. For permission to reproduce the image on the cover, Hogarth's *The Bench*, I am grateful to the Syndics of the Fitzwilliam Museum, Cambridge. The following material is reproduced by permission of the copyright holder: 'Mending Wall' from *The Poetry of Robert Frost*, edited by Edward Connery Latham © 1969. Reprinted by permission of Henry Holt and company, LLC.

My greatest debt is to my wife, Jane Courtney, for her love and good counsel, and to our children, Patrick, Michael and Anna. Their love of words and stories, their questioning of law (and literature) have been an indispensable counterpoint to the writing of this book.

Introduction to law and literature: walking the boundary with Robert Frost and the Supreme Court

In April 1995 the American Supreme Court decided the case of *Plaut* v. *Spendthrift Farm Inc.*[1] The case began in 1987 when Mr and Mrs Plaut and some other investors in Spendthrift Farm alleged that it had committed fraud and deceit when selling stock, contrary to Section 10(b) of the Securities and Exchange Act of 1934. The District Court in Kentucky held that this suit was time barred, following a recent Supreme Court decision in the case of *Lampf* which declared that such suits must be commenced within one year after the discovery of the facts constituting the violation and within three years of the violation itself. After this judgment became final, Congress enacted a new Section 27A(b) of the Securities and Exchange Act, providing that any action commenced before *Lampf*, but dismissed thereafter as time barred, could be reinstated. The Plauts moved for reinstatement accordingly, but the District Court held that Section 27A(b) was unconstitutional. This decision was confirmed by the Court of Appeal, and by the Supreme Court.

This case, like all legal cases, involves a story.[2] While it begins as a story of disappointed investors attempting to obtain redress for a wrong that has damaged them, the conflict shifts onto a new level after the failure of the initial suit. With the attempted reinstatement, both Plaut and Spendthrift Farm in effect become proxies for a contest between the judiciary and Congress. The Plauts' motion for the reinstatement of their action was defeated not in terms of securities law, but on constitutional grounds. Three courts found that Section 27A(b) contravened the Constitution's separation of powers in that it required federal courts to reopen final judgments entered before its enactment. The Constitution forbids the legislature to interfere with courts' final judgments. Congress had trespassed into the judicial realm with this law, which was therefore held to be invalid.

This legal story acquires a distinctly literary element in the judgments of the Supreme Court. Writing the opinion of the majority of the Court, Justice Antonin Scalia concluded his account of the legal authorities with a summary that relied equally on metaphor and logic: 'In its major features . . ., [separation of powers] is a prophylactic device, establishing high walls and clear distinctions because low walls and vague distinctions will not be judicially defensible in the heat of interbranch conflict' (356). In expounding legal principle and justifying his decision, Justice Scalia employs the rhetorical tools of metaphor and narrative. His metaphor of the wall represents the judicial power in the Constitution as a fortified city under assault from a hostile Congress or Executive. His exposition of the law rests on an implied, imagined narrative of battle. There is nothing extraordinary about Scalia's procedure here: this is a normal instance of judicial reasoning in a run-of-the-mill case. Judges and lawyers routinely seek to clarify their pronouncements and arguments about the law by resorting to metaphors and stories. They do so because law is inevitably a matter of language. The law can only be articulated in words. While the order of a court will be imposed on the body or the property of the parties to the case, it will originally have been spoken as a sentence. This is the fundamental connection between law and literature.

However, the legal language of *Plaut* v. *Spendthrift Farm* also manifests an unusual degree of engagement with the literary realm. Having invoked the metaphor of the wall, Justice Scalia seeks support for his formulation of the law by citing a well-known literary analogue: 'separation of powers, a distinctively American political doctrine, profits from the advice authored by a distinctively American poet: good fences make good neighbors' (240). Scalia assumes that he and his readers share a common culture and that they will be able to recognise his allusion to Robert Frost's poem, 'Mending Wall'. What is most interesting about this part of his opinion is its recognition that law is an aspect of this 'distinctively American' culture that he invokes. The judge grounds the authority of the law of separation of powers not just in legal precedent, but in the national cultural heritage. Political theory, history and literature combine to authorise and authenticate this law, and locate it in a larger narrative. While most judgments refer only to statutes and past cases, implying the independence and autonomy of law, Scalia's allusion exposes how legal values and concepts are embedded in a broader and more diverse web of meanings. In this incidental rhetorical flourish, he makes a rare acknowledgment of the formative power of cultural context upon the law, confirming Robert M. Cover's insight that, 'No set of legal institutions or prescriptions exists apart from the narratives that locate it and give it meaning.'[3] Moreover, Justice Scalia's use of poetry is revealing: he brings it into the public sphere, as a kind of ally of law. Literature and law, it seems, can work together in the production of cultural ideals and values.

Another member of the Court, Justice Stephen Breyer, concurred with the majority decision but qualified their statement of the doctrine, and in doing so questioned their understanding of the poem. He cautioned against 'the unnecessary building of such walls' as 'in itself dangerous, because the Constitution blends, as well as separates, powers in its efforts to create a government that will work for, as well as protect the liberties of, its citizens' (359). He finds that past cases provide other metaphors than the wall: citing *Springer* v. *Philippine Islands* he argues that the doctrine does not 'divide the branches into watertight compartment', nor 'establish and divide separate fields of black and white'. In refining the meaning of 'separation of powers', Breyer also takes issue with the majority's use of Robert Frost's poem to bolster their decision: 'One might consider as well that poet's caution, for he not only notes that "Something there is that doesn't love a wall," but also writes, "Before I built a wall I'd ask to know / What I was walling in or walling out"' (359). The poet's belief in walls is not as clear-cut as Justice Scalia believed.

This unusual judicial dispute over the meaning of a poem was reported in the *New York Times* and in *Mediator*, the bulletin of the Law and Humanities Institute.[4] To quote the latter: 'It is always a treat, and a rare one at that, to see the Supreme Court intertwine legal and poetic judgments.' The Law and Humanities Institute aims to foster an understanding of law's interrelations with literature. Underpinning its celebratory note on the case is a belief that poetry has a proper, but generally unacknowledged, role to play in the public debates, that literature has something to offer the law in its resolution of social conflicts. By evidencing the 'intertwining' of legal and literary language so clearly, the case of *Plaut* v. *Spendthrift Farm* provides an excellent introduction to the study of law and literature.

However, it is not only the justices' common interest in the poem which is significant; their different interpretations of it are even more instructive. While Robert Frost's 'Mending Wall' is widely known, a substantial quotation will assist our understanding of the text and its relevance to the law. Two farmers walk along their common boundary 'at spring mending-time', replacing the fallen stones of the fence:

> There where it is we do not need the wall:
> He is all pine and I am apple orchard.
> My apple trees will never get across
> And eat the cones under his pines, I tell him.
> He only says, 'good fences make good neighbors.'
> Spring is the mischief in me, and I wonder
> If I could put a notion in his head:

'*Why* do they make good neighbors? Isn't it
Where there are cows? But here there are no cows.
Before I built a wall I'd ask to know
What I was walling in or walling out,
And to whom I was like to give offense.
Something there is that doesn't love a wall,
That wants it down.' ...
He moves in darkness as it seems to me,
Not of woods only and the shade of trees.
He will not go behind his father's saying,
And he likes having thought of it so well
He says again, 'Good fences make good neighbors.'[5]

Justice Scalia and Justice Breyer uncannily re-enact the roles of the two farmers. Scalia repeats the proverb, 'good fences make good neighbours', and attributes it to Robert Frost, completely neglecting the context of the poem. Breyer asks the sceptical questions while rebuilding the wall, noting that Frost doubts the wisdom of the wall, whilst agreeing with Justice Scalia to apply the separation of powers doctrine to this case. Breyer's opinion exposes a rift between the poem and the law: to agree on the law but disagree on the poem either cancels out the significance of the poem, or it undermines the metaphoric wall of the separation of powers doctrine.

In exploring this contradiction, we can begin by examining the judges' assumptions about poetry. Justice Scalia seems to see poetry as didactic, as a repository of quotable moral and political truths, 'what oft was thought but ne'er so well expressed'. What he calls the 'advice' offered by Frost conforms with the wisdom of American political doctrine; indeed the law 'profits from' the poetic statement. In this view poetry is sententious: its moralising maxims harmonise with the task of applying legal rules. Modern poetry does not fit this description, and Frost's poem is primarily a narrative in which two opposite viewpoints on the events being recounted are aired. Frost discouraged moralistic readings of this poem in a 1944 interview, saying there was no 'rigid separation between right and wrong. "Mending Wall" simply contrasts two types of people.'[6] The following year he emphasised this ambivalence: 'Twice I say "Good fences" and twice "Something there is –".'[7] Justice Breyer picks up on the anti-sententious note in Frost's poem, in which the speaker is tempted to undermine his neighbour's belief in the value of fences, by questioning, '*Why* do they make good neighbors?' Breyer still wants some sort of guidance from the poem, but in correcting Scalia, he is faced with the unconventional implication that the boundary fence does not matter. This would have startling implications for the separation of powers, not to mention the law of real property. Faced with these difficulties, Breyer can only emphasise 'the poet's caution'. We might call this the 'minimalist' position; but we should nonetheless recognise his awareness of the complex meanings of the poem, and his refusal of any straightforward application of poem to law. The combination of literary text and legal context is a volatile one. Can you imagine the consequences if Justice Breyer followed through the implications of his reading of Frost's poem and devalued the legal precedents? I read his 'caution' as putting a narrow interpretation on the poem, and in effect as maintaining the wall between law and literature.

The existence of this wall can be elucidated by a closer reading of Frost's poem. Frost described 'Mending Wall' as a 'parable', but kept 'the secret of what it means' to himself.[8] However, we may approach a statement of its meaning by noting that the poem's speaker sees a contest between unknown forces in nature that dislodge the stones and inherited cultural practices which demand the rebuilding of the structure. He aligns himself with scepticism and freedom, and his neighbour with custom and traditional authority. The language of each is appropriate to his ethic, one tentative and exploratory, the other proverbial and inherited:

> He only says, 'Good fences make good neighbors.
> Spring is the mischief in me, and I wonder
> If I could put a notion in his head.'

The speaker's complaint against the man of maxims is literature's challenge to law: the challenge offered by a self-consciously creative domain, where alternative voices can be heard, where hypothetical situations can be explored and where the settled questions of society can be reopened through the medium of fiction. He imagines a different world and poses questions: what if ... ? why ... ? His mischievous approach matches Jonathan Culler's description of literature as 'an institution based on the possibility of saying anything you can imagine ... [F]or any orthodoxy, any belief, any value, a literary work can mock it, parody it, imagine some different and monstrous fiction.'[9] Equally, the other farmer is speaking the law. He accepts the rule that 'good fences make good neighbors'. The proverb is a catchy phrase that carries the force of belief, that compels acceptance and a certain course of action. He does not question its truth but respects its authority as something handed down from his forefathers. For him, the proverb is sufficient and complete: nothing more, nothing else, need be said. In recognising the archaic origin and 'darkness' of this mental enclosure, Frost intuits key features of all authoritative language. 'The authoritative word', according to M. M. Bakhtin, 'is located in a distanced zone, organically connected with a past that is felt to be hierarchically higher. It is, so to speak, the word of the fathers ... It is a *prior* discourse. It is therefore not a question of choosing it from other possible discourses that are its equal. It is given in lofty spheres, not those of familiar contact.'[10] From Mount Sinai to the bench and bar of the world's Supreme Courts, the law is emphatically an instance of the authoritative word. Like the neighbour, it permits 'no play with its borders'.[11]

The repair of the wall is a declaration of the importance of the boundary as a marker of the limits of property, of what land each can call his or her own and what is acknowledged as the other's. However, in debating the value of walls the poem symbolises not only the law's upholding of private property, but its fundamental reliance on boundaries. As the editors of a recent guide to socio-legal studies observe:

> In its basic operations, law attempts to create, police, and occasionally transgress social, spatial and temporal boundaries. The pre-eminent declaration of a legal system – its announcement of its own existence – establishes jurisdictional boundaries within which its authority prevails. This definition of a geographical space is matched by the declaration of temporal boundaries (statutes of limitation, ages of minority and majority, retroactive or prospective application of statutes or case law) within which legal authority is exercised. Within law's spatio-temporal grid, complex systems of classification are established, creating boundaries that define individuals, communities, acts, and norms: Who is a criminal? A citizen? A victim of negligence? A person or group entitled to legal protection or remedy?[12]

The inseparability of laws and walls was recognised by the ancient Greeks. Plato invokes 'Zeus the protector of boundaries' to authorise the first of his agricultural laws: 'No man shall disturb the boundary-stones of his neighbour, whether fellow-citizen or foreigner.'[13] Hannah Arendt traces the importance of the wall as a symbol of law from Heraclitus to Montesquieu and insists that its borders are always under pressure, due to 'action's inherent tendency to establish relations, force open limitations and cut across boundaries'.[14]

An understanding of 'Mending Wall' in this context reveals what was at stake for the Supreme Court in *Plaut* v. *Spendthrift Farm*: the policing of temporal and institutional boundaries that had been deliberately transgressed; the defence of intrinsic legal and judicial functions. Little wonder that Justice Scalia imagined the two branches of government as warring states, far removed from the civil dialogue and co-operation of Frost's farmers. The more tempered approach of Justice Breyer is shown in his adoption of the literary 'side' of the argument, his willingness to evaluate the need for the wall: 'Before I built a wall I'd ask to know / What I was walling in or walling out, / And to whom I was like to give offense.' Like the speaker in the poem, he upholds the wall in its customary place despite his openness to change. 'Mending Wall' sets the language of proverbial truth against the language of possibility. What the 'Supreme Court Poetry Seminar' suggests is that while both languages are available at law, the former is more likely to prevail. This book will explore instances of legal creativity, as well as the experience of those offended by its demarcations and exclusions. The questions posed by Frost's speaker and invoked by Breyer are among the vital questions literature can ask of law.

If we follow Culler in thinking of literature as 'an institution based on the possibility of saying you can imagine', must we conclude that, unlike law, literature is hostile to boundaries? A moment's reflection suggests not. The distinction between poetry, fiction and drama; the subdivisions of each of these genres – including novel and romance, sonnet and haiku, tragedy and comedy; the evaluative distinctions between high and low art – poetry as against doggerel, drama and melodrama, or Graham Greene's division of his fiction into novels and entertainments; and the fundamental boundary between literary and other writing are all examples of literature's dependence on external and internal boundaries for its identity and its everyday functioning. Yet we can readily see that these boundaries seem made to be transgressed, at least by modern writers: the verse-novel, the dramatic monologue, tragicomedy, the non-fiction novel are only the most obvious of many experiments in form and discourse. The Italian writer and critic Claudio Magris, a native of the city of Trieste, on the border of what used to be 'Western' and 'Eastern' Europe, has reflected on the relationship between writing and boundaries:

> Boundaries between states and nations, established by international treaties or by force, are not the only kind. The pen that scribbles on from day to day . . . traces boundaries, moves, dissolves and restores them . . . Literature is intrinsically a frontier and an expedition in search of new frontiers, to shift them and define them. Every literary form is a threshold, a zone at the edge of countless different elements, tensions and movements, a shifting of the semantic borders and gram-matical structures, a perpetual dismantling and reassembly of the world, its frames and its pictures.[15]

Magris acknowledges the value of boundaries as well as their limits in this capacious and socially alert description of literature. In his view literary texts can question traditional borders and distinctions; writing is an engagement with and an extension of existing boundaries. His passionate and idealistic reflection is useful for its insight that boundaries are dissolved and re-formed in and by literature. Whether Magris's argument is overstated, whether all texts produced in the literary field possess the openness and exploratory quality that he claims, may be questioned.[16] His insistence on literature's 'tracing' of boundaries, its drawing attention to borders and their effects, however, is illustrated with great clarity by many texts, including Frost's 'Mending Wall'.

For literary scholars and critics, too, a consciousness of the role of frames and boundaries has transformed their studies:

> Foregrounding the issue of boundaries has reminded us that literature is not something given once and for all but something constructed and reconstructed . . . Not only is the canon of literary works in any genre fashioned by a simultaneous perambulation and transgression of boundaries but the very concept of the literary is itself continually renegotiated. Any study of literature, then, is necessarily bound up explicitly or implicitly with an interrogation of boundaries: their identification or definition, the regulation of what may cross them and at what times and under what circumstances, the alarms that go off when unauthorized crossings occur, and so on.[17]

This awareness of barriers and their effects, especially the realisation of modes of inclusion and exclusion, abounds in traditional and modern literary representations of law, as the most cursory review shows. Sophocles' *Antigone* begins with the dilemma created by the unburied body of Polynices, declared a traitor by his uncle Creon, and condemned by his edict to rot outside the city walls. Antigone elects to defy that law, and cross the boundary marking his expulsion from the polity, with fateful consequences for herself and her society. The action of Shakespeare's *The Merchant of Venice* shows how the racial and religious difference of Shylock the Jew forms an ethical barrier for the Venetians which is reinforced by laws subjecting him to special penalties as a so-called alien. Kafka's brief and mysterious parable 'Before the Law', imagines the citizen seeking the aid of the law as eternally waiting outside its walls, never gaining admittance, let alone justice. Works like these may question the boundaries established by the law, or they may simply reflect such boundaries. In either case, it is the ability of literary texts to represent and draw attention to such boundaries and how they function that produces their greatest insights into law.

The judicial appropriations of Frost's 'Mending Wall' suggest that law and literature are adjoining fields, divided by a boundary fence that keeps breaking down, despite regular maintenance. The common ground of language resists the forms and divisions imposed on it, opening 'gaps even two can pass abreast'. This resistance creates opportunities for dialogue between the two disciplines, for licensed or unlicensed wanderings across the border, for 'subversion' as well as surveillance.[18] Frost directs our attention to the nature of borders, and to the various relations and exchanges they make possible. Claudio Magris has observed how the experience of a border can shift: 'at one moment it is a bridge on which to meet, at another, a barrier of rejection'.[19] As we shall see throughout this book, the border between law and literature has sometimes functioned as a bridge, promoting dialogue, and at others served as a barrier inhibiting it.[20]

However frequent the exchanges, however open the frontier between literature and law, it does not imply that the two fields are identical. Just as 'He is all pine and I am apple orchard', so we can think of literature and law as different uses of language. Brook Thomas makes this point forcefully in his closely reasoned 'Reflections on the Law and Literature Revival': 'Without a doubt legal texts can have literary qualities. But in the last analysis their function is different.'[21] A useful approach to the variety of functions or uses of language is provided by the philosopher Ludwig Wittgenstein's concept of 'language-games'. Among the 'multiplicity of language-games' listed in his *Philosophical Investigations* are 'Giving orders, and obeying them – ... Reporting an event – ... [and] Making up a story, and reading it –.' He explains that 'the term "language-*game*" is meant to bring into prominence the fact that the *speaking* of language is part of an activity, or of a form of life'.[22] As distinct linguistic forms of life, law and literature speak different kinds of sentences: one commanding obedience under threat of punishment, the other inviting pleasurable recognition and assent. The speaker of legal sentences has an 'imperative to issue exclusive judgments', to quote Thomas again;[23] while the creator of literary texts may suspend judgment in favour of inclusivity and dialogue, as the Frost poem shows.

If these obvious and fundamental differences appear at first glance to locate the two language types at a distance from each other, the example of *Plaut* v. *Spendthrift Farm* shows how the legal form of life produces several kinds of sentence, narrative and hortatory as well as imperative. Equally, despite W. H. Auden's poetic disclaimer, 'For poetry makes nothing happen: it survives / In the valley of its saying / Where executives would never want to tamper', the example of 'Mending Wall' shows how a statement which has the integration, compression and mnemonic quality of literary language ('*Good* fences make *good* neighbors') can encode values and govern conduct, can enchant judges and provoke dissent outside the apparently sequestered 'valley of its saying'.[24] As different forms of life, they enable different understandings of the world, or to give due weight to the organic metaphor they construct reality differently.

Auden was probably right in thinking that not many business executives read poetry (or bought his books). Since the deaths of Tennyson and Kipling it has become an increasingly specialist activity. However, specialisation does not imply seclusion. Gillian Beer points to the inevitableness and plurality of cultural encounters in society: 'Train-spotters, mothers of babies, astronomers, horse-riders have each their special knowledges and vocabularies; but none of them lives as train-spotter, mother, astronomer, horse-rider alone. Each inhabits and draws on the experience of the historical moment, the material base, the media, and community in which they all dwell.'[25] Although Beer's interest is in border crossings between science and literature, her vision of multiple relations, roles and vocabularies, and her insistence that these can only be understood in the light of the particular 'historical moment' in which the individual lived are equally useful to the interdisciplinary study of law and literature. Understandings of literature and of law have changed throughout history, and Beer argues that interdisciplinary activity promotes change: 'Interdisciplinary studies do not produce closure. Their stories emphasize not simply the circulation of intact ideas across a larger community but transformation: the transformations undergone when ideas enter other genres or different reading groups, the destabilizing of knowledge once it escapes from the initial group of co-workers, its tendency to mean more and other than could have been foreseen.'[26] In this book we shall explore many such stories of transformation in a variety of cultures, and reveal the 'diverse articulations which obtain in different historical and geographical loci'.[27]

For almost three decades the opportunity of cross-border travel broached by Frost's persona has been exploited by a fertile interdisciplinary project in Law *and* Literature.[28] One of the fundamental propositions of this movement was succinctly put by Richard Weisberg and Jean-Pierre Barricelli in a pioneering essay: 'Law is associated with Literature from its inception as a formalized attempt to structure reality through language.'[29] Several such structures and associations have been identified by scholars working at the border of the two fields, including:

(i) literary representations of legal trials, practitioners and language, and of those caught up in the law;

(ii) the role played by narrative, metaphor and other rhetorical devices in legal speech and writing, including judgments;

(iii) how the supposed freedom of literary expression is contained and regulated by laws;

(iv) the circulation of legal ideas in literary culture, and vice versa in various periods and societies;

(v)   the effects of social ideologies such as race and gender in legal language;

(vi)   theory of interpretation;

(vii)   the use of theatricality and spectacle in the creation of legal authority;

(viii)   the cultural and political consequences of new technologies of communication, such as writing, the printing press and the Internet;

(ix)   legal storytelling or narrative jurisprudence.

Thus the border between law and literature has become a bridge, which will enable even more connections to be discerned, and, if Beer is correct, produce further transformations in both fields.

Not all participants in the 'Law and Literature project' have shared this expansive vision. Robert M. Cover, whose article '*Nomos* and Narrative' (cited above) inaugurated narrative jurisprudence, subsequently issued a forceful caveat against the idealistic assimilation of law with literature. 'Judges,' he insisted, 'sit atop a pyramid of violence.'[30] The texts of the law have immediate bodily consequences for the condemned. This fact ensures the difference between the two fields. The case for the negative in the 'continuing debate' over law and literature has been forcefully presented by Richard A. Posner, a judge and legal academic. Posner undertakes a practical analysis of the potential benefits of this interdisciplinary activity for the understanding of law. Working within his own disciplinary framework, he evaluates the utility of literary texts and interpretative theory for the study of law. Though well read and appreciative of the humanistic value of literature, he concludes that neither its examples nor its theorists have much to offer law in practice. The differences between the two institutions, their varying tolerance for individual creativity and openness to multiple interpretations, among others are too great. In effect Posner reinforces the boundaries of the law and stresses the need for specialist knowledge as a pre-requisite to contributing to its development. 'The biggest danger in any disciplinary field is amateurism.'[31] The two exceptions to this enclosure within the existing contours of the law are the study of the regulation of literature by law, and the study of legal rhetoric as a means of improving forensic argument. On balancing the possibilities and dangers he can only profess 'warm though qualified enthusiasm' for this interdisciplinary project in his conclusion.[32]

The idea that law and literature structure reality through language remains central to an understanding of their relations. One writer who has examined this capacity in both fields is the sociologist Pierre Bourdieu. Like Gillian Beer, Bourdieu uses the term 'field' in a scientific sense, as a force field, as 'a method of representing the way in which bodies are able to influence each other'.[33] In the course of analysing 'the juridical field' Bourdieu describes the power of the law in linguistic terms: 'Law is the quintessential form of the symbolic power of naming that creates the thing named, and creates social groups in particular. It confers upon the reality which arises from its classificatory operations the maximum permanence that any social entity has the power to confer upon another, the permanence we attribute to objects'.[34] A classic example of the law's power to create a new social group by inventing a new name is that of 'pensioner', a new social identity brought into being in Britain by the Old Age Pensions Act of 1908. A more striking example of performative language, or the 'linguistic capacity to make things true *simply by saying them*' is provided by Bourdieu's translator, Richard Terdiman: 'the monarch's power to ennoble commoners simply by dubbing them and proclaiming that they are now titled'.[35] Language is integral to 'the entire practical activity of "worldmaking" (marriages, divorces, substitutions, associations, dissolutions)' that makes up everyday work in and under the law.

The creative work of naming and bringing forth new visions for society is associated in the modern world with literature, and Bourdieu acknowledges this power in his study of 'the field of cultural production'.[36] Citing his favourite examples from nineteenth-century France, Flaubert and Manet, he attributes to writers and artists 'the properly symbolic power of showing things and making people believe in them, of revealing in an explicit, objectified way the more or less confused, vague, unformulated, even unformulable experiences of the natural world and the social world, and bringing them into existence'.[37] Manet, with his paintings of 'the urban landscape in its ordinary triviality' exemplifies the artist as creator, one who inaugurates a 'real symbolic revolution', offering 'new categories of perception and evaluation of the world'.[38] Bourdieu's developed sense of where power resides in society prevents him from idealising or overvaluing the role of the artist: 'the symbolic revolution is doomed, most of the time, to remain confined to the symbolic domain'. However, he avoids pessimistic undervaluations of the 'Poetry makes nothing happen' kind, quoting Sartre's dictum that 'words can wreak havoc'. The field of cultural production is part of the social world, but it has a relative autonomy which allows for a greater freedom of expression, and which provides the conditions for writers and artists to 'bring into public and thus official and open existence, when they show or half-show, things which existed in an implicit, confused or even repressed state'.

As a sociologist Bourdieu is alert to the relative power of different speakers in all social spaces, including the legal and cultural fields, which are therefore sites of political conflict. He is also interested in tracing the power relations between fields, and his account of the juridical field begins by refuting theories which stress the autonomy of law. Just as Robert Cover identifies law's dependence on an underlying matrix of social narratives, so Bourdieu insists on the influence of existing social institutions and understandings upon legal world-making: 'It would not be excessive to say that [law] *creates* the social world, but only if we remember that it is this world which first creates the law.'[39] This insistence on the social context of the law and its speech acts lends a political realism to Bourdieu's sense of the capacity of legal language to make new worlds. The symbolic acts of the law tend to reinforce the status quo, or to announce changes already emerging in society. He recognises the transformative potential of symbolic acts, but also that utterances alone cannot achieve social change: 'the will to transform the world by transforming the words for naming it, by producing new categories of perception and judgment ... can only succeed if ... they announce what is in the process of developing'.[40] To revert to our example of old age pensions and the consequent emergence of a new form of social identity, the pensioner, the Act put forward by Lloyd George in 1908 grew out of a complex of factors, including longer lifespans for skilled workers, new economic understandings of the causes of poverty, debates about the theory and administration of charity, and the recognition of a national interest in the health of the population.[41] Overall, Bourdieu's realism harmonises with that of Robert Frost's persona, who knows that his questioning will have no effect unless his neighbour can begin to formulate new ideas about the fence for himself.

Not only does Bourdieu's subtle account of world-making through language confirm the relationship between law and literature; it also shows how close that relationship is. Barbara Leckie has integrated Bourdieu's writings on the two fields, and she concludes that 'the law could not likely effect its revolutions without the literary and [a]esthetic "revolutions" to which it is inextricably wedded ... Symbolic revolution then forms the link between law and literature.'[42] This insight directs us to particular instances or cases of 'symbolic revolution', moments of crisis in which the struggle over certain words or forms of representation can be traced in both the legal and the literary fields, stories in which symbols developed in one migrate to the other. In undertaking such a study we must examine in detail the institutional organisation of each field at particular times, the social and political networks of important practitioners, and the language and the forms of representation employed in a variety of texts around the border between literature and law.[43]

Yet if we return to the story of Robert Frost and the *Plaut* case, we observe a link between law and literature which is by no means a revolutionary one. The persona in 'Mending Wall' speaks hypothetically of removing the fence but significantly continues to repair it thoroughly. He is no demolisher of traditional orders. Likewise, Bourdieu recognises that writers may put their symbolic power 'at the service of the dominant',[44] and consciously or unconsciously reproduce existing understandings of society by recycling dominant symbols, forms and discourses. Frost's poem balances a language of conservatism against a potentially revolutionary one. Its interest is in staging a dialogue, and thereby raising a question. Frost exercised a similar caution when it came to the revolution in poetic form being carried out by his contemporaries, Ezra Pound and T. S. Eliot, refusing the radical dream of 'free verse' and instead adapting traditional narrative and poetic forms to the everyday speech and situation of rural New England. His compromise brought him the respect of many of his poetic peers (though not Eliot), and a wide public audience, particularly through his inclusion in school and university curricula. He was awarded four Pulitzer Prizes, the last in 1943, twenty years before his death. William H. Pritchard comments that these years 'were those of a man whose productions as a poet, for the first time in his career, took a position secondary to his life as a public figure, a pundit, an institution, a cultural emissary'.[45] Frost accepted an appointment as Poetry Consultant to the Library of Congress in 1958. By then, according to Mark Richardson, 'he had achieved a celebrity and popular prestige unprecedented for an American poet'.[46] His visibility in the fields of culture and power was enhanced in 1960, when he read a poem at the inauguration of President John F. Kennedy. The poem, 'For John F. Kennedy His Inauguration', which included an older work, 'The Gift Outright', sees the poet welcome the opportunity of consorting with politicians as presaging 'a next Augustan age',

> A golden age of poetry and power
> Of which this noonday's the beginning hour.[47]

In literary history the 'Augustan age' refers to the reign of the Roman emperor Augustus, when the poets Horace, Virgil and Ovid flourished, and to the period in eighteenth-century English culture, when writers such as Pope, Johnson and Swift revered and emulated the values and forms of the original Augustans. The Augustan age stands then for a conservative and aristocratic culture committed to the imitation of Nature and of inherited literary forms. As a cultural ideal it sits oddly with the ceremonials and the realities of a democratic republic; as an anachronistic ideal it still provides us with a glimpse of another, older form of social organisation in which literature and law were not separated by a wall or regarded as natural enemies. In Frost's America, however, despite his involvement in a campaign to free Ezra Pound from detention on charges of treason, and a state visit to President Khrushchev, the dream of a new Augustan age proved a short-lived fantasy. As Pritchard puts it, 'The final lesson appeared to be that poetry and power only went together in poems.'[48]

Robert Frost's reputation as 'the quintessential American poet'[49] was not diminished, however, and so it was that the aphoristic sentences of 'Mending Wall' could be abstracted from the subversive musings of his persona and used to defend the law's boundaries in the Supreme Court case of *Plaut* v. *Spendthrift Farm*. The openness of the literary text made it useful to Justice Scalia as the capstone of a strong conservative defence of separation of powers, and equally useful to Justice Breyer as the strategic tool for a moderate reformist critique. The poetic quotations are like seeds or windfall apples blown across the wall into the neighbouring field of the law. Their circulation proves that the absolute separateness or autonomy of the two domains cannot be sustained. The study of law's language opens up the cultural context, the ideological choices and the rhetorical work which underlie the pronouncement of the authoritative word. The law and literature project adopts a critical perspective towards both its constituent fields – and their border. This book aims to illuminate the constant traffic at that border, the many interactions between law and literature, and the transformations of each that result.

A Critical Introduction to Law and Literature is organised into two parts. Part I, 'Eminent domains: the text of the law and the law of the text', examines the two fundamental relations between the fields, literature's insistence that law is inescapably a matter of language and law's assumption of its right to regulate literature. 'Eminent domain', the compulsory purchase of private property by government acting in the name of the public good, is used metaphorically in the sense pioneered by Richard Ellmann in his study of the ways writers use the works of other writers: 'conflicting sovereignties which now encroach and now are encroached upon'.[50] Chapter 1 studies various attempts to extend the domain of literature into that of law and explores the implications of treating law as language. Chapter 2 focuses on the ways law has asserted control over verbal expression or performance or the reproduction of texts in the literary field, through such doctrines as obscenity, blasphemy and sedition, defamation and copyright. Part II, 'Law and literature in history', presents a chronological series of studies in border crossing between the two fields from the Renaissance to the present day. The ensuing chapters offer the evidence for the claim made in this introduction that law and literature have engaged with each other continually, albeit in different ways and in different degrees. So manifold are these connections that a comprehensive treatment is beyond the scope of this introduction. Accordingly, each chapter is organised around a distinct area of legal innovation and is related both to literary developments and to wider historical changes. Chapter 3 deals with the emergence of contract in the Renaissance. Chapter 4 explores the moral panic over crime in eighteenth-century England. Chapter 5 uses the case of Caroline Norton as a focus for examining the debate about the legal and political position of women in Victorian England. Chapter 6 views the new tort of negligence as a symbolic revolution in law paralleled in the cultural field by images of human vulnerability in a machine age. Chapter 7 employs a post-colonial approach to examine the significance of Western ideas of the rule of law in formerly colonised nations. Chapter 8 studies the legal and literary activity generated in America by *Brown* v. *Board of Education.*

Each of these studies forms a chapter in a larger narrative, of the history of the relationship between the two institutions. At one level, that story can be told as a tale of increasing estrangement and specialisation, but along with that institutional separatism goes a counter-narrative of dialogue and border raids. By telling both stories, the present study aims with Claudio Magris to shift the 'semantic borders' between law and literature.

PART I

Eminent domains: the text of the law and the law of the text

CHAPTER I

Law's language

On 11 May 1987, the Gitksan and Wet'suwet'en peoples of north-western British Columbia brought suit against the government of the province, seeking legal recognition of their ownership of their traditional homelands. After a highly publicised trial lasting four years, the Chief Justice of the Supreme Court of British Columbia, Allan McEachern, delivered judgment on 8 March 1991. His decision denied that these indigenous peoples had proprietary rights to the lands in question, despite their continuous occupancy since before the coming of whites. Instead, the judge upheld a claim by the Crown, declaring 'that the Plaintiffs had no right, title or interest in and to the Claim Area, and the resources thereon, thereover or thereunder'.[1] The issue of Aboriginal land rights is a hotly contested one in settler societies such as Canada and Australia, in which contemporary understandings of the complexity of indigenous cultural traditions and colonial history conflict with vested economic interests in the land. Consequently, Chief Justice McEachern's judgment attracted much criticism for its outdated colonialist assumptions about race and culture, but it also garnered support from major social institutions. One of the most interesting manifestations of this support occurred when the provincial government published the decision in book form, under the title *Reasons for Judgment: Delgamuukw v. The Queen*, and distributed it widely throughout British Columbia.[2]

All judgments are published, in the sense that the text is read out or handed down to the parties, is preserved as a transcript in the court archives and may well be reported in the press or in the official Law Reports. However, in this case the enunciation of the law seemed to demand a more extensive dissemination throughout society. The means chosen, the printing and binding of the legal text as a book, may have been intended, consciously or not, to add weight to the judgment, by combining the authority of the law with the aura of literature. Although the intention may be obscure, the decision to bind and distribute these *Reasons for Judgment* gave this legal utterance a higher than usual profile, and an appearance of finality in what was an on-going political debate. This publication was a rhetorical act, an attempt to persuade or influence the citizens of British Columbia of the importance of the decision. If *Reasons for Judgment* can be seen as an attempt to ensure that the authoritative word of the law found a place in the broader sphere of the public culture, then it alerts us to two aspects of the literary field: first, that like law, it makes use of a canon of great works and an evolving concept of tradition, in which texts from the past are consulted for illumination of the present; and secondly, that the authority of canonical works in the literary field is open to searching critique. For the publication of the book only intensified the criticism of the judgment. This outcome is exemplified by the 'close reading' of the Chief Justice's text undertaken by Dara Culhane:

> By 'close reading' I mean studying the texts not only for their literal or 'factual' content, but also to understand the various ways they communicate meanings directly and subtly, by using language in particular ways; by writing and speaking in rhetorical styles; by deploying metaphor and evoking images and emotions; by using grammar, and constructing each text as a whole along specific lines. That is to say, I read these documents as cultural texts, using the tools of anthropological and cultural criticism. And since particular texts do not make sense outside the broader context in which they are written I . . . also studied related work in the fields of anthropology, history, law and northwest ethnography.[3]

Although this is an unusual case, it exposes the rhetorical and linguistic character of all legal decisions, their necessary proclamation of an author-itative statement to a hitherto divided audience. In this respect it reveals a fundamental connection between law and literature that is frequently overlooked, the verbal character of the law and its processes. The recog-nition that law is inescapably a matter of how language is used, and the 'close reading' of its structures and meanings, its genres and contexts, have been major items on the agenda of Law and Literature studies. At one level it is obvious that laws are expressed in words, and that lawyers, litigants and judges routinely engage in the close reading of legal texts as a necessary part of applying the law. However, this kind of instrumental analysis is nar-rower than the interdisciplinary close reading practised under the umbrella of Law and Literature. Legal interpretation tends to focus on the literal meanings of words, and to assume that the meaning of an utterance is a product of the utterer's intention. It views language simply as a medium of communication. As the above quotation shows, however, there are a number of other ways in which meanings arise: by implication; through metaphor; and in the context of the utterance. Thus Law and Literature brings the concepts of literary theory and 'cultural criticism' to bear on legal discourse and interpretation. It seeks a more comprehensive understanding of how language and law interact. It reads legal texts as 'cultural texts', and is attentive to the full range of their linguistic effects. This framework may be troubling for some lawyers, for it reminds us, as Austin Sarat and Thomas R. Kearns note, 'that law can never escape the intricacies and imprecisions, as well as the promise and power of language itself'.[4] In this light, legal language may lose its finality and stability of meaning and become open to reinterpretation and critique, as Culhane's analysis of Chief Justice McEachern's judgment shows. In this chapter I will first describe some of the more important approaches to the language of the law, and secondly undertake a case study of some judicial texts on women and spousal murder in response to domestic violence.

RHETORIC AND LAW

The study of legal language is not new. Indeed it is as old as the ancient Greeks, who recognised the category of forensic oratory as one of the three kinds of rhetoric, along with deliberative (political) and epideictic (ceremonial display) rhetoric. Although in our society, with its print and digital technologies, there are many more occasions and kinds of rhetoric, the law-courts remain one of the primary scenes of rhetorical activity, and rhetoric, 'the art of persuasive communication', is as important as ever.[5] Aristotle in his *Rhetoric* defines it as an analytical discipline, not just a set of techniques to be performed: 'its function is not persuasion. It is rather the *detection of the persuasive aspects of each matter.*'[6] Consequently, Aristotle and the rhetoricians who followed him analyse not only the substance and presentation of arguments, but the impression created by the speaker and the composition of the audience. Aware of complaints that the art of rhetoric might be abused by speakers with little regard to truth, Aristotle insists that it is an 'offshoot of dialectic and of the study of ethics'.[7] This connection becomes clear when he presents an informed analysis of the enduring situation of legal pleading, the need to relate general laws to particular facts.[8] The significance of rhetoric for the practice of law and the pursuit of justice was crystallised in ancient Rome, where unlike Athens, litigants could employ lawyers to present their cases. Two such advocates, Cicero and Quintilian, produced treatises that developed the theory and practice of rhetoric, enshrining eloquent argumentation at the heart of Roman trials, political life and education.[9] This classical tradition was revived for the school curriculum and professional legal education during the

Middle Ages and Renaissance. Rhetoric was central to the teaching methods of the Inns of Court, and hence to the writings of the lawyers.[10] An exemplary case is that of the famous judge, Sir Edward Coke, who 'had in his library Aristotle's and Quintilian's rhetorics, several grammars and books of logic ... some Cicero and a book of elocution'.[11] However, the new technology of printed books was transforming the culture of the word, lessening the role of memory and orality, and thereby changing the orientation of rhetoric. As John Hollander notes, Renaissance rhetoricians really began to focus on literary texts, 'and their powers of persuasion were directed towards acts of interpretation and internalised judgment' in a transaction between writer and reader, rather than advocate and tribunal.[12] This new interest is clearly signalled in the published 'Lectures on Rhetoric and Belles Lettres' of such eighteenth-century writers as Hugh Blair and Adam Smith. Nonetheless, writers and lawyers down to this period were immersed in the rhetorical tradition during their formal schooling. Its imprint can be seen in the language of Blackstone's *Commentaries on the Laws of England* and the American *Declaration of Independence*.[13]

A number of factors, including the emergence of a separate category of the aesthetic with its elevation of imaginative writing above the discourses designed to influence action that were the special study of rhetoric, and the specialisation of knowledge and the professions in the second half of the nineteenth century, led to a decline in the significance of rhetoric in literary and legal education in the last two centuries. The discipline of rhetoric lost its eminence to literary criticism, and its study was 'fragmented', with genres such as advocacy manuals and self-help books like *How to Win Friends and Influence People* presenting themselves as specialist productions rather than as instances of a larger tradition. Notable works that updated or invoked classical rhetoric were published by writers such as Kenneth Burke, and by Wayne Booth and other Aristotelian critics centred at the University of Chicago, but the late twentieth century was more noteworthy for histories of rhetoric and calls for its revival.[14]

However, not surprisingly, this tradition as nurtured at Chicago provided the seedbed for the integrated study of Law and Literature. Here in 1973 James Boyd White published *The Legal Imagination*, the first of many books in which he advocates a humanistic approach to law based on the centrality of reading and writing in the work of the profession. White argues that language is used in law, as in literature, to constitute a community of writers and readers, to build a rhetorical community.[15] Thus he proposes analogies between the writing of a poem and that of a judicial opinion, for both are exercises in communication between a writer and his/her audience, attempts to secure assent to a particular representation of social reality. White emphasises not just the persuasive element in legal and literary rhetoric, but the 'constitutive' element, the capacity to build unanimity among participants in the discourse. He argues that law is a 'culture of argument' and, following Aristotle, stresses the ethical and rational norms that govern the presentation of claim and counterclaim.[16] Thus, law is ultimately 'a system of textual authority', one in which argument aims at the best interpretation of authoritative texts.[17] White demonstrates his thesis through readings of judicial opinions and statutes as well as literary texts. The hallmark of his writing is an openness to the exploration of meaning, a commitment to dialogue and latterly a belief in the importance of inclusiveness in the law. For example, in *Justice as Translation* he analyses the treatment of claims of racial inequality in American judicial opinions. Despite his convincing demonstration of the common rhetorical ground between law and literature, White's approach may present too idealised a vision of legal argument. Consider the following passage from *Heracles' Bow*: 'The law can be seen as a culture that we remake whenever we speak as lawyers . . . [O]ur enterprise is a radically ethical one, in which self and community are perpetually reconstituted.'[18] This reading is, in the words of one of his titles, an 'act of hope', for achieving a community around a trial or an authoritative judgment may be more difficult to achieve in fact than in word. Although White is aware that rhetoric has a political dimension as well as an ethical one, his analysis often pays insufficient attention to the realities of power, to inherited ideas of racial or gender difference, for example, 'huge stabilities' that prevent or delay change in the law and the community.[19]

Another scholar who has made a major contribution to the study of legal rhetoric is Peter Goodrich. Whereas White strives to develop an 'internal' perspective on law, one close to the way lawyers think, Goodrich draws on external frameworks, such as linguistics, literary theory and psychoanalysis, to present critiques of legal language. Goodrich picks up on the critical possibilities in the tradition of rhetoric presided over by Aristotle. His excellent introductory study of law as language, *Reading the Law*, presents a brief history of rhetoric in the context of law, and an anatomy of the key features of legal rhetoric. His thesis is that certain traditional rhetorical forms are embedded in the deep structure of modern legal reasoning, and can be analysed in judgments.[20] Goodrich's subsequent work fleshes out the history of English legal discourse, investigating the texts produced at significant moments in the formation of the common law.

In 'Antirrhesis: Polemical Structures of Common Law Thought', for example, he argues that argumentative strategies of denunciation conceived in theological debates during the Renaissance have been incorporated into the discourse of common-law advocacy, shaping forensic argument even today.[21] In addition to tracing the dominant metaphors and their implications, Goodrich also analyses lesser-known texts, especially legal treatises that were never canonised as leading textbooks. Books such as Abraham Fraunce's *The Lawiers Logike* represent the 'road not taken' by the common law, in effect its repressed possibilities.[22]

One of the strengths of Goodrich's work is that he updates the rhetorical tradition by bringing to the analysis of law's language the insights of modern forms of knowledge such as semiotics and post-structuralist theory. In consequence, he vividly realises the connection between power and legal language: 'The legal tradition founds the legitimacy of social speech; it institutes an order of lawful discourses and prohibits those heterodoxies of speech and writing that are deemed to threaten the security of legal meaning or the order of legal and political reason.'[23] Consciously situating his analyses outside this linguistic order, he produces radical critiques of law:

Neither a statutory text nor a case nor a textbook nor a practitioner's manual invites any dialogue or opinion. They are stylistically gauged to state the law through an awesomely boring and repetitive panoply of citation, quotation, footnoted references, names of cases, names of statutes, names of judges, . . . – all presented, it must be added, in a tongue that has never suffered the blandishments of usage anywhere but in court and in its diverse tiers of reportage.

Goodrich's playful use of hyperbole leads him astray here. Discourses are not watertight containers impermeable to new usages from outside. The opinion of Powell J. in *Bakke* v. *Regents of the University of California* (which will be discussed in chapter 8 below) is cast in this classic legalistic style, but it also negotiates with contemporary political discourses concerning racial justice and entitlement.

Goodrich's studies have inspired others to pay attention to the rhetorical devices employed in legal speech, to the particular tropes such as metaphor and personification. While these may seem decorative, they encode implicit values and habitual ways of thinking and are therefore worthy of study. Examples include studies of bodily metaphors in judicial opinions of the High Court of Australia, of the persistence of metaphors of expulsion and abjection in discussions or orders of imprisonment, and of the shift in modern law from aural to visual metaphors in modern legal discourse.[24]

LAW AS LITERATURE

The tradition of belles-lettres or fine writing, which emerged from rhetoric in the eighteenth century and was eventually rebadged as literature, has had its own engagement with legal texts. In a foreword to a 1961 collection, *The Law as Literature: An Anthology of Great Writing in and about the Law*, the English advocate and judge Lord Birkett wrote, 'Words are said to be the raw material of the legal profession, and the assiduous study of words, and the proper use of words have always been part of the lawyer's most desirable accomplishments.'[25] From this rhetorical description, Lord Birkett went on to make an evaluative, aesthetic claim: 'Many of our judges have been great masters of the spoken and the written word, and the Law Reports are not only a great treasury of law but they are a great treasury of literature.' This endeavour to enrol key legal writings in the canon of literature has represented for many twentieth-century lawyers the most intuitive method of connecting law and literature. And yet this intuition depends on a particular understanding of literature, derived from a classical liberal education. Thus Lord Birkett defines literature as 'writing of great excellence destined to live beyond the immediate hour'.[26] His assumption that beauty or felicitous expression is the core of innate literary quality, and that it will abide the movement of social change, draws upon his classical education, for in the same foreword he quotes from the *Greek Anthology* to define the book he is introducing as 'a garland of diverse flowers'. Within this apparent diversity, however, a recurrent preoccupation emerges, that of the defence of individual liberty. The texts chosen include Gandhi's address to the court on his trial for sedition, the opinion of Holmes J. on whether the pacifist views of an immigrant were grounds for barring her entry in *Schwimmer* v. *US*, and excerpts from the trial of South African newspaper editor Patrick Duncan, under the apartheid laws. Another judicial contributor to this tradition of the law as literature, Lord Elwyn-Jones, cites the forensic advocacy of Thomas Erskine in the treason trials of the 1790s and the judicial opinion of Lord Atkin denying unfettered executive power in the Second World War case of *Liversidge* v. *Anderson*.[27]

Such examples make it clear that a liberal political ideology is an implicit element of this approach to the literary value of legal writing: in them eloquence is tied to the defence of personal freedom under the rule of law. In this form of law-and-literature, the privileged textual genre is the judicial opinion, and as the examples by Atkin and Holmes suggest, often the chosen texts are dissenting judgments in appellate courts. In such cases there is a disconnection between literary value and legal pronouncement, suggesting that such legal aesthetics is really concerned with the language of justice, rather than law. Some of Holmes's dissents were later adopted by the Supreme Court, acquiring literary and legal power.[28]

This literary approach to legal writing entered a more professional phase in the 1970s, following the emergence of the Law and Literature movement in universities. Here the major theorist is Richard H. Weisberg. Weisberg and Jean-Pierre Barricelli, in their 1977 survey of Law and Literature for the Modern Languages Association of America, adopted the term 'law as literature' to describe this aspect of the interdisciplinary endeavour. The term stuck as a shorthand way of describing the poetics of legal writing, the formal study of its literary quality. Weisberg coined a neologism, 'poethics', to define what he saw as the ideal legal writing, one that united poetic language with an ethical achievement of justice, a combination of the beautiful and the good. In Weisberg's *Poethics*, great language enables a great understanding of the law. His model judge is Cardozo, in opinions such as *Hynes*.[29]

The question we may ask, however, is whether literary art can be employed in the service of an unjust result. Perhaps the best example of this is the opinion of Oliver Wendell Holmes in *Buck* v. *Bell*. In this case Holmesian eloquence is invoked to allow the compulsory sterilisation of a young woman, Carrie Buck, who was (wrongly) believed to be cognitively impaired. In Holmes's pungent distillation of eugenics, 'Three generations of imbeciles are enough.'[30] Richard Posner, for whom eloquence is a means of adding rhetorical value to a judicial opinion, has allowed that this may be literature despite its unsavoury finding.[31] Posner, who is generally an opponent of Law and Literature, approves the 'law as literature' connection. His work has the merit of insisting that literary value should not depend on ideological agreement, but he offers a rudimentary account of the criteria of value.[32]

The best studies of the literary qualities of legal texts are those by Robert A. Ferguson, who is also a keen student of Holmes's writings. His two essays, 'On the Judicial Opinion as a Literary Genre' and ' "We Do Ordain and Establish": The Constitution as a Literary Text' demonstrate the integrated contextual research and analysis of form of the literary historian. Ferguson uses Bakhtin's concept of the 'authoritative word' in discussing the formal and generic qualities of the judicial opinion, arguing that its hallmarks are a monologic voice, an interrogative mode and a declarative tone. In a formulation reminiscent of Goodrich's, he argues:

The one thing a judge never admits in the moment of decision is freedom of choice. The monologic voice of the opinion can never presume to act on its own. It must instead appear as if forced to its inevitable conclusion by the logic of the situation and the duties of office, which together eliminate all thought of an unfettered hand.[33]

In his reading of 'The Constitution as Literary Text' Ferguson stresses the importance of a contextual approach, examining the constitutional debates, the drafting process and the other written constitutions which served as models for the framers in their quest for the new nation's 'political scripture'. Such a reading values the legal text 'in all its generic strength, manipulative brilliance, cunning restraint, and practised eloquence' – not for its eloquence alone.[34]

In the last fifteen years, the validity of 'law as literature' has come under challenge on precisely the issue of its hidden ideological values. Armed with the insights of feminism and post-colonial studies, critics have pointed out that the canon of great legal-literary works assembled in anthologies or discussed in articles is highly partial in the voices and perspectives it offers as articulating the human experience of law. Given the history of Western society, with its patriarchal traditions and its imperialist domination of other lands, the canonisation of a select group of advocates and judges, however eloquent, has unconsciously foregrounded the concerns and experiences of white people, and men in particular.[35] This critique of 'Law as Literature' was first articulated by Judith Resnik and Carolyn Heilbrun: 'what (and who) is given voice; who privileged, repeated and invoked; who silenced, ignored, submerged and marginalised. Law and literature have shared traditions – of silencing, of pushing certain stories to the margin and of privileging others.'[36] The story with which I began this chapter, the attempt to recast Chief Justice McEachern's *Reasons for Judgment* as literature, is an instance of this critique. Dara Culhane notes the operation of European ideologies and values, and the privileging of white witnesses in the judicial text. As a considered essay on a vital question of law in a post-colonial society, it fails to offer a just representation of the issues.

The way forward for this approach to 'law as literature' is to address this critique, to acknowledge that canons of great writing are critical constructs which serve the cultural interests of their proponents, to be open to the range of voices and stories encountered in the context of the law, and especially to the voices and stories of the other. On this basis, a new 'legal aesthetics' is being formed, in which the literary realm is not valued for conserving cultural tradition, but for its capacity to imagine alternatives. Adumbrated in the work of Costas Douzinas and others, it has so far taken fictions as its key texts.[37] The possibility of a new legal aesthetics, traceable in the writings of the law, is also one of the questions to be explored in the present work. In the next two sections I shall examine other major responses to the critique of 'law as literature'.

LINGUISTIC STUDIES OF LAW

Thus far in this chapter we have concentrated on the language of the judicial opinion. Yet there are other important genres of legal language besides this, such as statutes, codes and forms of pleading. These have tended to be analysed using the tools of structural anthropology and linguistics. An early contributor to this effort was A. S. Diamond. In his *Primitive Law: Past and Present*, Diamond drew from his comparative legal anthropology the beginnings of a grammar of legal utterance. Studying the codes of Anglo-Saxon law and of West African societies, he pronounced some general rules concerning their 'natural language':

All genuine codes are couched in the natural language of statutory legislation, namely conditional sentences in the third person, the protasis containing the facts supposed, and the apodosis the sanction. Nowhere is there to be found a rule of law in the second person. The arrangement of topics, such as it is, is the natural arrangement of statutory legislation, namely according to the *external* subject matter of the rule – homicide, wounding, theft ... Throughout the primitive law, arrangement is never according to the internal principle.[38]

One of the evident ambitions of this social-scientific approach is its wish to discover universal rules. Also to be noted as a consequence of this confident articulation of universals is an assumption that certain forms are 'natural'. More recent scholars in this linguistic tradition have questioned this assumption, on the basis that all human systems of meaning are culturally, not naturally, based. They do not search for universal rules, but analyse the processes of meaning-making in particular legal systems. Pierre Bourdieu, for example, studies the 'juridical field' in modern Western society. He too aspires to 'a rigorous science of the law' but is more concerned to analyse how the legal system works, and its social effects, not to pronounce linguistic rules.[39] He describes 'juridical language' as having a 'rhetoric of impersonality and neutrality'. His account shares Diamond's grammatical precision but is more interested in the consequences of the forms: 'The *neutralisation effect* is created by a set of syntactic traits such as the predominance of passive and impersonal constructions. They are designed to mark the impersonality of normative utterances and to establish the speaker as universal subject, at once impartial and objective.'[40] Here linguistic analysis is one of the tools of a critical sociology of law. The language of the law is an important key in understanding how the institution operates, how a '*universalising attitude*' necessary for legal interpretation and judgment is inculcated. Thus, legal language is not studied for its own sake, but for the light it sheds on legal practices.

Another methodology deriving from linguistics, which developed in the 1970s, is legal semiotics, 'the study of law as a system of signs and methods of signification'.[41] It too examines the underlying structures of legal sentences, from a critical not a descriptive basis. According to J. M. Balkin, 'it studies the recurring forms of argument used to justify legal doctrines'. What this means in practice is the moves that the plaintiff and defendant can make in, say, a negligence claim, and the limited range of possible meanings created by those moves. Balkin argues convincingly that legal semiotics is really a contemporary version of rhetoric, that the 'forms of argument' of semiotics are the 'topics' of classical rhetoric. Among the practitioners of this school, it is perhaps most useful to note the name of Bernard S. Jackson for his work on legal narrative.[42]

Equally importantly, semiotics is not confined to the analysis of verbal communication. As Goodrich has said, 'language . . . must now be taken to include all the other systems of signs – of architecture, dress, geography, ceremony', for, 'It is through symbols, through the forms of appearance and representation of law in the public sphere, that a public generally recognises law as either a legitimate or simply a *de facto* sovereign social power.'[43] There is a brilliant analysis of the signs of the law by Roland Barthes, a semiotician *avant la lettre*, in his essay 'Dominici, or the Triumph of Literature'.[44] Barthes analyses the language of the judge and prosecutor, their deportment, the architecture of the courtroom and the placement of the accused Dominici in this theatre of justice. Barthes's essay is quoted in a more recent semiotic analysis of the law report of an English criminal appeal. Alison Young examines the generic conventions of the law report, and the linked signification of gender, illness and normality in the judges' discussion of shop-lifting.[45] With this kind of investigation into the ideological work of legal signs, semiotics remains a powerful resource for the critical understanding of how legal meanings are generated.

NARRATIVE JURISPRUDENCE

Narrative, or storytelling, forms one of the intersections of law and literature. Its importance for the novel, autobiography, film and other cultural forms is easily seen. However, the ability to construct and tell a convincing story is also a crucial part of the trial lawyer's rhetorical toolbox. Trials can be viewed as a contest between two competing versions of a traumatic incident. Certain kinds of narrative, such as confession, are performed in literary, legal and other contexts, across disciplinary boundaries.[46] Many of the judicial opinions admired for their literary qualities begin by telling the story of the case.[47] 'Narrative', as Peter Brooks has observed, 'is indeed omnipresent in the law.'[48] On this recognition, an important branch of the study of law's language has been built.

Variously called 'legal narrative studies' or 'narrative jurisprudence', it began with Robert Cover's magisterial 1983 article, '*Nomos* and Narrative'. Cover argued that, 'No set of legal institutions or prescriptions exists apart from the narratives that locate it and give it meaning. For every constitution there is an epic, for every Decalogue a scripture.'[49] As a legal historian, Cover realised that laws could be fully understood only in their cultural contexts; and he saw contexts not in terms of empirical facts, but of myths, stories by which communities made sense of their world. Recognising the pluralistic societies of the modern nation-state, Cover saw that while the law could be seen as an 'authoritative text', its 'meaning is always "essentially contested," in the degree to which [it] is related to the diverse and divergent narrative traditions within the nation'.[50] His argument invited readers and writers to view legal interpretation and adjudication as activities shaped not just by the words on the legal page, but by the protagonist's sense of verbal and communal history and purpose. Trials, for Cover, were contests over narrative, not just at a surface level of evidence presented and contradicted, but at a deeper level of established versus alternative social visions.

A case which illustrates Cover's hypothesis is *Dudley and Stephens*, in which sailors adrift at sea drew lots to select one of their number to eat, rather than face starvation. On being rescued and returned to land, they were charged with murder and convicted. The case is often included in casebooks of criminal law as authority for the rule that necessity does not excuse a crime. Yet behind the bland summary in the casebook, as Brian Simpson has shown in a gripping history, is a complex narrative in which two legal worlds met, one an acknowledged tradition of the sea, invoked in the candid admissions of the rescued sailors, and the other an impulse of the modern state, grounded in Christian natural law and an imperialist self-image of civilised rationality. Victory in this ideological contest was achieved not only through Ciceronian rhetoric, but also Machiavellian manipulation.[51]

Cannibalism and the Common Law represents a fruitful meeting between social and legal history, and the rekindled interest in narrative within historiography.[52] Narrative jurisprudence, however, developed under that name less as a form of history than as a mode of intervention in contemporary legal situations. Its critical, indeed political, orientation was made plain in a 1987 symposium on narrative and law in the *Michigan Law Review*, in which it was argued that a concentration on storytelling within the law could aid the legally oppressed.[53] As a mode of legal critique, it combines the analysis of stories presented in court, the detection of suppressed or excluded voices and the telling of new stories, previously unheard at law. Narrative jurisprudence studies the court record, identifying the kinds or genres of stories told, analysing the discourses employed by various participants, focusing too on the evasions and slippages, and the non-verbal utterances such as crying or fainting. The text here is not just the judge's opinion, but the entire transcript, in which the contest over representation of the original events unfolds in detail. To this analytical unmasking of the interplay between legal discourse and power is added the telling of an unheard story, of an unredressed injury. By incorporating these stories as stories, and reflecting on the possibilities of narration, scholars in narrative jurisprudence go beyond the transcript, and beyond the usual confines of legal discourse. The resort to stories over other forms of rational discourse derives from their ability to involve the reader in individualised factual detail. They represent what Robin West calls, 'an attempt to make the reader aware that these injuries *happen*'.[54]

Narrative jurisprudence has attracted theorists from among both legal and literary scholars, but has drawn especially from feminist and critical race studies. The latter movement will be discussed in my final chapter. Among the leading feminist practitioners are Martha Minow, Susan Sage Heinzelman and Robin West. In ' "Going Somewhere": Maternal Infanticide and the Ethics of Judgment', Heinzelman analyses two infanticide cases in contemporary Texas, and a modern Irish poem on the same subject. The case of Susan Bienek was a trial fought on competing stereotypes of the 'good' and the 'bad mother', in which the actual circumstances of her life and mental condition at the time of the event were unable to be voiced. Heinzelman contrasts the drive to a narrow, punitive judgment prescribed by this narrative with the more ethical and ambivalent judgment asked of the reader of Seamus Heaney's poem 'Limbo'. Lest it be thought that such comprehensiveness is restricted to the realm of literature, she shows that in the other case, of Juana Léija, a lawyer and a cultural expert were able to place the criminal act in a complex narrative of the accused's marital history, psychological state and cultural beliefs. This narrative was presented to the court, enabling an ethical judgment to be formed in which the sentence facilitated individual and community healing.[55]

The genres of legal stories have been a particular interest to these scholars. Much of their work has been directed to demonstrating how certain kinds of stories are favoured by the courts, indeed are woven into the subtext of the law. Robert A. Ferguson's pragmatic observation that 'the competition in story-telling caters to the lowest common denominator with competing stereotypes about crime as the gauge for choices to be made' is illustrated in Heinzelman's first case.[56] Robin West suggests that the capacity to 'debunk stock stories' is what has attracted feminists to narrative jurisprudence.[57] One of the 'stock stories' that West notes occurs in the criminal law of self-defence:

> The criminal law of justified self-defence is also squarely based on a stock story . . . of the nature of violence: a stranger is accosted in a public place, such as a bar or street, and if possible, retreats, but if retreat is impossible, he justifiably defends himself. The intricate rules in criminal law governing the justified use of force to defend oneself are tailored to this story. They do not fit well – or at all – violent encounters that depart from it . . . for example, the violent encounters between intimates that occur in a home.[58]

West argues that the legal rules would be very different if they had been developed around a narrative of domestic violence, rather than that of a bar-room assault. In the final part of this chapter I will discuss two legal texts that depend on or take issue with this stock story.

Narrative jurisprudence is a broad movement, and its goal of seeking justice through supplementary storytelling and making the law a more inclusive forum is not confined to taking up contemporary cases. The narrative study of cases past leads to an increased understanding of the culture inherited by the present. Robert A. Ferguson's narrative analyses of the slave rebellion trials of ante-bellum America combine narrative theory and historical research to provide rich accounts of the social dramas that are trials.[59] Through a study of the *Eichmann* and *O. J. Simpson* trials, Shoshana Felman has argued that in the late twentieth century, history itself was put on trial. The historical character of the arguments in these trials and others like *Brown* v. *Board of Education*, the fact that the actions of the participants are placed in a narrative history of racism, suggests that 'the court provides a stage for the expression of the persecuted'.[60] This is the possibility taken up in narrative jurisprudence. Yet Felman is aware that this new possibility may be refused by the courts: 'The law – and the court itself – is not entirely (and not by definition) on the side of justice; they partake of the violence of history.'[61] Indigenous peoples like the Gitksan and Wet'suwet'en peoples of British Columbia have found that the redemptive possibilities of legal narrative are not always fulfilled.

CONCLUDING EXAMPLES

To conclude this chapter, I would like to examine two examples of legal language, the opinion of Lord Goddard CJ approving a jury direction given by Sir Patrick Devlin in the English Court of Criminal Appeal case of *Duffy*, and that of Madame Justice Bertha Wilson in the Supreme Court of Canada in another criminal appeal case, *Lavallée*. Some of the concepts discussed above can be illustrated in relation to these two judgments, the 'stock story' underlying defences to crimes of violence.

The *Duffy* case of 1949 is published in the law reports for doctrinal purposes only; as a 'classic direction' to a jury on the law of provocation. It represents the traditional common-law approach to this question. Only a minimal narrative of the circumstances, replacing the names of those involved with their legal roles, is given. It states that the appellant 'had been subjected to brutal treatment by' her husband, had wanted to leave but been prevented, had gone and changed her clothes and, when the husband was asleep, had killed him using a hatchet and hammer. Devlin J. addresses himself to what is not provocation, and distinguishes between moral and legal discourse:

A long course of cruel conduct may be more blameworthy than a sudden act of retaliation, but you are not concerned with blame here – the blame attaching to the dead man. You are not standing in judgment on him. He has not been heard in this court. He cannot now ever be heard . . . It does not matter how cruel he was, . . . except in so far as it resulted in the final act of the appellant. What matters is whether this girl had time to say: 'Whatever I have suffered, whatever I have endured, I know that Thou shalt not kill.'[62]

As with the feminist analysis of self-defence, provocation was constructed around implicitly masculine cultural and social norms. It is defined here around a notional paradigm or 'stock story' of an assault that produces in its victim a sudden and temporary loss of control that is expressed in violence. There must be a temporal link between one assault and the response, and there must be some sense of proportion, a fist for a fist, despite the loss of control. In conceiving of provocation thus, the common law presupposed as 'natural' a reaction to violence that is in fact enculturated, and that is inseparable from ideas of masculinity. It also presupposed an approximate equality of physical strength. In short, the law constructed its idea of a person from a masculine cultural model, and its idea of the interaction from a set of male social practices. The result was a hidden bias, an unacknowledged structural fault that excluded battered women from a defence that could have allowed the circumstances leading up to their actions to be taken into account. Under this law, Mrs Duffy is offered Lord Goddard's 'sympathy', but nothing more; the law had to be 'vindicated'.[63]

If we focus now on Lord Goddard's way of speaking about the law, and he speaks *ex tempore* and in a familiar register, the report shows the ideology of the law as an objective body of doctrine, the idea that, in the words of Stanley Fish, 'the law wishes to have a formal existence'.[64] Lord Goddard's phrase, 'That is as good a definition of the doctrine of provocation as it has ever been my lot to read', implies that there is a fixed concept, that the judge is paraphrasing or expounding an already-formulated, already known law. The law exists – it is implied – as an objective body of such doctrines, separately from the judges, separately and before any particular case. Further, provocation and all other legal rules together add up to a coherent body called 'the law'. The Chief Justice's phrase, 'vindicating the law', not only says that the law must be obeyed, but that the law has a unified existence, a life of its own, which can be promoted or, presumably, harmed by misuse. If not quite personified, it has the unity and complete-ness of a distinct body.[65]

We may also note the use of the passive voice, also entirely conventional: 'That the appellant was properly convicted of murder according to law there can be no doubt.' This discourse, 'was properly convicted', locates the source of the judgment away from the particular Mr Justice Devlin, or the jury, and and on to the impersonal force of the law. The strategic uses of this grammatical form are well expressed by Herman Melville in his exposition of the legal reasoning used to convict the morally innocent Billy Budd: ' "Would it be so much we ourselves that would condemn as it would be the martial law operating through us?" '[66] No subjectivity or partiality, no personal frailty or lack of insight can be admitted, because the people involved are simply administering the objective law. Yet the com-plete exclusion of such personal factors is unlikely in reality.[67]

It is also worth thinking about the textual form of this judgment. There was argument in the Court of Appeal about the adequacy of the form of words quoted above, but they are approved as 'a classic direction', one that deserves to be remembered. The text is published to announce this, to enshrine Devlin's words as an authoritative statement precedent. In addi-tion to its legal value, one might also enquire whether the text might be invested with aesthetic value, given its graceful and clear expression, enlivened by a biblical allusion. Any such attempt would be doomed, in my view, because of the shift in public opinion, the sense that justice demanded a different outcome, one more responsive to the specific con-ditions of Mrs Duffy's life. Even in the aftermath of the decision, it is doubtful if this text would have been canonised, as it lacked an eloquent affirmation of the liberty of the accused.

Having noted the construction of an impersonal, objective voice of the law, we can confirm Peter Goodrich's observation that legal discourse is monological: the text does not invite dialogue. The common law works by preserving certain formulae in its archive of authorities and its institutional memory. This report highlights the acceptance of a new formulation into that memory bank.

Finally, Devlin J. quotes from the Ten Commandments, 'Thou shalt not kill', and in doing so he grounds the common law on the Judeo-Christian moral law. (In the 1960s he became famous for this position in a book, *The Enforcement of Morals*, and a debate with the legal philosopher H. L. A. Hart.[68]) This biblical allusion accounts in no small part for the rhetorical authority of his text. It is not just his own clarity of exposition, or even his forceful distinction between what is and what is not provocation, his setting the boundary. It is also that he invokes in passing a source of right and wrong that has traditional authority in Western culture. Despite the objectivist claims of the text, this ethical appeal to a higher law gives us a glimpse of the historical and ideological forces underpinning the common law. I refer here not to religion or the content of the law, but to its patriarchal transmission, as God's word, mediated by Moses, is quoted by Devlin, and approved by Goddard and two other appellate judges, as Law.

This text, then, is a good example of what Bakhtin called 'the authoritative word': 'The authoritative word is located in a distanced zone, organically connected with a past that is felt to be hierarchically higher. It is, so to speak, the word of the fathers . . . It is a *prior* discourse. It is therefore not a question of choosing it from other possible discourses that are its equal. It is given in lofty spheres, not those of familiar contact.'[69] The biblical quotation seals this text as an utterance of the 'authoritative word', but even before that, the law is presented as 'a prior discourse', a pre-existing body of principle. In the refusal to let personal sympathy interfere with the correct operation of the law, Lord Goddard refuses the possibility of seeking justice through 'familiar contact'; instead his voice sounds from a 'lofty sphere', and the word is hierarchically elevated as the medium of the law.

Bakhtin's theory of language, in addition to noting the stratification of discourses, also emphasises their plurality and proliferation, or the centrifugal element in every language. Gerald L. Bruns, in a hermeneutic reading of the language of the law, argues that this latter aspect must also be taken in to account by students of legal discourse.[70] It is possible to regard the story raised but refused countenance in Duffy's case as an instance of just such an alternative discourse. This was a narrative that would not really make an impact on the law until the feminist critique of social institutions challenged the 'naturalness' and completeness of legal and other practices. Even then, the criminal law, and social opinion in the form of jury verdicts and media representations, resisted change, as Helena Kennedy's well-known book, *Eve Was Framed* shows.[71] The new discourse developed to tell this other story was 'battered woman's syndrome', and it was based on medical and psychological evidence of the effects of prolonged domestic violence within intimate relationships.

It was hoped that this evidence would enable a woman charged with killing an abusive partner to avail herself of provocation or self-defence, but it has mostly secured verdicts of diminished responsibility, an outcome that constructs the woman as abnormal. Writing of the *Ahluwalia* case, one of the best-known English attempts to raise this material, Fiona Raitt and Suzanne Zeedyk comment:

> Although Kiranjit Ahluwalia had suffered years of extreme abuse and was acting in fear of her life, the only explanation of her behaviour that the court would accept was that it was due to irrational, uncontrollable impulses brought on by psychological disorder. It was impossible for them to see it as 'reasonable,' in the way that men's behaviour is seen as 'reasonable' when they act in self-defence or are provoked.[72]

One case where this consequence was avoided was that of *Lavallée*. This Canadian case is a landmark in the development of the criminal law defences available to a battered woman, and in the law's taking notice of a different explanatory narrative of violence. The leading judgment in the case, written by Wilson J., sees what has traditionally been the law of the fathers analysed and rectified by a feminist judge.

To begin with a brief narrative to set the context: Lyn Lavallée was tried for murder, and acquitted after successfully producing evidence that she was acting in self-defence when she killed her partner, Kevin Rust. The Crown appealed against this verdict, on the grounds that the evidence of self-defence was the opinion of a psychiatrist that Lavallée suffered from battered woman's syndrome, that this was not a proper area of expert testimony, and that the psychiatrist's evidence was based on materials which had not been put before the court properly as evidence: it had not been tested by cross-examination; it was not given on oath; it was hearsay. The prosecution argued that the evidence of this psychiatric condition should have been excluded. They succeeded in this argument before the Appeal Court of Manitoba. Lavallée then appealed to the Supreme Court of Canada, the final court of appeal, and the ultimate authority for declaring the law in Canada.

Justice Wilson's judgment first tells the story of Lyn Lavallée's relationship with Kevin Rust, and the events of the night of his killing. It then goes on to describe the legal issues about expert evidence raised by the appeal and to examine in detail the reasoning of the lower court. Next it states the governing law about self-defence. It then summarises the issues that have to be decided and presents its own determination about the admissibility of this psychiatric evidence of the mental condition and psychological state of a woman subject to a long period of violence from a loved one. Wilson J. concludes that this is a case where the psychiatrist's evidence draws on expert, scientific knowledge, and that the psychiatrist's report can provide evidence of self-defence. Finally Wilson J. assesses whether the specific requirements for self-defence have been proved by the psychological evidence. Structurally, then, following the narrative element, there is a progressive narrowing of the focus from general doctrine to the particular case.

The judgment is therefore dominated by legal reasoning, by citations of relevant statutes and cases. However, when we compare this judgment with that of Lord Goddard in Duffy's case, we can see a different understanding of law, a different approach to the authoritative word. Where Goddard stresses the fixed and prior existence of the law, its completeness, its need to be vindicated, Wilson insists that, 'Laws do not spring out of a social vacuum.'[73] There is a more sociological and historical understanding of law at work here, a sense that law is the instrument of social values, and a recognition that social attitudes towards violence in marriage have changed. As a result, the law is presented not as a separate and transcendent discourse, but as one implicated in and shaped by other social forces:

The gravity, indeed the tragedy of domestic violence can hardly be overstated. Greater media attention to this phenomenon in recent years has revealed both its prevalence and its horrific impact on women from all walks of life. Far from protecting women from it the law has historically sanctioned the abuse of women within marriage as an aspect of the husband's ownership of his wife and his 'right' to chastise her. One need only recall the centuries-old law that a man is entitled to beat his wife with a stick 'no thicker than his thumb.' (872)

Importantly, Wilson J. introduces the discourse of domestic violence into the criminal law, forcing it to acknowledge previous failures of protection: 'One consequence of this attitude was that "wife battering" was rarely spoken of, rarely reported, rarely prosecuted, and even more rarely punished' (872). The injustice produced by this culture of silence is being redressed through law. 'Legislative initiatives designed to educate police, judicial officers and the public' are noted, evincing the Supreme Court's acceptance of an instrumental, educative, reforming view of law's function, directed both at the institutions of the criminal justice system and at society (872).

The authority of the law can be rested on its being an instrument of social justice, and individual justice, rather than on its antiquity. With this different foundation goes a new openness to influences outside legal discourse. Law is not pictured here as a self-contained and self-justifying body of principle that speaks with mysterious oracular power through judges, but as an institution that must respond to other social discourses. Justice Wilson's text exemplifies this openness by its full and welcoming citation of medical and psychological literature about cycles of violence in families. She does not simply follow the expert witness Dr Shane's testimony, but she cements the general legal value of evidence of that kind by going back to the research herself, and by quoting from legal feminist scholarship that explains the implications for legal doctrine.

The result of this new orientation and this willingness to quote non-legal sources, and bring them into the text of the law is that a quite different sense of reasonable force emerges. Self-defence as a legal doctrine has a requirement that the level of force used in defending oneself must not be disproportionate to the assault offered. In the traditional language of the law, juries were asked to consider what would a 'reasonable man' do in the circumstances? What level of force would he respond with? The reasonable man was the standby of legal objectivity, a mythical figure upon whom juries and judges could project their notions of a reasonable action or reaction in any situation. He was the universal legal subject, the personification of rationality and due care and controlled agency who could be wheeled in as the ideal citizen, and against whom any other citizen's acts might be measured. Until recently, the gender of the reasonable man was not regarded as important; gender was a matter of indifference to a legal system that prided itself on its neutrality, its objectivity. However, Justice Wilson trenchantly demonstrates the fallacy of this assumption:

If it strains credulity to imagine what the 'ordinary man' would do in the position of a battered spouse, it is probably because most men do not typically find themselves in that situation. Some women do, however. The definition of what is reasonable must be adapted to circumstances which are, by and large, foreign to the world inhabited by the hypothetical 'reasonable man'. (874)

Here, the legal construct is given a gendered identity and made to confront its distance from actual experience. It cannot be invoked without importing a completely unsuitable standard of force. A new gender-specific standard of reasonable force has to be formulated by the law.

In this judgment the law is being reformed so that the voices of women hitherto silenced can enter the discourse. Lyn Lavallée chose not to give evidence at her trial. Her story was heard through her statement to the police, and through the evidence of the psychiatrist. In ruling that the latter evidence was admissible as expert testimony, the court recognised that scientific knowledge of the psychological effects of domestic violence was 'beyond the ken of the average juror' (873). Moreover, this material was necessary to displace 'popular mythology' from the jurors' minds. The judge summarises the condemnatory and prejudicial nature of these beliefs concerning domestic violence: 'Either she was not as badly beaten as she claims or she would have left the man long ago. Or, if she was battered that severely, she must have stayed out of some masochistic enjoyment of it' (873). The court reposes a modernist faith in the rhetorical power of social science data to dispel the traditional beliefs of the culture. In terms of narrative jurisprudence, it seeks to replace an older story in which the woman is presumed to be morally or sexually suspect with a new story that details the emotional landscape of the relationship and thus coherently explains the causes of the woman's own resort to violence. In stressing the credibility of this alternative story, Wilson notes the high degree of parallelism between the circumstances of Lavallée's killing and those of the cases studied by the psychologists, quoting Dr Lenore Walker: 'Most of the time the women killed the men with a gun; usually one of several that belonged to him. *Many of the men actually dared or demanded the woman use the gun on him first, or else he said he'd kill her with it*' (882; emphasis in judgment). This 'remarkable observation' uncannily predicts the last words of Kevin Rust.

Finally, in its style as well as its doctrine, this judgment offers some-thing new, a willingness to speak in a personal voice. Wilson J. is unafraid to use the first-person pronoun: 'I note in passing a remarkable observa-tion' (882); and 'I emphasise at this juncture that it is not for the jury to pass judgment on the fact that an accused battered woman stayed in the relationship' (888). This shift from an oracular to a human voice of the law matches the ethical transparency of the opinion, and its view of the law as an instrument of social policy. However, this 'I' is used sparingly, among the voices of earlier judicial authorities, and statutory phrases, in ways that do not diminish the usual 'rhetoric of impersonality and neutrality', or the appearance of inevitability demanded by the genre.[74] Rhetorically, this stylistic balancing works to ensure that the new story is accepted as the 'authoritative word' by a still-divided community.

Taken together, these two cases chart a shift in legal discourse, and in social understandings of justice and gender, over half a century. Though it favours precedent and traditional formulae, law's language also engages dynamically with other social forces. The search for an appropriate legal utterance is integral to the quest for justice. For this reason, the texts of the law are sometimes to be celebrated, and always to be studied.

CHAPTER 2

Literature under the law

In June 1971 after unsuccessfully defending the editors of the underground magazine *Oz* on charges of obscenity, the writer and barrister John Mortimer declared from the steps of London's Old Bailey that, 'There cannot be a limit on the writer.'[1] The notion that literature is a zone of free expression, that 'there cannot be a limit on the writer', is an idealist one. As we shall see in this chapter, it represents a long-held ideal in Western literary culture, and one that has been vigorously opposed. Not only the force of law, but inherited systems of ideas concerning both social values and literary forms, and the economics of publishing have all worked, admittedly in varying degrees, as 'limits' on writers. Consequently, it is important not to regard literature and law as 'polar opposites', one a space of freedom and the other an institution of social control.[2] Rather, this chapter will look more closely at the laws that regulate and control literature as a vital perspective in understanding the relationship between these two discourses.

More recently, Antony Julius has written generally of these laws that 'bear on literary creativity':

There is no discrete body of law relating to literature. There are instead a miscellany of laws regulating literature, some statutory, some judge-made, some criminal, others civil. The law of defamation, copyright law, laws prohibiting obscenity and blasphemy, bear – in variously restrictive and overlapping ways – on literary creativity. But there is no legal code which takes literature as its subject; the 'law of literature' lacks coherence, and is without system or structure. It is in a state of disarray; it oppresses without bringing order.[3]

As a lawyer, Julius foregrounds the constitutive power of the law, its capacity not merely to order, but to construct and enable all manner of human activity, including literature. This possibility, that law might function to promote rather than merely to constrain literature, forms a significant strand of the argument. Julius provides a balanced starting point for this discussion by combining an assumption that law need not be inimical to literature with a critical evaluation of current laws.

A succinct contemporary statement of the principles that should govern this area of law is provided by the International Covenant for Civil and Political Rights. Article 19 of the Covenant states:

(1) Everyone shall have the right to hold opinions without interference.
(2) Everyone shall have the right to freedom of expression; this right shall include the freedom to seek, receive and impart information and ideas of all kinds regardless of frontiers, either orally, in writing or in print, in the form of art or through any other media of his choice.
(3) The exercise of the rights provided for in (2) above carries with it special duties and responsibilities, and it may therefore be subject to certain restrictions, but these shall only be such as are provided by law and are necessary:
    (a) For the respect of the rights and reputations of others;
    (b) For the protection of national security, public health or morals.

The three areas of regulation listed by Julius, obscenity and blasphemy, defamation, and copyright, all come within the restrictions allowed under the Covenant. However, it is worth noting that the principle of free expression as a human right is not fundamental in the common-law tradition. The common-law position was enunciated by Lord Wright in a 1936 Privy Council case, *James* v. *Commonwealth*: 'free speech does not mean free speech; it means speech hedged in by all the laws against defamation, blasphemy, sedition and so forth; it means freedom governed by law'.[4] A major Australian legal reference source puts the position clearly: freedom of expression is 'a negative right or freedom in that it exists only where there is no legal restriction. The many restrictions on freedom of expression which arise from both common law and legislation may be regarded as implying the existence of a basic or negative right to both freedom of speech and freedom of action.'[5]

By contrast, freedom of expression *is* fundamental in the United States, where the First Amendment to the Constitution includes the provision that 'Congress shall make no law . . . abridging the freedom of speech, or of the press.' This positive freedom has not prohibited the development of laws relating to obscenity and defamation, as we shall see, but it has impacted on their scope.

In tracing the legal regulation of literature as one form of intersection between these two fields, it is important to stress that this has been a dynamic encounter. The boundaries of permissible speech and writing have always been transgressed by new and challenging texts, and legal regimes of containment have altered in their methods and principles. An understanding of current legal limits to freedom of creative expression demands a contextual and historical account of how various laws emerged and changed.

LITERATURE AND THE CRIMINAL LAW

Literary history is full of instances in which writers and their texts have transgressed the bounds of socially accepted expression, and have suffered the force of the law. In the year 93, the Roman poet Juvenal published a short satire on corruption at the Emperor's court, for which he was charged with treason. He was sentenced to *deportatio*, banished to a distant military outpost in Egypt, and, along with this, all his property was confiscated by the tyrannical Emperor Domitian. Three years later, Domitian was assassinated, and Juvenal's sentence was revoked, but as Gilbert Highet puts it, his 'fortune and career were gone'.[6] Between Juvenal's day and Vaclav Havel's imprisonment in our own era, many writers have been punished for expressing views that offended those in power.

The range of forbidden topics has varied according to the dominant ideologies of each society, but religion, sexuality and political authority have traditionally been sensitive areas. Legal doctrines concerning blasphemy, obscenity and sedition have developed accordingly. In this section, these three areas will be discussed separately, yet historically they are interrelated: the bawdy sexual representations characteristic of pornography have been a mode of attacking political and religious authority as well as exercises in libertinism; and in countries with an official, established religion, an attack upon the Church has been readily interpreted as an attack upon the State. In addition, the common-law term for these offences identified them as species of *libel*: obscene libel, blasphemous libel and seditious libel, although the requirement to prove a defamation upon an individual was soon dropped.

Despite this history of legally imposed boundaries upon expression, literature has from the Renaissance invoked an ancient liberty, to speak freely, citing the example of Juvenal and his fellow Roman satirists, Martial and Horace. The Renaissance scholar Annabel Patterson points to *The Mirror for Magistrates* (1559) as one of several literary arguments against censorship:

> This auncient freedome ought not be debarred
> From any wyght that speaketh ought, or wryteth.
> The authors meanyng should of ryght be heard,
> He knowethe best to what ende he endytheth:
> Wordes sometymes beare more than the hart behiteth.

Admit therefore the authors exposicion
If playne, for truth: if forst, for his submission.[7]

As well as claiming this 'auncient freedome', the passage also raises interpretative issues of great importance: the relevance of authorial intent in
assessing any criminalised utterance; and the capacity of language to bear
more than one intended meaning. The suggestion that a cryptic criticism
('forst') might be adopted in preference to a 'playne' one out of respect for
the law is a good debating point, if disingenuous. A dialectical relationship
has therefore existed between literary expression and social authority.
Many texts now canonised as literature were written within and against
legal restrictions, while the law has increasingly acknowledged that 'The
authors meanyng should of ryght be heard.'

Many aspects of modern Western culture began to emerge in the
seventeenth century. Among them were empirical science, parliamentary
democracy and the law relating to obscene publications. The common law
first grappled with the issue of indecent expression in the case of Sir Charles
Sedley in 1663. Sedley, a rake as well as a writer, got drunk with friends and
removed his clothing on the balcony of an inn near London's Covent
Garden theatre. He threw bottles over and relieved himself on the heads of
the crowd below, and then delivered a blasphemous speech to the accompaniment of lewd actions. 'In passing sentence against Sedley,' Leonard
W. Levy reports, 'Chief Justice Foster told him that the King's Bench,
being custodians of public morality, meant to punish "profane" actions
against Christianity.'[8] Levy notes that this was the first prosecution for
blasphemy as well as for obscenity. This criminalising of an indecent
performance was extended to the printing of obscene books in the 1727
case of *Rex* v. *Edmund Curll*. Curll had published a pornographic book
called *Venus in the Cloister*, and despite a stout defence, he was convicted of
the new offence of obscene libel. As Ian Hunter, David Saunders and
Dugald Williamson point out, this piece of judicial law-making was 'to
endure in English criminal law for 232 years, until the Obscene
Publications Act of 1959'.[9] The key factor in this development was the
court's belief that a printed work could through its distribution disturb the
'King's peace' by harming public morals. It was not mere Puritanism, then,
but anxieties about social order in the new print economy that led to the
crackdown on sexual expression in writing in the eighteenth century.

In 1857 when the Lord Chief Justice, Lord Campbell, was trying a case of
obscene libel, he became concerned by the trade in pornography in London
and introduced new legislation to supplement the common law. His

Obscene Publications Act empowered magistrates to order the destruction of books found to be obscene. As he spoke in Parliament, Lord Campbell held up a copy of Alexandre Dumas's *La Dame aux Camélias* and spoke of it in the following terms: 'He did not wish to create a category of offences in which this might be included, though it was certainly of a polluting character.'[10] As Walter Kendrick points out in his reading of this event, Campbell seemed to invoke three categories: 'the acknowledged classics' like 'Horace, Juvenal, Voltaire and Lord Byron', which were 'sacrosanct'; works of pornography; and works like Dumas's which lay in the middle, 'polluting', yet somehow outside the intention of the Act. Kendrick speculates that Campbell's ambivalence stemmed from a belief in artistic value, 'the elusive, redemptive spirit that the twentieth century would struggle over and over again to define'.[11]

However, in 1868, Lord Cockburn in the *Hicklin* case provided a definition of obscenity which cut the ground from under this fragile distinction: 'the test of obscenity is this, whether the tendency of the matter charged as obscenity is to deprave and corrupt those whose minds are open to such immoral influences and into whose hands a publication of this sort may fall'. The matter charged in this case concerned a pamphlet, *The Confessional Unmasked*, a piece of anti-Catholic propaganda. Despite the purveyor's religious intentions, the work was found to have a 'tendency to deprave and corrupt', and so was confiscated and destroyed. Ian Hunter and his co-authors rightly emphasise the influence of Victorian ideas of moral hygiene and sexual medicine in this definition, and the consequent pathologising of pornography.[12] The danger of the *Hicklin* test was its breadth, and, abstracted from the cultural milieu and interpretative assumptions of Lord Campbell, it soon began to be applied around the English-speaking world to challenging but serious works of fiction and poetry, and to texts providing guidance on contraception. Among its most zealous adherents was Anthony Comstock, who promoted new American legislation on obscenity in 1873, and then secured a Federal appointment to oversee its enforcement, which he held for four decades. Among his most famous targets were the plays of Bernard Shaw, the publication and performance of which Comstock sought to ban. Shaw defended himself and the progressive, experimental modernist movement by ridiculing the censorial mentality as 'Comstockery'. Comstock not only targeted the avant-garde but ranged across Campbell's three categories, seeking to ban acknowledged classics, provocative contemporary writing and pornography.

From the late nineteenth century the border between literature and pornography which Lord Campbell had acknowledged, and which

Anglophone writers of his generation had respected, began to be transgressed. Campbell's troubled tolerance of Dumas's *La Dame aux Camélias*
was forgotten in the 1888 trial of Henry Vizetelly for publishing translations
of the novels of Zola. Vizetelly was sent to prison. Meanwhile, the new
generation of English writers, like Swinburne, Wilde and Hardy, began to
resist the enforced asexuality of representation in English literature, and
under the banners of realism or aestheticism invoked the freedoms of their
French counterparts to treat sexuality more openly in writing. The decade
of the 1890s was marked by open challenges to Victorian orthodoxy in such
areas as sexual identity and gender politics. The Wilde trials offered one
answer to these challenges, as did the confrontations of Hardy and Swinburne
with editors wanting to censor their work. Disillusioned, Hardy withdrew
into poetry, but the battle between the law of obscenity and modernist
literature was joined by many new writers in the early decades of the
twentieth century, including Theodore Dreiser, D. H. Lawrence, Radclyffe
Hall and James Joyce.

Modernism can be viewed as a revolution of the word, a refusal of
existing codes and conventions of representation.[13] Lawrence and Joyce
were perhaps the most committed in their challenge to the authority of the
censor and Victorian morality. Joyce faced informal censorship when
printers refused to set *Dubliners*. Lawrence's *The Rainbow* was banned on
publication in 1915, and an exhibition of his paintings was closed down in
1926. Both not only claimed the freedom to represent sex, but did so in the
language of the streets. In their most controversial texts, *Lady Chatterley's
Lover* and *Ulysses*, swear-words mingle with other discourses and modes of
expression. Indeed, in analysing their consistent transgression of the boundaries of sexual representation, Allison Pease argues that modernists developed an 'aesthetics of the obscene', that they brought together the
previously separated traditions of the aesthetic and the pornographic.[14]
Not surprisingly, given their calculated deconstruction of the boundary
between literature and pornography, these works were subject both to
immediate censorship and to constant appeal by supporters claiming
their cultural value. Both were the subjects of landmark trials in the
development of obscenity law.

Ulysses is an exhaustive account of one day in the life of Leopold Bloom,
a Jewish advertising salesman. Bloom's mundane thoughts, words and
deeds are, however, patterned in ironic parallelism with the heroic story
of Homer's Odysseus. Its comprehensive inclusiveness and Bloom's complacent acceptance of various physical appetites left it open to censure.
Ulysses first began to be published in instalments in the American *Little*

Review in 1918. However, in 1920, after publishing the chapter containing Leopold Bloom's voyeuristic encounter with Gerty MacDowell, the editors were prosecuted, fined and enjoined not to publish any more excerpts. With book publication impossible in Britain, *Ulysses* was published in Paris by Sylvia Beach, proprietor of the Shakespeare and Company bookshop and a patron of Joyce's, in 1922. Copies sent to Britain were seized by Customs officials. For ten years it was available only in Europe, an illicit item for culturally minded tourists but attracting praise from fellow artists and critics.

In 1932, Random House in America imported a copy with a view to setting up an American edition. As anticipated, this copy, complete with a review article which was specially included inside the covers, was seized by Customs, and Random House disputed the legality of this action. In the ensuing trial, *United States* v. *One Book Called 'Ulysses'* in 1933, Judge John M. Woolsey made a number of key findings. Firstly, he decided to allow expert evidence of the literary merit of the novel from critics. Secondly, he placed great weight on this evidence in ruling that *Ulysses* was a work of art, and not a pornographic book. In addressing himself to whether the book fell within the legal definition of obscenity, Judge Woolsey inferred a purely aesthetic intention on Joyce's part and excluded any intention 'to stir the sex impulses'.[15] Then, the judge turned to the effect of the writing and crucially ruled that the book must be read as a whole, that the complained-of passages should not be read in isolation. On the basis of his own reading, he concluded that it did not 'stir the sex impulses', and was therefore not obscene. As a result, Random House was free to publish *Ulysses*. In doing so, the firm paid tribute to Judge Woolsey by including his judgment in their edition. This action emphasised the legal and social context in which literary texts were written and read. The judge's opinion is also an honoured piece of writing in 'the literature of the law'.[16] The fame and influence of this case have made it a subject for study in Law and Literature. In a thorough analysis of the judgment, Paul Vanderham shows that this ground-breaking decision achieved its very desirable result by means of 'well-intentioned lies'. He is especially critical of the absolute distinction between art and obscenity, and noting allusions to pornography in the novel, asks why a sensual interest cannot coexist with an aesthetic one. While its reasoning may be open to criticism, the aesthetic reading had a liberating effect, not just freeing *Ulysses* but providing grounds for publishers and writers to appeal against bans on other serious modern works that dealt candidly with sex.

Judge Woolsey's approach was adopted by a Philadelphia judge, Curtis Bok, in a 1949 case in which he cleared such major books as *The Studs*

Lonigan Trilogy by James T. Farrell, *Sanctuary* by William Faulkner and *God's Little Acre* by Erskine Caldwell. In a far-sighted section of his judgment, Bok also concluded that the First Amendment operated to protect such texts. However, he was ahead of his time: not only were books still being banned in other jurisdictions, but in 1957 the Supreme Court in the *Roth* case found that 'obscenity, whatever it may be, is not within the area of protected speech and Press under the First Amendment'.[17] However, within a decade, this jurisprudential thicket was to be cleared. The first step was taken in the 1959 trial over the American edition of *Lady Chatterley's Lover* by Judge Frederick van Pelt Bryan. Bryan drew on *Ulysses* and *Roth*: 'Both cases held that to be obscene, the dominant effect of the book must be an appeal to prurient interest – that is to say, shameful or morbid interest in sex. Such a theme must so predominate as to submerge any ideas of "redeeming social importance" which the publication contains.'[18] He read the novel as a whole and found its swear-words to be consistent with character, and its representations of sex integral to the development of the author's ideas on full human living. Thus, the novel had literary merit, did not appeal to the prurient interest and had social importance. Judge Bryan concluded on the constitutional question: 'It is essential to the maintenance of a free society that the severest restrictions be placed upon restraints which may prevent the dissemination of ideas.' He made a distinction which would become important for subsequent cases in the 1960s: 'A work of literature published and distributed through normal channels by a reputable publisher stands on a quite different footing from hard core pornography furtively sold for the purpose of profiting by the titillation of the dirty-minded.'[19] Counsel for the publisher in this case, Charles Rembar, subsequently argued the cases in favour of two long-banned novels, Henry Miller's *Tropic of Cancer* and the infamous eighteenth-century novel, *Memoirs of a Woman of Pleasure* (better known as *Fanny Hill*). In these cases he subtly altered the 'redeeming social importance' test to one of 'redeeming social value', and brought them successfully out of the 'hard-core' category. With these results, the long struggle for the explicit fictional representation of sex in America was won, a victory Rembar announced in a book called *The End of Obscenity*.[20]

Across the Atlantic, in Britain, the 1950s began with an 'anti-vice drive', and in 1954 prosecutions were begun in respect of five novels. However, the ideological conflict experienced in America was repeated, and the prosecutions were mostly unsuccessful. Protests and campaigns for reform eventually led to new legislation, the Obscene Publications Act of 1959. Under this act, the influence of modern ideas on sex, representation and freedom was demonstrable. It created a defence to a charge of publishing an obscene article, that the publication in question was 'justified as being for the public good' on such grounds as 'that it is in the interests of science, literature, art or learning, or of other objects of general concern'.[21] In addition, evidence could be adduced from experts to support arguments of literary merit, or other public good.

This new law was first tested in 1960, when Penguin Books were prosecuted for publishing *Lady Chatterley's Lover*. The trial before Justice Byrne and a jury lasted six days. The defence called thirty-five expert witnesses in support of the novel's literary merit, the prosecution none. Among the defence witnesses were writers like Rebecca West and E. M. Forster, critics like Raymond Williams and Helen Gardner, publishers including Allen Lane, the founder of Penguin, churchmen, lawyers and MPs. In reply to their affirmations of Lawrence's prophetic value as a great artist and critic of sexual repression, the prosecution could only count swear-words, question witnesses' expertise and read out explicit extracts. However, this appeal to a shared commonsense morality failed. When prosecuting counsel suggested in his opening address that the jury ask themselves,

would you approve of your young sons, young daughters – because girls can read as well as boys – reading this book? Is it a book that you would leave lying around in your own house? Is it a book that you would wish even your wife or your servants to read?

the jury looked bemused, and some observers took this communicative failure as evidence that the prosecution presented an outdated and class-bound view of English society and morality, with Lawrence symbolising a newer, freer and more egalitarian England. In the event, the jury returned a verdict of 'Not Guilty' after three hours. Penguin Books sold over 2 million copies of *Lady Chatterley's Lover* and produced an inspired legal-literary spin-off, an edited transcript of the case, *The Trial of Lady Chatterley*.[22] This, then, was an epoch-making trial, inaugurating what John Sutherland called a tide of liberalisation.[23] The result of the long process of judicial and legislative activity in England and America was to overthrow bowdlerism and Comstockery, and to enable literature to explore sexuality as readily as any other aspect of social reality.

Viewed from a greater historical distance, the *Lady Chatterley* trial represents another shift in obscenity law, from the medical-moral theory of *Hicklin* to an aestheticist approach to the text. Analysing the discourses used by the expert witnesses, Ian Hunter and his co-authors identify not 'objective and authoritative evidence of the standing and merit of a work' in this evidence, but 'a demonstration of the use of aesthetic *techniques* of ethical self-fashioning, including a stunning capacity to poetically deepen any sexual description, however pornographic'.[24] These critics, like Vanderham on the *Ulysses* trial, draw on a longer historical perspective, which includes the feminist critique of pornography. That critique first emerged in 1971 with the publication of Kate Millett's *Sexual Politics*, which showed the contempt for women manifest in *Lady Chatterley's Lover* and other recently de-censored books.[25] In two American cities, Minneapolis and Indianapolis, feminist campaigners formed an alliance with moral conservatives to pass anti-pornography ordinances. These laws were short-lived.[26] In a 1992 Canadian case, *R. v. Butler*, judicial notice was taken of the potential harm of pornography to women and children. The Supreme Court of Canada concluded that obscene publications might legitimately be restricted on the grounds of social harm, even though 'it might be construed as violating the Charter of Rights and Freedoms'.[27] While such attempts have been controversial, even among feminists, balancing such factors as social-science research into links between pornography and rape, human rights in the area of sexuality and pragmatic concerns about the effectiveness of bans, the regulation of pornography remains a live issue, although more focused on visual media and the Internet than on books.[28] This is most apparent with respect to child pornography. In the 1982 case of *New York* v. *Ferber*, the American Supreme Court unanimously outlawed such material. Justice Byron White said that, 'the prevention of sexual exploitation and abuse of children constitutes a government objective of surpassing importance'.[29]

Blasphemy is one common-law offence that seemed for much of the twentieth century to be a dead letter, but which was resurrected in the 1970s and became a vital topic in the 1990s when the Ayatollah Khomeini's fatwa was pronounced upon the novelist Salman Rushdie for his novel, *The Satanic Verses*. As the American constitutionalist Leonard W. Levy noted, 'A criminal law, even if only a vestigial relic, never dies until it is repealed or held unconstitutional.'[30] Historians of blasphemy, like Levy and Joss Marsh, also point to the blurred boundaries between it and its near neighbours, obscenity and sedition: 'Blasphemy is not just an irreligious crime; political considerations have often tinged prosecutions, as have considerations of the public welfare and morality.'[31]

Blasphemy emerged from the ecclesiastical law of heresy to become a category in the English criminal law during the seventeenth century. As Richard Webster writes, 'In 1676, during the trial of an apparently deranged man, who claimed that Jesus Christ was a bastard and a whore-master and that religion was a cheat, the Lord Chief Justice, Sir Matthew Hale, first laid down the principle that Christianity was part of the law of England, and that a threat to the Church was, by its very nature, a threat to the State.'[32] Despite the enormous changes in law and society since then, this crime remains. In the words of a standard modern textbook, 'Blasphemy consists in the use of language, written or spoken, having a tendency to vilify the Christian religion or the Bible; it is not blasphemy to attack any other religion.'[33] Hale's conferral of legal protection upon Christianity has been enormously influential, not only in extending the life of blasphemy into secular modernity, but in providing Christian apologists with a weapon against freedom of expression, in matters of sexuality and politics a well as in questions of religious belief.

Three hundred years later, in 1977, the last successful English prosecution was brought against the editor of *Gay News* for publishing a homosexual love poem, 'The Love that Dares to Speak its Name', by James Kirkup. In this poem one of the Roman guards at Christ's crucifixion is a homosexual, whose desires are prompted by the sight of His body. The prosecution was brought by Mary Whitehouse, as part of her long-standing crusade against pornography. The presiding judge directed the jury as follows:

The offence of blasphemous libel today occurs when there is published anything concerning God, Christ or the Christian religion in terms so scurrilous, abusive or offensive as to outrage the feelings of any member of or sympathiser with the Christian religion and which would tend to lead to a breach of the peace.[34]

The subsequent conviction and fine were upheld on appeal, though an additional sentence of imprisonment was revoked. The tide of liberalisation and secularism was not strong enough to encompass the frank expression of sexual dissidence in a religious context.[35]

The requirement of a likely breach of the peace in modern blasphemy laws indicates that doctrinal unorthodoxy in itself is no longer prohibited from expression. This qualification emerged in the nineteenth century, during one of the many campaigns against atheist publications. In 1883, another Chief Justice, Lord Coleridge, stated in the trial of G. W. Foote, editor of the *Freethinker*, 'I now lay it down as law, that, if the decencies of controversy are observed, even the fundamentals of religion may be attacked without a person being guilty of blasphemous libel.'[36] In her illuminating study of working-class atheism, Joss Marsh points out that Coleridge's concept of 'the decencies of controversy' was a class-based ideal, one which acknowledged intellectual debates in the quarterlies and treatises of the intellectual and cultural establishment but refused to recognise working-class journals with their parodies and satires, their plain statements of unbelief and critiques of religious ideology. After studying the clustering of cases across the century, Marsh argues that blasphemy laws 'were invoked at times of special political stress and cultural pressure'.[37] This argument is as true of the 1970s as it is of the periods Marsh studies, the 1810s, the 1840s and the 1880s. The printer Richard Carlile was imprisoned in 1819 for publishing Tom Paine's *The Age of Reason*, an ideological critique of the Bible first suppressed in the 1790s. Its reappearance in a new era of working-class discontent, which culminated in the Peterloo massacre, convinced the authorities that Paine's rationalism in religion and radicalism in politics was an incendiary combination for its working-class readership. In this case and in the later ones, the possibility that artisans might engage in debate about social institutions was perceived as 'a threat to the State'.[38]

In a notable trial of 1841, Edward Moxon, the publisher of Wordsworth and Tennyson, was charged with blasphemous libel for producing an edition of Shelley's early poem, *Queen Mab*. He was defended by the playwright, barrister and Member of Parliament, Thomas Talfourd. Although unsuccessful, Talfourd put up a strong case, arguing that the passages in the indictment needed to be read in the context of the whole work, that the work formed part of a legitimate edition of the poet's lifelong corpus, and that this was an estimable literary enterprise, not a blasphemous one. As Joss Marsh notes, the terms of Talfourd's defence would be echoed one hundred years later, by the lawyers defending Penguin Books for publishing D. H. Lawrence's *Lady Chatterley's Lover*.[39]

The English law of blasphemy was updated in a notable case of 1917, *Bowman* v. *Secular Society*, in which the House of Lords found that the aims of the Secular Society did not contravene the blasphemy law. Lord Sumner found that 'the gist of the offence of blasphemy is a supposed tendency . . . to shake the fabric of society generally', and he concluded: 'My Lords, with all respect for the great names of the lawyers who have used it, the phrase "Christianity is part of the law of England" is really not law; it is rhetoric.'[40] While the present study would suggest that all law is rhetoric, this pronouncement is also notable for its philosophical materialism, as if the secular movement of twentieth-century Western history has been registered in the law. Further evidence for this proposition comes from the fact that there were no successful prosecutions for blasphemy from 1921 till 1977.

The decline of blasphemy represents a victory for liberalism and secularism in the West. In this context, literature itself has come to acquire quasi-sacred status. However, other societies have resisted these aspects of modernity and have demanded that writers respect their religious scriptures and traditions. With contemporary transnational communications and the movement of people across borders, the principles of literary liberty and religious respect were bound to come into conflict. The publication of Salman Rushdie's novel *The Satanic Verses*, in 1988, is the most recent *cause célèbre* of blasphemy in literature. This novel included in its scenes and its language material gravely offensive to Muslims, prompting book burnings in Bradford, a ban in India, riots and a death sentence on its author by the Ayatollah Khomeini of Iran. Representations were made by British Muslims to ban the book, but these failed. They also instituted a prosecution for blasphemy, but the Divisional Court ruled that the offence only applied when the object of ridicule was the Christian religion. In the face of these disappointments, protests against the book escalated. Rushdie himself was placed in police protection. Writers in England and America defended his freedom to express his artistic vision, but in an unfortunate by-product of the affair, Rushdie's exercise in provocation strengthened the position of fundamentalists and extremists in the Muslim world. Racial violence against Muslims increased, with several being killed, including two moderate Imams in Belgium, and many dozens injured in the first year after publication. Only a summary of this complex story of law, language and competing beliefs can be told here, but it does suggest that the law is at present inadequate and should either be amended to include scurrilous attacks on all religions, or repealed and replaced by a new offence of inciting hatred against any religious group.[41]

The third category of criminalised utterance at common law is sedition. The leading English authority on libel and slander, Peter Carter-Ruck, defines seditious libel thus: 'Any words, whether written or spoken which are calculated to disturb the internal peace and government of the country and which are published with that intention constitute a seditious libel.' He invokes the comprehensive definition given by *Stephen's Digest of the Criminal Law*, where it is stated that a seditious intention is an intention

to bring into hatred, or contempt, or to excite to disaffection against the person of Her Majesty, her heirs or descendants, or the government and constitution of the UK as by law established, or either House of Parliament, or the administration of justice, or to excite Her Majesty's subjects to attempt, otherwise than by lawful means, the alteration of any matter in Church or state by law established, or to raise discontent or disaffection in Her Majesty's subjects, or to promote feelings of ill-will and hostility between different classes of such subjects.[42]

The law of seditious libel developed in its modern form in the late seventeenth and early eighteenth centuries, after other methods of controlling press criticism of government, such as licensing and treason, had proved inefficient.[43] The wide scope of this offence caught many writers, including Daniel Defoe in 1704. With the emergence of civil society, literature became a means of soliciting political change, and sedition a valued tool for resisting it. The radical parliamentarian and founder of the critical journal *The North Briton*, John Wilkes, was prosecuted in 1763 but escaped by pleading parliamentary immunity. With the American and French revolutions, sedition trials became the frequent recourse of a British government desperate to resist constitutional change.[44]

Seditious libel was part of the law exported to the British colonies. One of the most notable developments in the law occurred in America in 1735, during the trial of John Peter Zenger. This case 'established the fundamental principle that a true statement could not be punished as a seditious libel, no matter how vociferous the criticism of the government'.[45] Zenger claimed a 'liberty to know, to utter, and to argue freely', the very freedoms later incorporated in the First Amendment.[46] Despite this enactment, sedition remained a recognised legal restraint on speech in the United States. Its use by government peaked during and after the First World War. The modern, restrictive concept of sedition was first enunciated in a powerful dissenting judgment by Justice Oliver Wendell Holmes in the *Abrams* case of 1919. Holmes urged that sedition prosecutions could only be justified under the Constitution if a 'clear and present danger' existed: 'it is only the present danger of immediate evil or an intent to bring it about that warrants Congress in setting a limit to the expression of opinion where private rights are concerned'.[47] Finally accepted in 1969, this view of the law today seems the only approach compatible with liberal democratic principles. Carter-Ruck reports that the last British prosecution took place, unsuccessfully, in 1947.[48] The law of sedition was used widely by the British in India in a vain effort to suppress the independence movement. The most celebrated trial was that of 'Mahatma' Gandhi in 1922, for three articles he had written. Gandhi pleaded guilty, and in his closing speech critiqued the racial bias of British justice and the exploitation of India by the British Government. He ended by inviting the severest penalty for himself:

I am here, therefore, to invite and submit cheerfully, to the highest penalty that can be inflicted upon me for what in law is a deliberate crime and what appears to me to be the highest duty of a citizen. The only course open to you, the judge, is either to resign your post, and thus dissociate yourself from evil if you feel that the law you are called upon to administer is an evil and that in reality I am innocent, or to inflict on me the severest penalty if you believe that the system and the law you are assisting to administer are for the good of the people of this country and that my activity is therefore injurious to the public weal.[49]

Gandhi was sentenced to six years' imprisonment.

DEFAMATION

Article 19 of the International Covenant on Civil and Political Rights recognises that respect for the reputation of other people operates as a limit to freedom of expression. The making of derogatory statements against another person has long been proscribed by legal systems throughout the world. Carter-Ruck notes that provisions against defamation occur in the Bible, in ancient Roman law and in the Anglo-Saxon codes. He uses as his starting point a definition from a lay publication, *The Caxton Encyclopedia*: 'The publication of a statement tending to discredit a person in the eyes of reasonable members of society generally.'[50] The implication of this definition is that defamation is a private matter, a civil wrong; however, from its inception there was a recognition that attacks upon reputation had consequences for the public weal. The category of criminal libel, then, has also been a significant force in the development of laws that bear upon writers and writing. Criminal libel is generally traced back to medieval statutes enacted to punish 'devisers of tales whereby discord or occasion of discord have thence arisen between the King and his people or great men of this realm'. The first such statute, known as *Scandalum Magnatum*, was passed in 1275.[51] Similar laws were enacted in the following centuries, but by the sixteenth century such 'tales' were seen as an affront to the individual referred to, as well as an undermining of public order. In this context, duelling and civil claims for redress against defamation became widespread. The historian Lawrence Stone has pointed to the existence of a 'cult of reputation' at this time:

One of the most characteristic features of the age was its hyper-sensitive insistence upon the overriding importance of reputation. Many of the punishments of the day, the stocks, the pillory, the apology read out in the market-place, were based upon the theory that public humiliation was a more effective penalty than a swingeing fine. The extraordinary seventeenth-century code of the duel, under which men felt impelled to risk their lives to avenge a casual word, was merely a cancerous growth from the same cells.[52]

M. Lindsay Kaplan argues that a 'culture of slander' was rampant in early modern England, affecting both law and literature:

Whether slander increased as a result of anxiety over reputation brought on by other factors, or if it in fact contributed to this unease ... it is clear that the desire to preserve reputation in early modern England positioned defamation as a central consideration of the period. This anxiety also appears in contemporary discussions about maintaining authority and order on both the local and national levels. The capacity of discordant words to disrupt the peace or jeopardize the stability of the realm was an increasing concern of the English state by the end of the sixteenth century.[53]

In the early seventeenth century, James I was sufficiently exercised by the persistence of libellous gossip that he supplemented his edicts against it with poetic interventions in the 'culture of slander'.[54]

Carter-Ruck suggests that as duelling attracted criminal penalties, the civil action of libel developed apace.[55] Rosemary Kegl has analysed the gender distribution of plaintiffs, noting that women preponderate in the cases of sexual slander brought before the ecclesiastical courts, while men form the majority in the secular courts, where allegations concerning probity in business could be heard. 'Historians usually interpret the disproportionately large number of women who appear as plaintiffs in church defamation cases as an indication both that women were more vulnerable to sexual slander than men and that, unlike men, their reputations were dependent primarily on their sexual behaviour.'[56] By 1647 a firm sense of the kinds of damage through words that the common-law courts would redress had emerged. The formulation in *March's Actions for Slander* was, according to Carter-Ruck, approximately the same in principle as the law of slander as we know it today:

All scandalous words which touch or concern a man in his life liberty or member, or any corporal punishment; or which scandals a man in an office or place of trust; or in his calling or function by which he gains his living; or which tend to the slandering of his title or disinheritance; or to the loss of his advancement or preferment, or any other particular damage; or lastly which charge a man to have any dangerous or infectious disease.[57]

The destructive effects of slander were explored in many literary works, while the cultural importance of reputation is perhaps best evidenced by the praise extolled in Shakespeare's *Othello*:

> Good name in man and woman, dear my lord
> Is the immediate jewel of their souls;
> Who steals my purse steals trash; 'tis something, nothing;
> 'Twas mine 'tis his, and has been slave to thousands;
> But he that filches from me my good name
> Robs me of that which not enriches him,
> And makes me poor indeed.[58]

Othello is one of the many narratives of slander in the literature of the time. As well as representing the consequences of defamation, however, poetry and drama came under suspicion as forms that allowed the criticism of individuals. The poetic theorist George Puttenham defended poets as 'trumpetters of all praise and also of slaunder (not slaunder but well-deserued [i.e. deserved] reproch)'.[59] Legal writers were unimpressed with this sort of equivocation, with the transvaluation of damaging statements as literary truth telling, and tended to impute slanderous intent to the poets. Sir Edward Coke CJ in a 1606 case, for example, assimilated the two types of utterance when he defined libel as 'an epigram, rhyme, or other writing'.[60]

Suspicion about poetic libel was especially aroused by satire, which became a genre of increased importance after the Restoration. Michael Seidel reports how in this period 'satire, libel, lampoon and slander were inextricably mixed'.[61] Writers like Dryden, Swift and Pope validated and modelled their poetic critiques on the work of Roman satirists like Juvenal and Horace. According to Seidel,

satirists and lampoonists were ingenious in figuring ways to represent current state affairs indirectly: lampoons of court officials, pasquinades on current events, mock court-session poems, instruction poems to historical painters, mock pope-burning procession verses, dialogue poems, dream visions, pseudo-monologues, songs, odes, dramatic epilogues and prologues, verse essays, and formal verse satires were part of the abundant satiric literature of the Restoration. Every significant writer of the period contributed to that abundance.[62]

However, the poets kept within the law by disguising their targets under false names and by an artistic commitment to wit that complicated the criticism and gave aesthetic pleasure to the audience. Indeed, in opening his *Imitations of Horace* (1733), Alexander Pope disputed Coke's conflation: '*there is not in the world a greater Error, than that which Fools are so apt to fall into, and Knaves with good reason to encourage, the mistaking of a* Satyrist *for a* Libeller; *whereas to a* true Satyrist *nothing is so odious as a* Libeller'.[63]

In 1792, at the height of the French Revolution, when political tensions in England were producing repressive laws, Fox's Libel Act provided some measure of protection for free speech. Under this act, the right of a jury to determine whether a statement or publication was libellous was confirmed. Although directed at criminal libel trials, the act's declaration of the functions of judge and jury was taken to apply to the common law as well. The presence of a jury was instrumental in the acquittal of many radical writers in the ensuing decades. Juries also had the role of assessing damages in civil defamation cases. Fox's Act is a landmark in the history of press freedom.

Newspapers and periodicals became ever more important and respectable forums of debate as the nineteenth century advanced, and the law of defamation reflected this. An important development for literary culture was the acceptance that cultural criticism came within the defence of 'fair comment' on matters of public interest. An 1863 case, *Campbell* v. *Spottiswoode* established that a work of art or literature may be criticised in a review, 'but the critic must not use the occasion to make a personal attack upon the artist or author, for usually the work cannot warrant an attack of this nature'.[64] The scope of fair comment was tested in 1877, when James Whistler sued John Ruskin over the following remarks on his painting 'Nocturne in Black and Gold: The Falling Rocket': 'I have seen, and heard, much of Cockney impudence before now; but never expected to hear a coxcomb ask two hundred guineas for flinging a pot of paint in the public's face.' The jury returned a verdict for Whistler but only awarded him a farthing in damages. He did not recover costs, and as a result was bankrupted. In 1888 the Law of Libel Amendment Act facilitated public debate in the media by according privilege to 'fair and accurate contemporaneous reports of judicial proceedings published in newspapers', and reports of public meetings.[65]

By the beginning of the twentieth century, the transition of libel from a predominantly criminal to a predominantly civil cause of action was complete, and its scope expanded to comprehend imputations made in fictional contexts. The case of *Hulton* v. *Jones* (1910) was brought by a barrister named Artemus Jones, who read a light sketch published in a newspaper about the resort of Dieppe, in which was included a fictional character, a churchwarden from Peckham bearing the name of Artemus Jones. This character was seen holidaying in Dieppe with a woman other than his wife. The plaintiff was not a churchwarden from Peckham and had not been to Dieppe, but the court found in his favour on the basis that acquaintances of his who had read the sketch had thought it was referring to him. The imputation of adultery was damaging to his reputation, and the newspaper had taken no care to check whether the name belonged to any real person. The intention of the writer was irrelevant; reasonable readers could elicit a meaning that undermined the plaintiff's reputation. This case opened the door to claims of libel by fiction, in which the identification of characters with living people was alleged to have induced hatred, ridicule or contempt for the latter. The disclaimer commonly printed in the prefatory pages of a novel, 'This is a work of fiction, and any resemblance to any person living or dead is merely coincidental', confirms the genre but does not shield the writer or publisher against suits for defamatory content. Some such 'fictional' libels have been proven, as in a case involving Laurie Lee's autobiographically based novel *Cider with Rosie*, in which an implicit allegation of arson at a local piano factory drew a writ from its owners.

They recovered damages, and Lee altered his piano factory to a boilerworks in subsequent editions.[66] A similar case in America concerned the portrait of a clinical psychologist in a 1971 novel called *Touching* by Gwen Mitchell. A living practitioner was identified with the fictional protagonist and with the nude encounter therapy sessions he conducted, and brought a successful suit.[67]

In post-modern culture, where distinctions between history and fiction, and past and present are blurred, and where literary texts often present radical critiques of the centres of power, the conscious debunking of famous people may result in defamation. The former Indian Prime Minister Mrs Indira Gandhi is a character in Rushdie's *Midnight's Children*, both under her own name and under the soubriquet The Widow. This is an inventive, linguistically rich comic novel about India since independence. Mrs Gandhi is severely criticised in the novel, but while unable to complain about the invective piled on The Widow, she sued the novel's publishers over a personal claim that her son Sanjay had accused her of neglecting her late husband, who had died of a heart attack. She won the case, obtaining a public apology, an order that the passage in question be deleted from all future editions of the book and an order that Rushdie and his publisher pay her legal costs.[68]

Another manifestation of post-modern literature is the unparalleled interest in autobiography and memoir among readers and critics alike. While literary theory has tended to stress the fictive elements in these genres, and in the notion of personal identity, the law of defamation continues to privilege the factual and to uphold the reputations of real individuals. In a recent Australian case, two members of the Federal Cabinet and their wives sued the publisher Random House Australia over a story told in a political memoir by scriptwriter, novelist and playwright Bob Ellis. Despite the montage structure and anecdotal basis of the book, the court found that the sexual meaning of the story told about the plaintiffs would be interpreted as true, and impact negatively on their reputations.[69]

In *New York Times* v. *Sullivan* (1964) the American Supreme Court reviewed a suit brought by the Police Commissioner of Montgomery, Alabama, against the newspaper for publishing an advertisement protesting against the police's treatment of Martin Luther King and his fellow civil rights activists. The Alabama Courts upheld a jury award of $500,000 against the *New York Times*. In a groundbreaking decision, the Supreme Court set aside this order, and held that the advertisement was protected under the First Amendment. Mindful of the importance of free speech in a democracy, the Court declared that 'public discussion is a political duty', and that a public official could not succeed in a libel suit unless he or she proved not only that the statement in question was false, but that the defendant knew it was false, or proceeded with reckless disregard as to whether it was false or not.[70] Thus a new defence, the public figures defence, was added to the American law of defamation in an attempt to prevent crippling damages from being inflicted on the press in a context of deep-seated political and social conflict.[71] Although this law has been criticised, its adoption in other countries might prevent political figures from exploiting the current law to prevent adverse publicity, as the now-disgraced Jeffrey Archer did in England.[72]

The *Sullivan* ruling was extended to criminal libel in the Supreme Court case of *Garrison* v. *Louisiana*. With this recognition of the democratic interest in open political expression, the offence of criminal libel became hard to sustain. As Justice Brennan noted, 'under modern conditions, when the rule of law is generally accepted as a substitute for private physical measures, it can hardly be urged that the maintenance of peace requires a criminal prosecution for private defamation'.[73] Justices Black and Douglas were more direct: 'under our Constitution, there is absolutely no place in this country for the old, discredited English Star Chamber law of seditious criminal libel'.[74] Despite these exhortations, criminal libel has remained on the statute books in many states, and prosecutions, while rare, are not unknown. Even in democracies without a Bill of Rights, such as Britain and Australia, the political culture is hostile to criminal libel. No prose-cution has been mounted in Australia since 1950, when the Communist Party member Frank Hardy was charged over his *roman à clef* about political corruption in Melbourne, *Power Without Glory*. The central character in the novel, John West, is based on the businessman John Wren, but the case was brought by Mrs Wren over a claim in the novel that she had an affair which produced an illegitimate child. If this sounds more like a case for civil than criminal libel, the context of the Cold War partly accounts for the public prosecution. It was, in addition, a tactical move by Wren to punish Hardy without exposing the truth and public interest of his claims about Wren himself from being adjudicated upon. The tactic failed, for the defence argued that the portrait of Mrs Wren needed to be seen in context and thus introduced other sections of the book into evidence, to be duly reported by the press. Hardy was acquitted, and the novel became a bestseller.[75]

As new media of communication are invented, the law of defamation is adapted to ensure the preservation of individual reputation. Such an adaptation occurred in 1916, when Princess Irina Youssoupoff successfully sued MGM over a representation of herself in the film *Rasputin – The Mad Monk*. In a move that has become familiar, Hollywood producers introduced a fictitious love element into a historical narrative, thereby compromising the exiled princess's reputation. More recently and more radically, the invention of the World Wide Web and the emergence of digital technology have presented new possibilities for creative expression, and with them, new ways of reading and writing. One such form is hypertext, in which blocks of text are connected by various electronic links and can thus be read in different sequences. Its effects are described by Ilana Snyder: 'Hypertext differs from printed text by offering readers multiple paths through a body of information: it allows them to make their own connections, to incorporate their own links and to produce their own meanings.'[76] A growing body of theoretical and creative work on and in the new media is already demonstrating their potential to transform cultural production and participation. One of the recurrent values articulated in this literature is that the Internet should be a zone of freedom. Theodore Holm Nelson, who coined the tem 'hypertext', markets his *Project Xanadu* (which aims to combine an electronic archive of all existing books with a new online publishing system) as 'the most audacious and specific plan for knowledge, freedom and a better world yet to come out of computerdom'.[77] Beneath such hyperbole lies a real concern with freedom of expression, and an awareness that 'hypertext networks have immense political ramifications'.[78] In this medium defamation presents new challenges to the law. The balance between the private right not to be traduced and the public right to a free exchange of ideas is hard to strike in a hypertext environment. In *Godfrey* v. *Demon Internet Ltd*, a defamatory email contribution was published on an internet discussion group and was not removed when the plaintiff requested it. Was the defendant a publisher, within the terms of the Defamation Act 1996, or merely an innocent disseminator? Given the voluminous traffic on its many sites, and the on-going nature of communication in the medium, what was the internet service provider's responsibility? The trial judge found that the defence of innocent dissemination ceased to apply once the defendant chose to leave the offending statement on its site.[79] Demon entered an appeal but settled before the appeal was heard. The case would be differently decided in the United States, where legislation has been passed to protect internet service providers from such libel suits.[80] An Australian case addresses a question raised by the transnational reach of the Internet: if an online journal contains defamatory matter, where is the journal published – in the place where it was written, or where it was read? This question, and the related one regarding jurisdiction came before the High Court of Australia in *Dow Jones* v. *Gutnick*. The court held that libellous statements in *Barron's Online* had been published in the Australian state of Victoria when downloaded.[81]

COPYRIGHT

In 1704, fresh from his imprisonment and determined to succeed as a professional writer, Daniel Defoe wrote *An Essay on the Regulation of the Press*. In this work, he advocates a new law governing writing and publication, a code that would define the areas of prohibited expression, and the penalties for breach, and that would above all secure for writers the property in their work and protect them from literary piracy:

> The Law we are upon, effectually suppresses this most villainous Practice, for every Author being oblig'd to set his Name to the Book he writes, has, by this Law, an undoubted exclusive Right to the Property of it. The Clause in the Law is a Patent to the Author, and settles the Propriety of the Work wholly in himself, or in such to whom he shall assign it; and 'tis reasonable it should be so: For if an Author has not the right of a Book, after he has made it, and the benefit be not his own, and the Law will not protect him in that Benefit, 'twould be very hard the Law should pretend to punish him for it.[82]

Defoe's essay was an intervention in a political debate over how best to regulate the expanding book market.[83] In this new commercial context, he argued, a regime of compulsory licensing of publications, such as had been in place until 1694, was no longer appropriate. It was open to partisan abuse, and arbitrary enforcement, and was inimical to the promotion of knowledge. In the event, his suggestion of a comprehensive law was not taken up, and Defoe himself was to spend more time in prison. But the idea of an 'exclusive right to the property' in a book and the argument for laws preventing unauthorised profiting from it were highly persuasive in an emergent market economy. Within five years, Parliament was debating its first copyright law.

Before proceeding to the history of copyright, it is useful to place the emergence of this concept in context. Defoe's argument that writers have a property right in their texts and are exclusively entitled to the profits of their verbal creativity may not strike us as controversial or even novel, but that is because our ideas of literature and authorship as involving an original creation which can be owned have been shaped by the concept of copyright itself. Copyright is one of the clearest instances of the interrelation of legal and literary ideas, of literary concepts feeding into legal doctrine, and legal categories then shaping cultural practice. Not surprisingly, it is one of the focal points of Law and Literature studies.

The *Oxford English Dictionary* foregrounds the centrality of ideas of originality and authorship in modern copyright doctrine: 'The exclusive right given by law for a certain term of years to an author, composer, designer, etc. (or his assignee), to print, publish, and sell copies of his original work.'[84] Although these assumptions seem more or less natural to us today, a quick glance at other societies shows that they are quite specific to Anglo-American culture. In ancient Egypt, originality in art was not encouraged or rewarded; rather, any deviation from previous work was prohibited. Similarly, in traditional Chinese culture the highest value was to produce as exact an imitation of the work of an older artist as possible, thereby enhancing the tradition. In Western Europe until the Renaissance, writers tended to retell stories and rework known tropes, rather than to aspire to originality. Most if not all of Shakespeare's plays are combinations of plots and motifs drawn from existing works, as the researches of Kenneth Muir and others have shown.[85] Shakespeare's version of *Coriolanus* draws heavily not just on the original Latin biography of the hero in Plutarch's *Lives*, but on Thomas North's translation of this text. This and many other examples have led Stephen Orgel to answer the charge of plagiarism sometimes directed at Renaissance artists and writers, and to propose a culture of imitation, in which there was an 'enviably easy intercourse between writer and writer, between scholarship and creativity', and apt formulations were considered as 'the common property of the world of letters'.[86] Only after the seventeenth century 'did quotation marks serve to enclose an utterance as the exclusive material of another'.[87] Before then, they drew attention to passages worthy of copying. Collaboration was commonplace in the writing of plays, with well-known partnerships like Beaumont and Fletcher, and temporary ones like those between Shakespeare and Fletcher, and Shakespeare and Thomas Middleton. Plays were owned by theatre companies, and it was a notable moment in the emergence of modern notions of authorship when Ben Jonson bought his plays back, and edited them for print publication in 1612.[88]

Ben Jonson is a transitional figure: in addition to printing his plays, he had an aristocratic patron and circulated his poems in manuscript. Thus, he belonged to the culture of courtly letters, whilst foreshadowing the rise of professional authors in a market economy. The transformation of literary culture, in which writers sold their verbal wares for money, depended on the availability of printing technology to meet the demands of an expanded reading public beyond the upper classes. Alongside these material developments went intellectual changes, especially ideas of property and identity. John Locke's *Two Treatises of Government* (1690) defined property as a natural right belonging to the individual, in terms which profoundly influenced law and society in eighteenth-century Britain.[89] Locke's definition of how property is created,

> Whatsoever he removes out of the State that Nature hath provided, and left it in, he hath mixed his *Labour* with it, and joyned to it something that is his own, and thereby makes it his *Property*,

was applicable to writing as much as to farming or manufacture. In the literary economy, invention was newly privileged over imitation, and the elements of originality and individual creation began to crystallise around the idea of the writer as author.

The new copyright law, the *Statute of Anne*, was passed in 1710, and had as its full title, 'An Act for the Encouragement of Learning, by Vesting the Copies of Printed Books in the Authors or Purchasers of such Copies, during the Times Therein Mentioned'. 'Copies' in this title was ambiguous, and meant both copyrights, and the manuscript of the work.[90] The full title also indicates that booksellers along with authors were owners of copyrights, and thus targets of the law. Indeed, Lyman Ray Patterson, the historian of copyright, argues that this law was not really focused on authors but was 'a trade-regulation statute enacted to bring order to the chaos in the book trade by the final lapse in 1694 of . . . the Licensing Act of 1662, and to prevent a continuation of the booksellers' monopoly'.[91] The act allowed existing copyrights to be extended for twenty-one years, a limited extension of the booksellers' proprietary interests, but added a new copyright for authors or their assignees in new books for a term of fourteen years, at the end of which the right reverted to the author, if still alive, for another fourteen years.

The effect of this act was to curtail the perpetual copyrights held by the London booksellers under the previous regime, to allow new players into the field and to confer on authors a property right in their writings. In practice, the last right was usually assigned to a bookseller, and it was booksellers who took up the cause of authors' rights as a way of protecting their own commercial interests in the courts. After the expiration of the twenty-one years, the London booksellers found their provincial rivals printing and selling their titles, and undercutting their prices. In a series of cases before the courts, they argued that authors had a perpetual copyright under common law, which the *Statute of Anne* had not modified, and that as assignees, they retained the exclusive right to print all older works.

Their competitors, especially an Edinburgh practitioner named Alexander Donaldson, argued against any common-law right. The 'Great Question of Literary Property' exercised the entire public sphere, until it was settled by the narrowest of margins in the House of Lords in *Donaldson v. Becket*.[92] This case decided that the *Statute of Anne* had dissolved the author's perpetual copyright at common law, and that copyright was to be regulated by statute.[93]

While authors had a considerable stake in the debates over literary property, they were really only bit players in the eighteenth-century struggles over copyright. In the following century, however, they were to become the very subjects of the discourse. This shift is a result of the cultural movement known as Romanticism. Although the beginnings of the Romantic age are usually dated by reference to the revolutions in America or France, or to the publication in 1798 of Wordsworth and Coleridge's *Lyrical Ballads*, an important preparatory step in the formation of Romantic ideas of authorship was the publication of Edward Young's *Conjectures on Original Composition* in 1759. In this influential work, Young laid the foundations of Romantic aesthetics by praising originality and genius over imitation: 'The mind of a man of Genius is a fertile and pleasant field, pleasant as *Elysium*, and fertile as *Tempe*; it enjoys a perpetual spring. Of that spring, *Originals* are the fairest Flowers: *Imitations* are of quicker growth, but fainter bloom.'[94] A generation later, the artist as genius and the originality of truly artistic composition were the cornerstones of a new approach to poetic practice and theory in England and Germany. In the preface to the 1800 edition of *Lyrical Ballads*, Wordsworth argued that, 'all good poetry is the spontaneous overflow of powerful feelings; but though this be true, poems to which any value can be attached were never produced in any variety of subjects but by a man who being possessed of more than usual organic sensibility had also thought long and deeply'.[95] In this manifesto for the new poetry, Wordsworth redefines the genre as an outpouring of the author's personal, and superior, sensibility, a fusion of thought and emotion, a unique and powerful expression of self. The problem for such an author is that he (and the gender is emphasised) may not be appreciated by readers, may not make a commercial success. In the 1815 edition of his *Poetical Works* Wordsworth confronted this reality whilst affirming his genius: 'every author, as far as he is great, and at the same time *original*, has to create the taste by which he is to be enjoyed'.[96] This vision of the solitary struggle of authorship, what Peter Jaszi and Martha Woodmansee call 'the heroic self-presentation of Romantic poets', belied the close involvement of Dorothy Wordsworth in her brother's poetic output, yet it became central to the further development of copyright law.[97]

In 1836, Thomas Talfourd, an admirer of Wordsworth and a friend of Dickens, sought to reform the period of copyright protection so as to strengthen the value of the 'literary property' held by authors. Wordsworth invested an extraordinary amount of energy in supporting Talfourd's parliamentary campaign, travelling to London to lobby politicians, writing letters to individuals and editors of journals, composing poems on the subject and providing arguments for Talfourd to use. Not only did the Romantic ideology of the author provide the rationale for viewing literature as property, but the example of Wordsworth himself was invoked as evidence of the justice of a new copyright term of the author's life, plus sixty years. Opponents of the bill pointed to Wordsworth's self-interest, and his egotism in assuming the attentions of posterity. More constructively, they mounted arguments based on free trade and the value of 'useful knowledge' over poetry. As a result, the bill was withdrawn or defeated several times, before an acceptable compromise was put forward in 1842, involving a term of forty-two years.[98] The passage of this bill involved 'an intense dialogue between the legal and literary cultures'.[99] Above all, poetic theory was enshrined in law, and what Mark Rose has called 'the author–work relation' was embodied in the institution of copyright, endowing the author 'with legal reality' in a form that has proved resistant to cultural change or critique ever since.[100]

Copyright was among the eighteenth-century ideas incorporated into the American Constitution, and Congress enacted its first copyright statute in 1790. This act set up a term of fourteen years for existing and new works, with a like renewal for living authors of new works. It also confined the law to works published in America by Americans, a provision which enabled foreign works to be pirated, much to the chagrin of Charles Dickens fifty years later. The first major copyright dispute, *Wheaton* v. *Peters* (1834), concerned the published reports of Supreme Court decisions. Similarly to Wordsworth's poems, the reports had not proved immediately popular, but were expected to gather a slowly increasing readership over the years. Peters, on succeeding Wheaton as court reporter, produced a cheaper reprint of his and other previous reports, as part of his own series, ignoring Wheaton's assertion of copyright. The case has been called 'the American counterpart to *Donaldson* v. *Becket*' in that it dealt with the question of statutory versus common-law rights and held that copyright was exclusively governed by the statute.[101] In a case that was evidently 'close to the bone', the Supreme Court held that no reporter could have copyright in its judicial opinions, although commentary thereon was copyrightable.[102] In a detailed study of the case, Meredith L. McGill has shown that the Court privileged public interests over authorial property rights: '*Perpetual* private ownership and control was unacceptable in a culture that regarded the free circulation of texts as the sign and guarantor of liberty.' That the texts in question were law reports only intensified the claims of republican ideology. In America, unlike England, 'the central tenets of republicanism, which ally the printed text with the public sphere, qualify the impact of principles of "possessive individualism" on the development of literary property and, in concert with developments in print technology and publishing practice, work to postpone the emergence of the modern property-owning author until late in the century.'[103]

One famous writer who discovered the limits of legal recognition of her literary property was Harriet Beecher Stowe, whose genius was recognised, but whose copyright was found not to be infringed by a German translation of *Uncle Tom's Cabin*.[104] Eventually, more expansive conceptions of both 'work' and 'author' were accepted as law. In 1884, a studio photograph of Oscar Wilde was found to demonstrate the originality and creative artistry of an authored work worthy of copyright protection.[105] Two decades later, the adaptability of copyright law to new technologies was confirmed when a circus poster was held to be protected.[106] In 1951, the mezzotinting of paintings by Old Masters was found to involve sufficient individual skill as to be copyrightable.[107] As Peter Jaszi rightly observes, such decisions result in a ' "minimalist" and "democratised" vision of authorship'.[108] The Romantic theory of the author has continued to operate as copyright law's underlying theory of creativity through all the technological advances of the twentieth century, from motion pictures to computer software, despite the fact that corporate and industrialised modes of production are a world away from the 'solitary reaping' of Wordsworth.[109]

Another important trend in twentieth-century copyright law across the Anglo-American jurisdictions is the extension of the duration of copyright. In 1911 the UK Copyright Act radically altered the term of copyright to the life of the author plus fifty years. A similar extension was enacted in the United States in two stages, with the 1909 Act providing for a term of twenty-eight years, with a possible extension of equivalent length, and the 1976 Copyright Act stipulating a term of life plus fifty years. During the 1990s, Britain and the United States added a further twenty years to this term, pursuing consistency in copyright protection with the European Union. The effect of the latest change has been a vastly increased respect for the private rights of the creators and owners of copyright, and a correspondingly diminished recognition of the cultural and economic value of having works in the public domain. This shift is well illustrated by the naming of the American legislation the Sonny Bono Copyright Term Extension Act, in honour of the singer turned congressman who was its most energetic proponent. Bono believed in perpetual copyright, but the Constitution expressly precludes this. The British amendment, the Duration of Copyright and Rights in Performance Regulations 1995, lacked a celebrity sponsor but operated retrospectively. This provision had an immediate impact on literary culture because a considerable body of Modernist writing had just entered or was about to enter the public domain. Major writers like Virginia Woolf and James Joyce, who had died in 1941, went out of copyright in 1992 and back into it in 1996. To counter any possible injustice, the regulations allowed a 'licence as of right' to persons who had proceeded with a publication in expectation of its coming into the public domain.

The estate of James Joyce has been especially assiduous in exercising renewed control over their literary property. A new edition of *Ulysses* was the subject of legal action; permission to use eighteen words from *Finnegans Wake* in a musical setting was refused; the author of a scholarly biography of Lucia Joyce was allowed to quote no more than five hundred words from the Joyce corpus. In these instances, neither the licence as of right nor the statutory defence of fair dealing (in America fair use) normally used by critics, scholars, journalists and other writers availed. So determined has the estate been to exploit its rights under law that lawyer and Joycean scholar Robert Spoo has suggested: 'Where censorship and obscenity laws were once the dominant legal forces shaping the sociocultural existence of *Ulysses*, today that role has been assumed by copyright and related intellectual property regimes.'[110] James Joyce was well aware of the multiple nature of authorship, of the role of intertextuality in literary creation. *Ulysses* picks up, quotes, reworks many snatches of literary text, advertising slogans, tropes and other expressions. It is therefore a travesty that his works should become the site of a blockade carried out in the name of copyright:

In the ecology of copyright, a work like *Ulysses* has its creative origins in the raw materials of the public domain. With the sanction of law, the work then comes under private control for a certain term, and, when the term has expired, the work returns to the public domain to increase those raw materials and to spur the creation of new works – and incidentally, new copyrights.[111]

The assertion of private rights over public interests in the production of new artworks and new knowledge, fostered by the prolongation of copyright, has, to quote Spoo, 'upset this ecological cycle'.

Another aspect of the privatisation of copyright law has been the addition of moral rights to the suite of laws governing literature in many common-law jurisdictions. Deriving from French law, the *droit d'auteur* or author's moral right was introduced into English law in 1988 as part of the Copyright Designs and Patents Act. Moral rights are specifically acknowledged in Canadian law, where, owing to the strong French cultural influence, there is a developed body of case law as well as the statutory provisions. In the United States moral rights are recognised under the Visual Artists Rights Act, but not otherwise. Under an amendment to the Australian Copyright Act passed in 2000, moral rights of authors, artists and architects were legislated. These laws have their philosophical basis in natural rights theory, as the Canadian Internet Policy and Public Interest Clinic explains:

The sale of a copyrighted work is not like the sale of any other article of commerce. With physical goods, all rights are relinquished on sale; there are no restrictions on what a new owner can do with the goods: keep, mutilate or destroy. However, an author who sells a manuscript 'retains a species of personal or moral right in the product of his brain'.[112]

Across the jurisdictions, two specific aspects of the author's moral rights are recognised, the right to attribution of authorship, and the right to integrity of authorship. The former involves a right to be named as author of the work (or to remain anonymous); the latter is a right to protect the work from derogatory treatment, to be consulted over any alteration to the work or to its location. Whether an author's rights have been infringed or not is to be judged by an objective test.

As a legal regime, copyright has been intended to secure a variety of ends: to bring order to the book trade; to promote the circulation of ideas and art; to provide an incentive for writers to invest time and labour in authorship and ensure they and their families derive a just benefit from their successes; and to protect owners of cultural property from unauthorised copying in 'an age of mechanical reproduction'.[113] This chapter has suggested that there has been a movement from a public-interest rationale to a private-interest one. A constant element across the history of copyright has been a dialogue between literature and law. It would be a mistake to think that that dialogue ended with Wordsworth's death in 1850. However, his influence has been enduring, for as Jaszi and Woodmansee note, 'the linchpin of Anglo-American copyright as well as of Continental "authors' rights" is a thoroughly Romantic conception of authorship'.[114] Jaszi and Woodmansee, a legal scholar and a literary scholar respectively, have been engaged in a collaborative project to update this dialogue. In 1991 through the Society for Critical Exchange, they organised an interdisciplinary conference on authorship and copyright, the papers of which were published as *The Construction of Authorship*, a book cited in these pages. As well as exploring the evolution of copyright in the context of cultural history, they and a growing number of colleagues have sought to influence the further development of intellectual property law. As well as a critique of Romantic ideas of authorship as obfuscating the realities of creative production in modern economies, they have also advocated the claims of the public domain, and the need for a truly internationalist perspective on intellectual property. In 1993 the Bellagio Declaration was issued following a conference on cultural property in the post-colonial era. Among other things, the lawyers and literary critics, computer scientists and publishers, environmentalists and cultural historians who participated declared:

In general, systems built around the author paradigm tend to obscure or under-value the importance of 'the public domain', the intellectual and cultural commons from which future works will be constructed . . . The aggressive expansion of intellectual property rights has the potential to inhibit development and future creation by fencing off 'the commons'.[115]

An alternative approach to intellectual property is being pioneered on the Internet by an organisation known as Creative Commons. A consortium of lawyers, computer scientists, artists and educators, Creative Commons has developed a system of licences under which works posted on the Internet may be used and even modified by non-commercial operators. In this way, works circulate in the public domain of cyberspace, generating an audience for their authors, but the authors retain the right to publish and to control commercial uses. In a further instance of their public-domain campaign, two members of Creative Commons, Eric Eldred and Lawrence Lessig, were the lead plaintiff and counsel respectively in *Eldred* v. *Ashcroft*, a challenge to the constitutionality of the Sonny Bono Act. Mark Rose, whose history of *Donaldson* v. *Becket* has been quoted in these pages, also filed an *amicus curiae* brief in the case. That case was unsuccessful, but the cause of the intellectual and artistic commons remains a vital one, as the recent experience with the Joyce copyrights shows.

This chapter has offered a critical history of some of the more significant ways in which the production and distribution of literature has been regulated by law. It would be wrong to conclude that the relationship between the two institutions has always been antagonistic. Although writers have pushed at law's limits to maximise the conditions of literary possibility, often at their own cost, lawyers like Thomas Talfourd and Judge Woolsey have used juristic creativity to protect the rights of writers and recognise the social value of literature. It would also be wrong to infer that the history of this interaction is one of progressive liberalisation. The authority of precedent in the common law has enabled anachronistic offences such as blasphemy, sedition and criminal libel to be resurrected in times of social and political crisis by authoritarian governments.[116] As a result, dissident writers have been and are being imprisoned.[117] Equally, however, social change does cause some forms of regulation to fall into disuse, and new ones to emerge in response to new needs. In Australia and elsewhere, for example, mass migration and the growth of ethnically mixed societies has led in recent decades to new proscriptions against racial vilification.[118] In all such instances of innovation and adaptation, the legal regulation of literary activity needs to weigh both public and private interests.

PART II

Law and literature in history

CHAPTER 3

Renaissance humanism and the new culture of contract

Francis Bacon, in *The Advancement of Learning*, divided history into ancient, medieval and modern periods, proclaiming, 'this third period of time will far surpass that of the Graecian and Roman learning'.[1] Bracketing off the medieval centuries as unworthy of notice, he and his contemporaries turned instead to ancient Greece and Rome as their true humanistic precursors. Characterising their own culture as a 'renaissance' or rebirth of classical learning, they believed that the study of Greek and Roman texts afforded a unique instruction in the acquisition of a fully rounded humanity. Shakespeare's Hamlet recognises, though in his despondency he cannot share, the optimism and idealism implicit in this humanism: 'What a piece of work is man! How noble in reason! how infinite in faculties! in form and moving, how express and admirable! in action how like an angel! in apprehension, how like a god!'[2] The moral values and rhetorical skills modelled in this educational programme were directed both inwardly, at the private cultivation of the individual, and outwardly, at effective participation in government as a counsellor or courtier.

In the field of literary studies, it is traditional to emphasise the cultural achievements of the age, to view works like *Hamlet* as 'only the most succulent of the fruits [grown] from deep roots in the training the humanists offered'.[3] However, more recent scholars have been concerned not merely to appreciate the flavours of such fruit, but to study its connections with the branches, roots and soil of Renaissance society and culture. The relationship between law and literature was an integral part of this environment. In this study of the period, we are, in Patricia Parker's words, 'dismantling the anachronistic division into academic disciplines that obscured the range of interlinking interests, discourses and practices in the period'.[4] As a lawyer and writer, Francis Bacon is an appropriate person to induct us in to this period and its 'interlinking interests'. Although best known today as a Lord Chancellor impeached for corruption, he was, Parker reminds us, 'at once formative in the articulation of early modern science (in texts that employed metaphors of other-world discovery), a prominent jurist, proponent of torture, and spy, as well as a writer of essays, an influence on the reform of language, and a public figure whose sexual relations with men were a contemporary open secret'.[5]

Bacon's statement, 'I have taken all knowledge for my province', might stand for the intellectual ambition of the period, but as a political metaphor, in which knowledge is an empire to be ruled, it is equally revealing.[6] Along with Galileo and Kepler, Bacon stressed the primacy of experiment and evidence in the framing of truth-statements. His famous aphorism, 'knowledge is power', encapsulates the usefulness of the new knowledge in affording humans an unprecedented level of mastery over nature.[7] Furthermore, the advances in astronomy, and the construction of a new cosmology, closely followed the voyages of discovery that led to the colonisation of the Americas, and the exploitation of those new provinces.

In understanding the links between knowledge and power in the Renaissance, it is useful to adopt a materialist perspective. The spread of classical literacy was facilitated by the invention of printing, and the replacement of parchment with paper. This technological change made the old texts and the new ideas available in a literal sense, which in turn expanded the audience of literate persons. There were also economic developments, new ventures in trade, new sources of valuable commodities such as gold, silk and spices, that created wealth and fed a new culture of display, in which the patronage of artists and the commissioning of paintings were within the means of merchants and aristocrats as well as the Church. As Lisa Jardine has shown, such artworks often celebrated through copious representation the 'worldly goods' of the patron or the subject.[8] One of the most useful contexts for understanding Renaissance English literature and law is an economic one: this was, in the words of legal historian Samuel E. Thorne, 'a strikingly active commercial society'.[9] The plays of Shakespeare and his fellow dramatists were part of a new and specifically commercial theatre in London. The transformation and expansion of the economy into a new capitalist formation created fears of social disruption: in a traditionally feudal society, how much land could a successful merchant buy? Should the wearing of expensive garments be restricted to the upper classes? Should the law proscribe the charging of interest on monetary loans in accordance with biblical injunctions? This chapter examines the impact of money and trade in the culture of the Renaissance, focusing particularly on the new law of contract. What were the 'interlinking interests, discourses and practices' that connected law and literature, and what was their effect on the representation of contract in writing whether poetic or legal or both?

THE INNS OF COURT

We can begin to answer these questions by studying the cultural geography of Renaissance London. Introducing a recent collection of essays entitled *Literature, Politics and Law in Renaissance England*, Erica Sheen and Lorna Hutson note 'how closely identified were the cultural spaces of both legal and literary writing'.[10] The most important of these locations was the home of professional education in the common law, the Inns of Court. There were – and still are – four such Inns: Gray's Inn, Lincoln's Inn, the Inner Temple and the Middle Temple, all having the authority to enrol students and to admit them as barristers. However, the Inns played a broader cultural role, as evidenced by a dedication Ben Jonson included in *Every Man out of his Humour*: 'To the Noblest Nurseries of Humanity, and Liberty, in the Kingdom: the Inns of Court'. This tribute suggests that an English legal humanism developed at the Inns. Its composition had less to do with specifically legal education, which as R. S. White has shown, was 'haphazard, unsystematic, and voluntarily undertaken', than with opportunities residence at the Inns offered for wider cultural participation.[11]

In keeping with humanistic ideas, many young men enrolled at the Inns who had no intention of practising law but were primarily interested in politics or in administering their family estates. During the sixteenth century, middle-class men, merchants' sons like John Webster, the future playwright, were enrolled, but the student body was overwhelmingly drawn from the aristocracy and gentry. For them, the Inns of Court worked to foster bonds between men of rank and the legal profession, to 'instil a sense of community' around a belief in the common law, and to provide a basic grounding in legal rules and reasoning for use in the management of property or business.[12] Among the means available to secure these ends were textbooks in rhetoric and regular theatrical productions. As a consequence, the Inns have been well described as 'the largest single group of literate and cultured men in London'.[13] Philip Finkelpearl has counted no less than twenty-eight 'important writers [who] lived there for some length of time', including Thomas More, Roger Ascham, George Gascoigne, Sackville and Norton, Abraham Fraunce, Sir Walter Raleigh, John Harington, Thomas Campion, John Donne, Francis Bacon, Sir John Davies, John Marston, John Ford, William Davenant, Sir John Denham, Thomas Carew, Sir John Suckling and William Congreve.[14] Some of these pursued careers in law as well as writing, such as More, Bacon and Davies; others became playwrights or poets, and also sought advancement through politics or the Church

(Donne, Raleigh, Marston, Denham); still others forsook the law for a life of fashion and the theatre (Congreve).

The collocation of law and theatre may be surprising to modern readers, but the Inns had a strong theatrical tradition. Law students were famous frequenters of plays, partly owing to their economic position and partly to the geographical proximity of the Inns and the theatres. Moreover the Inns invited theatrical companies to perform in their halls. Two of Shakespeare's plays are known to have had performances in the Inns, *Twelfth Night* and *The Comedy of Errors*. In addition, there was a tradition of annual Christmas 'revels' in which students elected a Prince, wrote and acted in parodies and stories of misrule, introduced mock laws and condemned one of their number, feasted, and danced.[15] John Rastell of the Middle Temple, brother-in-law of Thomas More, was a coroner and publisher of law books, and a playwright who built a stage at his own house.[16] A generation later, two members of the Inner Temple, Thomas Sackville and Thomas Norton, wrote a powerful tragedy, *Gorboduc*, which was part of the Christmas revels of 1561–2. Literary history records this as the first play to employ blank verse in English, while its author Sackville is also known in legal history as the judge Lord Buckhurst. This summary suggests there was a strong affinity between revelling and the law. Karen Cunningham has researched the nature and extent of this connection and found that it permeated the curriculum in term-time as well as the holiday festivities. Students were generally left to read privately in the law-books, and to attend court, but the Inns also convened 'moots', in which the legal principles applicable to real or imaginary cases were argued. Cunningham identifies four parts to mooting: '(1) the problem; (2) the question arising from the problem; (3) the disputation, arguments pro and contra; and (4) the solution, any authoritative answer given by the teacher.'[17] Based on small stories involving events at the margins of legal categories, mooting developed into a site for the display of ingenious novel arguments, an exercise in legal invention. It was therefore highly imaginative, a performative practice that called forth greater freedom of utterance than was usually allowed in the Tudor monarchy. Thus moots, like the theatre, provided a contained space in which to rehearse and debate difficult social issues.

Early in the sixteenth century, Sir Thomas Elyot pointed out the similarities between moots and classical rhetoric as part of a critique of legal language. To quote Lorna Hutson's summary of his argument: 'if only English lawyers did not have to read "fardelles and trusses of the most barbarouse autors", they would bring "the pleadyng and reasonynge of the lawe to the ancient fourme of noble oratours".'[18] Henry VIII's Chancellor,

Thomas Cromwell, was moved by this argument to institute weekly read-ings in rhetoric or political philosophy at the Inns. Rhetoric, as a trans-disciplinary training in eloquence and discourse, became one of the foundations for the close linkage between literature and law in the period.[19] Thomas Wilson, whose *Arte of Rhetorique* was perhaps the most popular rhetorical manual of the century, claimed that oratory had three aims – to teach, to delight and to persuade.[20] This formulation seems to unite Aristotle's concept of rhetoric as persuasion with Horace's idea that 'Poets aim at giving either profit or delight, or at combining the giving of pleasure with some useful precepts for life.'[21] Wilson gives instances of fables and stories that have proved effective in oratory, but his real interest is in political and forensic rhetoric. So useful did lawyers find his discussion that Gabriel Harvey described this book as 'the dailie bread of owr common pleaders'.[22] Despite many examples drawn from the law, Wilson exhibits a distrust of some forms of legal argument. Discussing ambiguity in language, he treats it not as a fact requiring a verbal contest of interpretations, but as a pretext for lawyers' tricks:

Sometymes a doubt is made, upon some woorde or sentence, when it signifieth diverse thynges, or maie diversely be taken, whereupon ful oft ariseth muche contencion. The lawyers lacke no cases to fill this parte full of examples. For rather than faile, thei will make doubtes often tymes, where no doubt should be at all. Is his lease long enough (quoth one): yea sir, it is very long, saied a poore husbande man. Then (quoth he) let me alone with it, I will finde a hole in it, I warrant thee. In all this talke, I excepte the good lawyers, and I maie well spare them, for thei are but a fewe.[23]

Unsettled by radical ambiguity, Wilson seeks to reinstate law as a fixed principle, grounded in a cosmic order. He writes in his chapter, 'Of Disposition, or the apte ordering of thynges', that, 'by an order we are born, by an order we live, and by an order we make our ende. . . . By an order Realmes stande, and lawes take force.'[24] As Patricia Parker has argued, the deep connection between law and rhetoric makes the latter 'an instrument of civil order', in which the rules of correct 'disposition' are deployed to control the potential anarchy of 'invention'.[25]

C. S. Lewis's belief that 'rhetoric is the greatest barrier between us and our ancestors' is worth bearing in mind as we turn to the connection of rhetoric and literature.[26] W. B. Yeats's claim, 'We make out of the quarrel with others, rhetoric, but of the quarrel with ourselves poetry', opposes each to the other.[27] Yet for Renaissance writers and readers such an opposition would have been unthinkable. Sir Philip Sidney, once a student at Gray's Inn, derived from Wilson and his classical sources a theory of poetry as 'an art of discourse, . . . within the bounds of rhetoric'.[28] Poetry, according to Sidney, aims 'to teach and delight', to move readers to virtuous action through its images or 'speaking pictures'. The poet is a maker, who promotes readerly judgment by 'representing, counterfeiting or figuring forth' the world in verbal images.[29] Fictional representations work not only on individuals, but on societies: 'what philosopher's counsel can so readily direct a prince as the feigned Cyrus in Xenophon; or a virtuous man in all fortunes, as Aeneas in Virgil; or a whole commonwealth as the way of Sir Thomas More's *Utopia*?' Sidney's *Apology for Poetry* proposes literature as 'an instrument of politics', a way of imagining community. George Puttenham, a precursor of Sidney's, proclaimed poets 'the first lawmakers to the people', as their works 'made for the persuasion of the public peace and tranquillity'.[30] Peter Goodrich expounds the mythical dimensions of this line of argument: 'The fallen state of nature was finally superseded and society established through the offices of poetry and rhetoric.'[31] Because both employed hypotheses involving narrative, through which 'an action comes retrospectively to be understood in all its complexity', enabling judgments to be made, poetry and legal eloquence worked to maintain as well as to constitute social order.[32]

We should beware of reading the culture of the Inns solely in terms of order, of extrapolating from discourse to communal practice. John Davies, later a judge in Ireland and a poet, was twice disciplined by the Benchers of the Middle Temple for misconduct associated with the revels. On the second occasion, in 1598, he was the butt of a libellous satire, for which he beat the prince of misrule, and was expelled.[33] In Elizabethan London, law students had a reputation for disorderliness, for 'an active and slightly sordid urbanity'.[34] The proximity of the Inns to theatres on the south bank of the Thames also gave ready access to the brothels, bear-baiting rings and taverns there. Complaints were made about prostitutes visiting members' rooms, and about the large number of non-members in the precinct. It was a varied, but decidedly masculine, culture, running the gamut of temporal and spiritual pleasures, as Wilfrid Prest has noted: 'If playgoing was the inns of court man's favourite recreation, listening to sermons and political gossip came a close second.'[35] Another element of the cultural geography, then, is political, through the Inns' closeness to Fleet Street, and to the residence of the ambitious Earl of Essex.

The rhetorical culture of the Inns therefore fostered links between law and literature which spread through personal contact and textual transmission well beyond that privileged cultural space. It also led jurists to think of legal writing as a cultural rather than a technical exercise, even, in the case of Sir Edward Coke, as a species of nation building.[36] The mingling of lawyers and writers prompted the diffusion of legal issues and terms in many literary genres. That legal discourse could exceed its limits, and lawyers turn their skills to self-serving ends, are made clear in an acerbic satire by John Donne. In a general complaint about London, he reserves his harshest criticism for a poor poet turned greedy lawyer: this man 'throws ... / His title of barrister on every wench, / And woos in language of the Pleas, and Bench.' Literary integrity is contrasted with legal ambition, which is represented as being 'worse than embrothelled strumpets prostitute'.[37] A poem like this is a useful corrective to idealisations of the legal-literary world of the Inns, not least because it shows the poet and his target participating in a masculine economy of malicious discourse.[38] Poetry has the last laugh, however, for while alleging sharp practice by the lawyer, the poem celebrates its own evasion of the libel law. As the leader of a new 'cynical, witty style' of poetry developed at the Inns, Donne was uniquely placed to observe the misuse of legal language by practitioners.[39] A literary outsider who memorialised the culture of the Inns was Isabella Whitney. Poverty forced Whitney to leave London, and in a mock 'Wyll and Testament' she enumerated the city's abundance and devised a humorous fantasy of supply and demand that inverted her own economic exclusion. The culmination of this cultural geography is a description of the Inns, with the lawyers and students represented as beneficiaries of 'all that London hath':

> For such as cannot quiet bee,
>   but strive for House or Land:
> At th'innes of Court I Lawyers leave
>   to take their cause in hand.
> And also leave I at ech Inne
>   of Court, or Chauncelrye:
> Of Gentylmen, a youthfull roote,
>   full of Activytie:
> For whom I store of Bookes have left,
>   at each Booksellers stall:
> And part of all that London hath
>   to furnish them withall.
> And when they are with study cloyd;
>   to recreate their minde:
> Of Tennis Courts, of Dauncing Scooles,
>   and fence they store shal finde.
> And every Sonday at the least,
>   I leave to make them sport.
> In divers places Players, that
>   of wonders shall reporte.[40]

Whitney stresses that the educational programme of the Inns was rounded and 'full of activity'. As well as preparing for the everyday disputes over property ('House or Land'), the legal apprentices were exposed to mental 're-creation' through the fictional 'wonders' of the theatre.

EQUITY IN COURT AND ON STAGE

How did this humanistic culture of law and literature manifest itself in legal doctrine and literary form? Karen Cunningham's conclusion, that, 'one need not have been at law school to speak the languages of legal practice, nor need he have been in the theatre to speak the languages of imaginative fictions', suggests that it is shared discourses, rather than individual biographies, that will reveal how deeply interrelated the two activities were.

In his suggestive article, 'English Law and the Renaissance', J. H. Baker argues that the humanism of the Inns of Court played a major part in the Tudor transformation of the common law.[41] One site of innovation lay in the law of contract. The details of this will be discussed below, but the intellectual preparation for this change depended on the acceptance of classical theories of equity. From its medieval foundation, the rigid formalism of the common law with its limited writs and causes of action prompted amendment through fiction and statute. It also led Edward III around 1330 to authorise the Lord Chancellor to hear claims that lay outside the common law. This medieval jurisdiction was fortified in the Renaissance period by the rediscovery of Aristotle's writings on equity.[42] In *Nicomachean Ethics* Aristotle defines equity as 'a rectification of law where law is defective because of its generality'. In cases where injustice would result from the application of the general rule, equitable justice allows 'a special ordinance [to be] made to fit the circumstances of the case'.[43] As Kathy Eden points out, equitable analysis is a 'gentle, corrective measure' that looks to intentions as well as acts: the intentions of the actor, and the intentions of the legislator.[44] This is confirmed in Aristotle's *Rhetoric*: 'it is equitable to pardon human weakness, and to look, . . . not to the letter of the law, but to the intention of the legislator; not to the action itself, but to the moral purpose; not to the part, but to the whole'.[45] Eden shows that this concept shaped the treatment of human action in both trials and plays in ancient Greece, and proved useful to Roman law and to Renaissance humanists alike.

In sixteenth-century England, the jurisprudential debate over the relationship between law and equity spilled over into a jurisdictional conflict between the courts of common law and Chancery, with the former complaining about the Chancellor issuing injunctions in cases decided by them. Thomas More, like his predecessor Cardinal Wolsey, saw his office as upholding 'the golden rule of equity' to all subjects. An increase in Chancery business resulted. Facing protests from his judicial colleagues, More urged upon the judges the validity of the equitable approach: 'if the judges of every court ... would upon reasonable consideration by their own discretions ... mitigate and reform the law themselves, there should from henceforth by him no more injunctions be granted'. When the judges refused, he stated the necessary corollary: if they drove him to the necessity of awarding injunctions 'to relieve the people's injury' they could not thereafter blame him for doing so.[46] Despite this initial reluctance, the concept of equity was soon circulating in and exerting influence on the common law. Christopher St German, its main proponent, drew on continental thinking, and argued that, 'equity is part of the law, not something outside it'.[47] Though controversial, this proposition produced some importation of equitable principles into the common law. It led to a new approach to statutory interpretation, the 'equity of the statute', in which courts construing the effect of a piece of legislation in a particular case took primary notice of the legislators' intention in passing the law, rather than the plain meaning of its terms.[48] In the area of common-law doctrine, the equity debate encouraged the development of new 'actions on the case', instances of creative law-making by courts. One such new 'case' was the action of *assumpsit* in the new law of contract.[49]

The making of such judgments was the province not only of lawyers, but of all practitioners of the rhetorical arts. Debates over abstract questions were supplemented and clarified by hypothetical situations, placing an issue in its full circumstances. This procedure enabled the 'equitable' judgments Aristotle recommended in his *Rhetoric*, and which Cicero called 'a new kind of Law', to be made by orators and writers.[50] In its turn, this rhetorical practice was especially valuable in the development of the Elizabethan theatre. Given the literary and theatrical connections of the Inns, we should not be surprised that equity became 'a privileged point of contact between the court and the stage' at his time.[51] Ina Habermann argues that to some extent, all drama of the period can be regarded as equitable:

Plays may contain special questions or hypotheses in the tradition of rhetorical deliberation, but they focus on individual stories, placing them in a broader moral and ethical framework. Moreover, rather than supplying a simple illustration of a problem, theatre gives an audience 'images to think with,' which enables an exchange that is dynamic and ultimately unpredictable.[52]

Consequently, equitable drama is 'interrogative' not didactic. Habermann's main examples of equitable drama are the tragedies of John Webster. Webster, as a product of the Middle Temple, knew the dramatic potential of trial scenes, but they were not essential. As Lorna Hutson and Victoria Kahn have shown, there is a fundamental correspondence between Aristotle's notion of a complex plot, 'which involves a movement from error [*hamartia*] to knowledge through inference from artificial proofs', and his definition of equity as 'corrective of the "error" of the positive law'.[53] Lorna Hutson has also demonstrated that the comedies of the Roman playwright Terence translated by Renaissance lawyers like George Gascoigne and John Rastell are also deliberative in form and interrogatively equitable.[54]

Perhaps the best-known example of the equitable drama of error is Shakespeare's *The Comedy of Errors*. As this play opens, a merchant of Syracuse is condemned to death for illegally entering Ephesus. The Duke of Ephesus listens to his story but determines to uphold the law: 'we may pity though not pardon thee'.[55] In the main plot another Syracusan merchant arrives and becomes embroiled in errors produced by mistaken identification with his long-lost twin brother, a citizen of Ephesus. The wife of the latter mistakes the former for her husband and bars the door against the wrong man. As the excluded husband threatens to break the door, a friend pleads with him in equitable terms:

> . . . your long experience of her wisdom,
> Her sober virtue, years, and modesty,
> Plead on her part some cause to you unknown.
> And doubt not, sir, but she will well excuse
> Why at this time the doors are made against you.   (III.ii.89–93)

The husband rejects this advice and stands on his legal rights. As a result, the errors are compounded, and the trouble deepens. Only when both twins are brought before the Duke in an impromptu trial in the final scene is the matter of identity and relationship proved. The brothers are also recognised by the Syracusan condemned at the outset as his sons, and his freedom is secured.

SLADE'S CASE AND THE CULTURE OF CONTRACT

The male protagonists of *The Comedy of Errors* are merchants, engaged in trade with other nations, in borrowing money, and buying goods and services from suppliers at home. Enmity between the neighbouring states of Ephesus and Syracuse, however, has created laws harsh in themselves and inimical to free trade: death for citizens of either state who enter the other. Although extreme, these laws reflect what Ian Ward has called the 'mercantilist motivations' of the era's economic thinking.[56] If we turn now from the equitable relief of unjust laws to the economic and social context, the 'errors' in the play, though comic, involve realistic disruptions to this mercantile economy, including the instituting of legal process for non-payment of debts. The comic resolution of the errors involves the discovery of kinship between citizens of the rival states. In its milieu of trade, debt and travel, the play bears witness to the new commercial context of Renaissance Europe.

This period saw the emergence of a new system of production and exchange, and the rise of a new class to economic power. With the gradual collapse of feudal society, workers had greater freedom to move, and to contract with employers, resulting in more fluid concepts of identity and a more individualistic ethos. The range and volume of trade increased through imperial conquest and colonisation, and through the advent of credit enabling large capital investment. This involved an extension of the concept of the market, from a site of local to one of international exchange, and from a defined event in one physical place to a continuous and ubiquitous institution.[57] The new market offered a wider selection of goods for sale, including luxury goods and imported items. It allowed transactions that were not necessarily immediate exchanges of money for goods, with terms for performance and payment spread over longer periods. Mercantile contracts enabled a widening network of relationships as they drew together investors and lenders, buyers and sellers, who were not otherwise known to each other outside the marketplace. (The word 'contract' derives from the Latin verb *contrahere*, to draw together.[58])

In the sixteenth and seventeenth centuries, these were radically new conditions of existence, superseding many traditional bonds, or supplementing them with rather more inchoate, temporary and instrumental relationships. It is tempting, though probably too simplistic, to represent this transformation from medieval to early modern society in terms of Sir Henry Maine's 1861 pronouncement that, 'the movement of progressive societies has hitherto been a movement from Status to Contract'.[59] As F. W. Maitland noted, Maine realised that the feudal system was governed by the law of contract.[60] However, it is still useful to distinguish between those 'status contracts' of loyalty and service, and what Max Weber called 'purposive contracts', entered into by autonomous individuals for limited goals. The latter type is characteristic of contracts in modern Western society. Indeed for Weber,

the most essential feature of modern substantive law, especially private law, is the greatly increased significance of legal transactions, particularly contracts, as a source of claims guaranteed by legal coercion. So very characteristic is this feature of private law that one can *a fortiori* designate the contemporary type of society, to the extent that private law obtains, as a 'contractual' one.[61]

Some older-style status contracts were preserved during this cultural shift, especially the contract of marriage. Nonetheless, the spread of contract discourse was such that it began by the seventeenth century to inform political philosophy in the idea of a founding compact for society. By the nineteenth century the idea of freedom of contract was so integral to the lifeworld of Western modernity that Weber could use it to describe the era in which he was writing. Yet, for the first generation of Europeans to work and live with this change, it was a radical innovation. According to the historian of market culture Jean-Christophe Agnew, 'Britons felt their way round the problematics of exchange' in the century leading up to the English Civil War in 1642.[62] He quotes one contemporary citizen who figured the upheaval through a commercial metaphor: 'The world is nothing but a shop of change.'[63] The questions raised for individuals and societies concerning their new identities, relationships and understandings of credit were rehearsed in the courts of law, the theatres and other forums.

The legal case that reformed contract law in England in response to these changing conditions was *Slade* v. *Morley*. In 1594 John Slade agreed to sell Humphrey Morley the crop from a particular field, and Morley to pay for it by St John the Baptist's Day. The grain was delivered, but Morley did not pay. Slade brought an action on the case in *assumpsit*, rather than a traditional action for debt. The latter would have allowed Morley to defend himself by bringing forward oath-helpers to support his own claim to have paid, since the original agreement was merely verbal. Instead, under the action of *assumpsit*, Slade argued before a judge and jury that Morley had promised to pay, and that this promise could be deduced by his own delivery of the goods under the contract. Within the common-law courts, the King's Bench had been willing to deduce such promises, and grant such actions, but the Common Pleas had not. The case was recognised immediately as a test case and was referred to the Court of Exchequer Chamber, comprising all the judges and barons. Sir Edward Coke appeared for Slade and Francis Bacon for Morley, and the profiles of these eminent counsel indicate the jurisdictional stakes. In effect, King's Bench was seeking power over what had been the ecclesiastical area of promise and contract, and validating what it saw as an equitable innovation in the law. This highly contentious case was not decided until 1602, after several hearings, and even then, Coke's argument was carried on the basis of a show of hands (six to five in favour), with no formal reasons for judgment. It was recorded by several law reporters, a sign that its legal significance was immediately evident. However, the only full report was by a partisan, Coke, who concealed the contingency of the result by citing his own arguments to the exclusion of those of Bacon. Chief Justice Popham's statement, 'every contract executory imports in itself an *assumpsit*, for when one agrees to pay so much money, or deliver any thing, thereby he assumes or promises to pay, or deliver it', became for ensuing generations of lawyers and students an authoritative ruling.[64] *Slade's Case* authorised the central element in Anglo-American contract law, that 'consideration' in the form of a *quid pro quo*, an exchange of something tangible, is a necessary part in a legally enforceable contract.

Before *Slade's Case* the law of contract had lagged behind commercial practice, so the decision represented a progressive, albeit contentious, step.[65] Law-and-Literature scholars have analysed how it relates to the wider changes in social conditions and intellectual debates of the period and have noted that its 'collapsing contract and promise into one', as David Harris Sacks puts it, turns contract into a speech-act, a linguistic performative.[66] The underlying 'moral psychology' of this move is also significant. Sacks argues that it reveals an ambivalent interest in mental states, a belief in their centrality and their opacity, related to the Reformation's emphasis alike on conscience and sin. Luke Wilson has also connected *Slade's* interest in intention with the new representation of interior states, and with a new concept of contractual time.[67] Equally, Sacks and Lorna Hutson link the evidentiary requirement of some external, tangible sign of intention in *Slade* to the expanded context of exchange. In a local market where buyer and seller were known to each other and to the community, the consequences of reneging on a verbal contract were obvious; the oath-maker and his compurgators had a powerful incentive to tell the truth, in the retention of their personal 'credit' among their neighbours. In the metropolis and overseas markets, these factors hardly counted: a new, objectively discernible form of consideration was required. Hutson describes how 'the so-called "doctrine of consideration" was actually a displacement of the pledge of faith into arguable motive'.[68] As religious sanctions waned in power, the evidential value of oaths and promises lessened relative to more secular or empirical evidence. The eclipse of the action for debt and compurgation was part of the modernising process. *Slade's Case* offers a window on the legal culture of the period, its openness to new ideas, and its way of assimilating these ideas into the common law. The 'prime authority' for *assumpsit* as a remedy was not a case, but a statement by a judge in Gray's Inn Hall.[69] This authority was not sufficient to effect a modernisation of the law. Instead, the argument for *assumpsit* was carried because it was able to be made in terms that resonated with emergent understandings of 'human agency, identity and obligation'.[70]

Contract, then, was one of the markers of change in the transition from medieval to modern society. Contractual thinking and contractual language carried increasing conviction across the culture. During the seventeenth century political philosophers such as Hobbes and Locke imagined a founding contract as the basis of social and political order. In 1610 there were negotiations for a formal Great Contract between Parliament and the King, aimed at fixing their respective rights. They failed, but the discourse of contract provided ammunition for political argument right up to the Civil War and the Glorious Revolution. John Selden, historian and member of Ben Jonson's Mermaid Club as well as the Inner Temple, who participated in the debate on the parliamentary side, discussed law in these terms in his *Table-Talk*: 'Every Law is a Contract betwixt the Prince and his people, and therefore to bee kept.'[71] Contractual terms appear, Luke Wilson notes, 'with striking frequency in the nontechnical literature of the period'.[72] One domain of especially high incidence is the theatre. In Marlowe's *Doctor Faustus* the enlarged scope of human desire and freedom of exchange offered by the culture – and the anxiety this created – are tested through the contract in which Faustus sells his soul to the devil. First performed in 1590 or 1591, the same decade as *Slade's Case*, *Doctor Faustus* supports Jean-Christophe Agnew's argument that the theatre became 'a representational laboratory for a world perplexed by a culture of liquidity'.[73] The new fluidity of identity is embodied in Faustus's shifts from scholar to arrogant mage to penitent sinner, seduced into a contract by the 'bogus and confused' legal terminology of Mephistophiles.[74]

Agnew draws a strong parallel between the drama's representation of social identity as precarious, and the instability 'that a boundless market had already introduced' into subjectivity.[75] He discerns between the theatre and the market a 'complex and mutually illuminating relation between the practical liquidity of commodity form and the imaginative liquidity of theatrical form'.[76] Evidence for this interaction exists in plays' use of contract discourse and in their emphasis on the 'fabrication of character'. The precariousness of identity and the ability of characters to 'fabricate' it are well illustrated in Shakespeare's *The Comedy of Errors*. Perhaps the best example of theatrical engagement with contract discourse occurs in Ben Jonson's *Bartholomew Fair* (1614). In the Induction to this play, Scrivener invites the audience to sign

> Articles of Agreement, indented, between the Spectators or Hearers, at the Hope on the Bankside in the County of Surrey, on the one party; and the Author of *Bartholomew Fair* in the said place and county, on the other party; ... the said Spectators and Hearers ... do for themselves severally covenant, and agree to remain in their places ... for the space of two hours and a half ... In which time the author promiseth to present them by us with a new sufficient play called *Bartholomew Fair*.

In addition to these duties, the contract grants the audience certain rights of judgment and demands their applause. Luke Wilson has observed that there is something 'preposterous', literally back to front, in demanding applause before a performance, but for all its comic play Jonson's legalese highlights the realities of the commercial theatre, and his immersion in a contractual culture.[77]

While the element of performance gave the theatre a special link with the world of contract, it was not the only genre adapted to that world. The sonnet, like the soliloquy on stage, exemplifies another aspect of the psychology that underlies the new law of contract, namely, the elaboration of an interior world of consciousness, self-reflection and moral judgment. Shakespeare's Sonnet 87 presents an excellent example, for here 'the character of an emotional relationship is expressed in terms of a legal contract':[78]

> Farewell! thou art too dear for my possessing,
> And like enough thou know'st thy estimate:
> The charter of thy worth gives thee releasing;
> My bonds in thee are all determinate.
> For how do I hold thee but by thy granting?
> And for that riches where is my deserving?
> The cause of this fair gift in me is wanting,
> And so my patent back again is swerving.
> Thyself thou gavest, thy own worth then not knowing,
> Or me, to whom thou gavest it, else mistaking;
> So thy great gift, upon misprision growing,
> Comes home again, on better judgment making.
> Thus have I had thee, as a dream doth flatter,
> In sleep a king, but waking no such matter.

Contractual discourse ('charter', 'bonds') quickly gives way to that of gift as it becomes clear that the relationship is over. The speaker recognises that there is no enforceable agreement between the parties, due to a lack of consideration: 'The cause of this fair gift in me is wanting.' Even the legal category of gift turns out to be an inexact metaphor, since the subject is taken away. These difficulties of definition suggest that the pun on the word 'dear' in the opening line is a problematic one, objectifying one who turns out to be a subject, the possessor of an independent will. Agnew's comment that a money medium can imbue 'social intercourse with a transactional quality' points to the source of the difficulty. In a commercial culture, the monetary metaphor is at once supremely attractive and ineradicably proprietary. In the end, both parties have operated under a mistake ('misprision').

One of the most extraordinary texts in the Renaissance literature of contract is a short prose romance, 'The Contract', by Margaret Cavendish, Duchess of Newcastle. Published in 1656, it concerns a marriage contract made during the childhood of its heroine by her guardian with the son of a local duke. Morally wayward, the young man signs the contract to please his dying father. After the death of the duke, he marries another woman. The heroine grows up in rural seclusion a beautiful, intelligent, principled and obedient young woman, who when she is presented at Court attracts both the ruler and her betrothed. Her guardian bars the latter in punishment for his breach of the contract and promotes the elderly ruler as suitor. Delitia, the heroine, falls in love with the other, now duke himself. In conventional romance fashion, she is faced with a conflict between passion and duty, while her beloved's marriage forms a legal obstacle. She and the duke devise a strategy, which includes a legal argument based on the validity of the original contract, to ensure that they may marry. Delitia shows the benefits of humanistic education for women in a compelling argument to the judges. However, the effect of this feminist representation is undermined by a patronising reply from the judges: '"it is happy for us that sit upon the bench that your cause is so clear and good, otherwise your beauty and your wit might have proved bribes to our vote"'.[79] As Kate Lilley, Cavendish's modern editor, shows, beauty is an unanswerable force in her writing, a conventional romantic trope which sits oddly with the challenging rationality of her ideas on education and her familiarity with the rhetorical tradition. 'The Contract' pushes the boundaries of the romance form, making it 'the scene of a woman's heroic agency and successful negotiation of the theatres of power'.[80] As a genre predicated on the triumph of desire over difficulty, romance is well suited to political imaginings. Cavendish was a Royalist, an attendant to Queen Henrietta Maria during her exile, and the marriage contract was a figurative device in political writings. Royalists sought to contain the revolutionary potential of the contract analogy by promoting the marriage contract, with its combination of sovereignty and mutual affection, as the proper model for the state. Victoria Kahn has shown how this romance, with its strategic manipulation of the law in the service of desire, has to make some complex moves to espouse the rightness of an inherited compact and the correctable error of wilful disobedience without compromising the heroine's integrity.[81] As Kahn suggests, there are parallels between Delitia's successful courtroom advocacy and that of Portia in *The Merchant of Venice*. These imaginary interventions point up the lack of independent recognition of women's needs under Renaissance law. Sheen and Hutson's point that women were 'ambiguously positioned in Renaissance law and ideology as aspects of men's private or domestic life' is well illustrated in Cavendish's own life. She appeared briefly and unsuccessfully before English tribunals to argue for the restitution of her husband's confiscated estates.

Shakespeare's *The Merchant of Venice* is a profound exploration of the new market culture. The very name of Venice evoked this economic system, and contemporary audiences would not have overlooked the 'social and juridical similarities' between the world represented on stage and that of late sixteenth-century England.[82] The play's central question is posed in terms of contract law: whether Shylock can obtain an order for the specific performance of the bond he and Antonio freely entered:

> . . . let the forfeit
> Be nominated for an equal pound
> Of your fair flesh, to be cut off and taken
> In what part of your body pleaseth me.[83]

The parties to this contract, the Venetian merchant, Antonio, and the Jewish moneylender, Shylock, negotiate with each other despite mutual hostility that is born of cultural and religious difference and economic rivalry. Their relations may be seen as a microcosm of the internationalised market, with its need and willingness to trade with outsiders as a means of securing a commercial advantage for one's own associates or kin; with its uncertainty and exposure to the risk of failure; and its interconnection with a legal system that recognises the economic value and the moral force of contracts.

Contract and commerce have become so naturalised in this society that they permeate even the courtship of Bassanio and Portia. Having chosen the correct casket, Bassanio waits until his position as her suitor is 'confirmed, signed, ratified' by her. Portia replies in commercial terms, signalling her wish to be 'more rich', to 'exceed account', referring to 'the full sum of me', transferring the capital that is herself: 'what is mine, to you and yours / Is now converted' (*MV* 3.2.166–7). Filomena Mesquita observes that the patriarchal wealth inherited by Portia is effectively imaged in the casket, and that Bassanio's 'capacity to climb the social ladder through the cunning use of another's capital, and indeed another's life, points towards forms of venture capitalism'.[84] Bassanio and Gratiano acknowledge the acquisitive element in suit through their allusions to Portia as the golden fleece and themselves as 'Jasons' (3.2.240).

Upwardly moving while profiting from Antonio's credit, Bassanio is representative of that liquidity of identity which Agnew sees as the hallmark of the new society. Portia's successful disguise and role-playing as the lawyer Balthazar afford another instance of this liquidity. Less theatrically, Jessica's elopement with Lorenzo involves a renunciation of her religio-racial identity. Even Launcelot Gobbo, in shifting masters, exemplifies the new mobility. In this changing world, happiness is not guaranteed by commercial success, as the vague depression afflicting Antonio at the start of the play confirms. Ian Ward has noted how Shakespeare's contemporaries sensed that 'the aggression of the emergent market and wider social dislocation' were related.[85] Deep-seated legal and ethical conflicts arose from new practices such as rack-renting and usury. Antonio's active opposition to the practice of charging interest and his intervention in the money market to undermine Shylock's business reflect a historical campaign against usury in Elizabethan England. Thomas Wilson, the rhetorician, argued in 1572 that it was 'against all law, against Nature, and against God'.[86] This biblical attitude was, however, waning, and in the previous year Parliament had attempted to control, rather than outlaw, the practice, by setting a maximum rate of interest. Fifty years later, in 1623, Francis Bacon weighed up the 'incommodities and commodities' of usury. In a memorandum of advice to King James, which he published two years later in the third edition of his *Essays*, Bacon concluded that usury had become an inescapable fact of economic life, which it was 'better to mitigate . . . by declaration, than to suffer it to rage by connivance'.[87] The double life of Bacon's text, as a Lord Chancellor's opinion and, with only minor changes, a reflective essay, highlights the regular traffic between law and literature at the time. *The Merchant of Venice* was written around 1597, when the issue was still being urgently debated.

Despite their differences, Antonio and Shylock both expect the bond to be upheld. Antonio articulates the Venetian ideology of the rule of law, which strongly echoes the arguments of Coke and contemporary jurists for the independence and predictability of the common law:

> The Duke cannot deny the course of law;
> For the commodity that strangers have
> With us in Venice, if it be denied,
> Will much impeach the justice of the state,
> Since that the trade and profit of the city
> Consisteth of all nations. (3.4.26–31)

A predictable law, accessible to all traders whether citizens or aliens, is necessary to the continued 'trade and profit of the city'. Therefore, private contracts are enforceable as law. Shylock justifies his stance in terms of the doctrine of consideration and matches his antagonist's understanding that Venice's reputation as a trading centre regulated by law is at stake:

> The pound of flesh which I demand of him
> Is dearly bought;'tis mine, and I will have it.
> If you deny me, fie upon your law:
> There is no force in the decrees of Venice. (4.1.101–2)

There have been many legal commentaries on the trial scene, from Rudolf von Jhering to Daniel J. Kornstein, and ranging in response from admiration to ire. We cannot do justice here to this tradition within legal humanism but refer readers to two excellent summaries.[88] It is generally agreed that when Shylock claims to 'stand here for law' (4.1.142), he represents the objective, impersonal application of rules in the common law or other legal systems. However, his claim pushes the limits of what this contractual society finds acceptable as a subject of agreement. The play presents an extreme case, and this scene, like a moot at the Inns of Court, presents the disputation and the solution.[89] Arguments for and against the literal enforcement of the bond are put. The contrary argument is an equitable one. Enforcement of the bond would produce an unjust result, the loss of a life. Bassanio appeals to Portia for what Aristotle calls 'a special ordinance': 'Wrest once the law to your authority; / To do a great right, do a little wrong' (4.1.211–12). Portia's appeal for mercy likewise draws on the discourse of equity: 'I have spoke thus much / To mitigate the justice of thy plea' (4.1.198–9). Thomas More, we recall, asked the common-law judges to 'mitigate and reform the law themselves'. R. S. White points out that the English jurisdiction of equity does not exist in Venice; otherwise, Shylock could not simply refuse to countenance it. Consequently, Shakespeare is not showing 'the *operation* of English equity or royal prerogative, but rather arguing for its underlying *rationale*'.[90] Shylock's choice of law over equity is achieved by a rejection of the power of rhetoric: 'There is no power in the tongue of man / To alter me' (4.1.236–7). Shylock can neither be persuaded by reasons nor moved by appeals to moral values. This refusal of rhetoric entails a rejection of the ideals of legal humanism and equitable drama.

The solution engineered by Portia is to apply the letter of the law with the utmost possible strictness, turning an equitable drama into a spectacle of law. Shylock may cut a pound of flesh, neither more nor less, and no blood, since that is not specified in the bond. Shylock's tactic is turned against him, and his apparent triumph becomes a comprehensive defeat. Such a structure of sudden reversal, in which strict construction meets stricter, and refusal of mercy is followed by granting of mercy, is characteristic of plots involving poetic justice:

> For as thou urgest justice, be assured
> Thou shalt have justice more than thou desirest. (4.1.311–12)

Portia does not speak in the dispassionate and calm tones of a legal oracle here; her assurance has overtones of a threat. Moreover, the idea of an excess of justice is contradictory, and signals an abandonment of restraint, a punitive intention. Portia's partiality, her relationship to Bassanio, and through him to Antonio, has often been the subject of comment, but one interesting factor in the scene is the intense affiliation between Shylock and the judge. His exorbitant praise, 'O wise and upright judge', and his breathless and intimate dialogue, 'Ay, his breast. / So says the bond, doth it not, noble judge? / "Nearest his heart": those are the very words', betray a kind of 'legal lust', an excited identification with the deployment of legal violence.[91] As the reversal comes into effect, Gratiano exhibits the same lust in mimicking Shylock. Law has become the pretext for vindictive uses of power, an instrument of domination.[92]

The ideological interests behind the law become evident when Portia reveals the terms of the statute against aliens. With this law, the pretence of an equal and neutral rule of law in Venice is shattered. Preferential treatment is given to citizens, and extraordinary penalties visited on outsiders who attack them. Although the usurer is necessary to the Venetian economy, and the money of strangers is welcome, the racial and cultural identity of the society is reinforced through law. The impetus towards new relationships and new identities set in motion by the market economy's engagement with the other is acknowledged by the progressive commercial law but limited by the unequal and racially biased criminal law. Anti-alien riots occurred in London in 1588, 1593 and 1595, just as the law of contract and the new market were developing.[93] *The Merchant of*

Venice registers both the possibility of an altered understanding of humanity and the resentment of change in the conflictual agreement between Shylock and Antonio. As the 'shared discourse' of contract ramified throughout Renaissance society, law and literature both promoted and interrogated it. Drama and rhetoric, doctrine and rules together developed with the institutional backing of the Inns of Court. This common location ensured an often symbiotic relationship between literature and the law. It is not enough, though, to celebrate the lives of More and Bacon, or those like Shakespeare who were invited to perform at the Inns. We must also attend to those critical voices excluded from this cultural centre, such as that of Isabella Whitney. The surviving compositions of women, working-class petitioners, and foreigners have been uncovered in recent years by new historical approaches. Their writings, obscure in their own times, reveal new perspectives on authority, on contract, on language and on identity to us, as we continue to live our lives in an ever-expanding market society.

CHAPTER 4

Crime and punishment in the eighteenth century

In one of the ruling ideas in eighteenth-century literary culture, poets were legislators. 'Poets are the unacknowledged legislators of mankind', the Romantic poet Shelley declared from exile in Italy.[1] Although this is the most memorable formulation of the doctrine, earlier poets omitted the qualifier, and assumed their role was an acknowledged one. A century before Shelley, Alexander Pope in his *Essay on Criticism* argued that literature was subject to traditional rules as part of the law of Nature:

> These rules of old *discover'd*, not *devis'd*,
> Are *Nature* still, but *Nature Methodiz'd*;
> *Nature*, like *Liberty*, is but restrain'd
> By the same Laws which first *herself* ordain'd.[2]

Homer was the first literary law-giver, and the writers of ancient Greece and Rome 'Receiv'd his laws, and stood convinced 'twas fit / Who conquer'd *Nature* shou'd preside o'er *Wit*.' In Britain, Pope found only a few writers who 'here restor'd Wit's *Fundamental Laws*', thereby justifying his own satires on the culture of his day.

A generation later, Samuel Johnson distilled this trope in his novel, *Rasselas*: his hero Imlac states that the poet 'must write as the interpreter of nature, and the legislator of mankind, and consider himself as presiding over the thoughts and manners of future generations'.[3] Johnson's friend, Oliver Goldsmith, saw poets as exerting a corrective influence in their own generations but insisted that they were legislators only by analogy:

new fashions, follies, and vices make new monitors in every age necessary. An author may be considered as a merciful substitute for a legislator; he acts not by punishing crimes, but preventing them; however virtuous the present age, there may be still growing employment for ridicule, or reproof, for persuasion, or satire.[4]

Goldsmith gives a modern twist to this trope, not simply through substituting the word 'author' for 'poet', but through his image of the author as a 'monitor', one who keeps watch over, and admonishes, a recalcitrant society.

In espousing a central role for literature in the maintenance of social order, the 'author-as-legislator' trope assumes an entrenched alliance between law and literature. It leads us to expect a continuation of the integration of discourses, and the institutional hospitality of law for literature and vice versa, that we have traced in the Renaissance period.[5] And indeed, as we shall see, there is abundant evidence in the genres of literary and legal writing to demonstrate the extension of this tradition. At the same time, certain developments in society, and as a result in literature and law, create tensions within this alliance, tensions that lead ultimately to the bifurcation of the two disciplines that we know today. In this chapter we will trace this complex process of engagement, in which literature and law attempt to support each other in the pursuit of a vision of order, yet the content of that vision produces opposition, conflict and separation between the two disciplines.

One of the most remarkable attempts to use literature as a 'merciful substitute for a legislator' occurred in the penal colony of New South Wales on 4 June 1789. On that day, the birthday of George III, the military governor permitted a group of convicts to perform a play, *The Recruiting Officer* by George Farquhar, as part of the celebrations. This event has been memorialised as the first full production of a European play in the Australian colonies, but its ironies are manifold. A group of prisoners, outcasts from their society, perform in support of the sovereign who expelled them. In the play they take on various roles of characters who hold important positions in the English governing class, including Justices of the Peace, military recruiters, squires and heiresses. According to one of its two modern treatments, Timberlake Wertenbaker's play *Our Country's Good*, the governor's rationale was reformative, to use the play to convert disaffected felons into citizens:

What is a statesman's responsibility? To ensure the rule of law. But the citizens must be taught to obey that law of their own will. I want to rule over responsible human beings, not tyrannise over a group of animals. I want there to be a contract between us, not a whip on my side, terror and hatred on theirs.[6]

In effect, Governor Phillip believes *The Recruiting Officer* can work to recruit orderly subjects for the state. Wertenbaker's play was originally developed and performed as a double bill with *The Recruiting Officer* at the Royal Court Theatre in London. The intertextual relation between the two plays works to echo recent theories of ideology, which argue that individuals are 'recruited' by ideologies to positions within the social order.

The convict production offers the modern reader an entry-point into the wider cultural environment of eighteenth-century literature and law, by inviting the question, why were British criminals sent to New South Wales? Leaving aside the strategic reasons for establishing a British colony in the south Pacific, the penal settlement in New South Wales was founded in response to a crisis in the criminal justice system at home. It was part of a long-term shift in British penal policy, a shift in the technology of punishment from the gallows to the prison, from terror to individual reform, to adopt the contrast that Wertenbaker puts into the mouth of Governor Phillip.

The inculcation of obedience through fear was the preferred approach of England's legislators for most of the century, as the number of offences for which capital punishment was prescribed increased threefold during this period. Many of these new capital offences involved small infractions of property rights. This draconian criminal law became known as 'the Bloody Code'. The enforcement of this law was designed to emphasise its majesty through ritualised displays of legal power at court sessions and most especially at the gallows.[7] From the middle of the century, the ineffectiveness and injustice of this policy led writers from the legal and literary fields to protest against it. The alternative proposed, imprisonment, was said to offer the possibility of reforming the mind of the criminal. In 1787, the year that the fleet set sail for New South Wales, Jeremy Bentham published his *Panopticon*, a comprehensive account of the architecture and internal organisation of the new prison concept.[8] Bentham thought that transportation simply placed the old regime of terror offshore, and delayed the development of a rational solution to the problem of crime. The old and new philosophies are debated in Wertenbaker's play, an indication of their continuing relevance. This chapter will explore the role of writing, as ally and dissident, in the crisis of crime and punishment at key points in the century.

LITERATURE AND CRIME IN THE 1720S

Eighteenth-century England affords historians and students a vista of contrasts. Law 'had come to replace religion as the main ideological cement of society', but lawyers were acerbically satirised.[9] Poets upheld an Augustan ideal of order based in nature, but this imaginative vision was promulgated against the background of a perceived crime wave. As the parliamentarians extended the death penalty to a myriad of misdemeanours, the literary legislators applied the weapons of satire to the vice and disorder around them. Writers actively intervened in political disputes, often on partisan terms, and even private conflicts were seen to have public, social significance. Pope wrote his mock-heroic poem *The Rape of the Lock* to restore harmony to two feuding aristocratic families. In setting the scene for his comic retelling of the story, he notes the swift dispensation of justice: 'The hungry Judges soon the Sentence sign, / And wretches hang that jurymen may dine.'[10] Injustices produced by law were a common subject for satire. Lady Mary Wortley Montagu used a literary forum to condemn a vicious husband whom the divorce laws supported. Her 'Epistle from Mrs Y[onge] to her Husband' imagines his wife presenting her case:

> This wretched Out-cast, this abandon'd Wife,
> Has yet this Joy to sweeten Life,
> By your mean conduct, infamously loose,
> You are at once m'Accuser and excuse.
> Let me be damn'd by the Censorious Prude
> (Stupidly Dull, or Spiritually Lewd),
> My hapless case will surely Pity find,
> From every Just and reasonable Mind,
> When to the final Sentence I submit,
> The Lips condemn me, but their Souls acquit.[11]

Civil wrong is here figured as a criminal 'Sentence', indicating the severity of social and legal penalties for the divorced woman. Moreover, the use of criminal discourse also indicates the era's preoccupation with crime.

The 1720s saw the first of the century's moral panics about increased criminality. Although modern historians have shown that the overall crime rate across the eighteenth century rose only at times of economic hardship or at the conclusion of wars, when large numbers of soldiers were demobilised, the contemporary discourse was dominated by perceptions of a crime wave sweeping over the country.[12] Among the signs of this panic was a proliferation of new ways of speaking about crime, both in the literary forms for representing it and in the legal forms for naming and punishing it.

In 1723 the Waltham Black Act, a compendious piece of legislation intended to protect property owners in and around the royal forests at Windsor, added forty-six new offences to the criminal law. So wide was the scope of the act that it was a virtual criminal code, and it inaugurated the century's leading penal strategy by making death the invariable punishment. Some of its sections criminalised previously acknowledged customary rights enjoyed by tenants on the lands. Even quite small acts could attract the severest penalties. For example it became a capital offence to interfere with the banks of a fish-pond. As E. P. Thompson showed, the Black Act was a piece of class legislation, an attempt to use the law to promote the proprietary interests of the Whig governors and to override both the rights and the protests of those adversely affected.[13] Although intended to deal with a specific, local situation, its terms were widely interpreted by judges, applied generally throughout the country and kept in force by Parliament long after its original purpose had been achieved. The Black Act thus became the prototype for the 'Bloody Code'.

As a massive and massively unfair mobilisation of state power, the code was resisted in various ways. The harshness of this form of legal creativity was mitigated by juries, who found ways of evading its violent consequences, by returning verdicts of not guilty in the face of judicial directions, by valuing property under the threshold required for the death penalty, or more traditionally, by appending recommendations of mercy to their verdicts. The crowd around the hanging tree at Tyburn, and the criminals themselves, could turn the ritual of execution, with its procession, criminal's last words and grim conclusion, into a carnival of disorder. Jonathan Swift captured this in 'Clever Tom Clinch Going to be Hanged' (1726–7):

> As clever Tom Clinch, while the rabble was bawling,
> Rode stately through Holborn, to die in his calling;
> He stopped at the George for a bottle of sack,
> And promised to pay for it when he came back. . . .
> And when his last speech the hawkers did cry,
> He swore from his cart it was all a damned lie.
> The hangman for pardon fell down on his knee;
> Tom gave him a kick in the guts for his fee.[14]

Clinch is based on the impenitent highwayman, Tom Cox, who kicked both hangman and chaplain off the cart rather than express contrition.[15] Despite its vigorous, earthy comedy, this poem is a conservative satire, critiquing the behaviour of Clinch and the 'rabble', not the content of the law.

Swift's reference to the sale of copies of Clinch's 'last speech' is historically apt. The processes of trial and execution became a zone of intense cultural activity, generating a wide variety of narrative forms, and contributing to literary as well as legal history. As Hal Gladfelder puts it, 'criminality and the law were lenses that brought into focus much of what was most disturbing, and most exciting, about contemporary experience'.[16] Narratives of actual crimes and criminals abounded from the late seventeenth century.[17] Two important publishing ventures show the mutual dependence between crime and literature: the *Ordinary of Newgate's Accounts* and the *Old Bailey Session Papers*.[18] These hugely popular series became important parts of the apparatus of social control, designed to supplement the scaffold by deterring readers from the temptations of crime. The Chaplain in Ordinary to Newgate Prison was granted the right to publish the criminal biographies and final statements of condemned prisoners. The *Session Papers* were trial narratives, which from the late seventeenth century gradually developed into full records of criminal trials. As they evolved, both these forms acquired a 'thickness of description' that provided their readers with more details of criminal lives than were needed for their didactic function. Details of circumstances, locations and individual personalities could compete with the normative categories of law, sin and repentance, by offering an engaging representation of the life-worlds of the condemned.[19]

The readerly interest of these narrative forms 'stimulated a taste for crime reporting by journalists'.[20] Crime stories were therefore an important element in the infancy of newspapers, and they remain so. One enterprising newspaper owner, John Applebee, employed an already well-known journalist and writer, Daniel Defoe, as a crime reporter. Defoe was able to interview criminals, including the legendary escapologist Jack Sheppard, and to acquire a detailed understanding of their milieux and modes of operation. Taking advantage of this access, he proceeded to write longer criminal biographies of Sheppard and Jonathan Wild, and fictional biographies, novels with criminal protagonists.[21] In moving so easily between crime reporting and novel writing, Defoe was by no means unique. Not only were other writers, mostly now forgotten, working in the same fields, but the fields themselves abutted one another. Grub Street, the desperate home of literary hack-workers, was in the heart of criminal London. The novel was a suspect form, dangerously modern and still suffering from the Puritan distrust of fiction as a species of lies. This anxious status was redoubled by the novelists' predilection for criminal subjects. The writers, of course, took steps to deny these charges, chiefly by pretending that their novels were 'true histories'. Thus the urgent and fertile production of stories about crime occurred in a discursive field that was still taking shape, in which the present generic boundary between fictional and non-fictional narratives was not well established. In short, the legal problem of crime proved integral to the development of the novel and helped shape literary history.[22]

The most engaging of these early criminal novels is Defoe's *Moll Flanders* (1722). A first-person novel, purporting to be the confessions of the much-married former thief and pick-pocket, *Moll Flanders* differs from the 'Last Speeches' and other forms of crime literature in the complexity of its heroine's representation. Defoe's ventriloquism in constructing a voice that adopts the penitent stance required by the Ordinary of Newgate and by his masters who dispensed pardons, whilst fascinating the reader with the most immediate narratives of her exploits, creates an ambiguous but engaging heroine. Are her professions of repentance and conversion sincere? Is Defoe being ironic in his impersonation of her? While different answers to these questions are open, it is clear that as a verbal creation Moll achieves a high level of authenticity along with her ethical dubiety. In another instance of the intertextual traffic between law and literature, Moll Flanders is based on a real transported pick-pocket, Moll King. In 1718 she was convicted and sentenced to death, but reprieved owing to pregnancy. She returned from America illegally and recommenced her old trade. Entering the orbit of the corrupt thief-taker Jonathan Wild, she was betrayed and once again sentenced to death, and once again reprieved.[23] Though their stories are not identical, their name, crimes and resilience are shared. A fictional 'letter' purportedly from Moll King published in *Applebee's Original Weekly Journal*, and commenting on her situation as a returned convict, is one of the disputed texts attributed to Defoe.[24]

Moll Flanders is narrated from the standpoint of a reformed criminal, in the voice of a penitent. Interspersed among her moral reflections, however, are traces of the idioms of her former life, which resurface to give relish and immediacy to the remembrance of her crimes. Describing her education in the arts of theft, she says, 'by the help of this Confederate, I grew as impudent a thief, and as dexterous as ever *Moll Cut-Purse* was'.[25] Pleasure and pride in 'getting away with it', in her professional success, compete with moralistic discourse. Similarly, when describing her initial resort to crime, Moll alludes to the Devil tempting her but also offers a more radical economic explanation for her behaviour: 'Poverty presses, the Soul is made desperate by distress, and what can be done?' (254). However, this circumstantial justification is only temporary, as her stealing continues. The Christian explanation of crime as sin supersedes the economic insight. Nonetheless, economic discourse is a significant factor in Defoe's world-view. Despite her eventual capture, conviction and punishment, crime pays for Moll Flanders. She saves the proceeds of her crimes and builds up a stock of capital with which to start her new life in comfort, and thence grows positively prosperous. As a thief, pick-pocket and prostitute, she participates in the new consumer economy, with its vastly increased supply of luxury items, like watches, silks and wigs.

In this fictional world, legal process is something to be evaded, and not only by Moll. Defoe lets his heroine off lightly. Her very success as a criminal means she is tried as a first offender, and thus her death penalty is commuted to transportation. The novel is more interested in punishment than trial, and its confessional form allows reflection on various penalties. The hanging of two fellow-thieves 'frightened me heartily' says Moll (269), but its deterrent effect was decidedly temporary. By contrast, transportation is the novel's preferred mode of punishment. Only formalised by statute in 1718, though previously offered on a voluntary basis, transportation to the colonies is rosily painted by Defoe as enabling a completely new start for the convict.[26] Moll's rehabilitation is signalled by her successful, legitimate involvement in the import and export trade. Thus the novel works to promote imperialism and a new penal policy whilst delighting its readers with the vicarious pleasures of crime.

FIELDING AND THE 1740S

The middle decades of the eighteenth century saw another wave of anxiety about crime. Henry Fielding, who as a young man witnessed the hanging of Jonathan Wild at Tyburn in 1725, immersed himself uniquely in the literary and legal discourses on crime from the 1740s. Fielding led a life in successive phases, as a young man about town, as a playwright, a lawyer and a novelist. In 1749 he was appointed to the magistracy, and he devised the Bow Street Runners police force during his term in office. Though he may appear to us as a representative of the integrated culture of law and letters, it was only when Walpole's Licensing Act of 1737 closed down the theatres that he enrolled in the Middle Temple, studied law and became a barrister. As a struggling advocate on the Western Circuit, he combined both professions, but did so in secret. As his friend James Harris recalled: 'At his Lodgings, upon ye circuit, he was often working on his Peices [sic] of Humour, which when business was approaching, soon vanished out of Sight, while ye Law Books and the Briefs, with their Receptacle ye Green Bag lay on ye Table ready deployed to inspire the client with proper Sentiments.'[27]

Early in this decade, Fielding wrote anonymous political satire and essays for journals such as *The Champion*, but in 1742, he published his first novel, *Joseph Andrews*. Styling his book a 'comic epic poem in prose' Fielding attempted a literary equivalent of his friend William Hogarth's achievement in art, the accurate representation of the manners and morals of their society. Rather than direct condemnation, he sought to elicit ridicule of folly and vice by satire. Like Hogarth, he professes allegiance in this work to realist canons of portraiture, not to the caricaturist's technique of exaggeration. *Joseph Andrews* tests the innocence of Joseph, Fanny and Parson Adams against the depredations of greedy publicans, uncharitable priests, cunning robbers and a host of self-serving 'People of Fashion' in a series of adventures on the road. Fielding's fusion of realism, satire and moralism is well illustrated when Joseph is robbed and left naked by highwaymen. Highwaymen were among the most feared criminals outside London. Joseph is found, but not immediately rescued, by a coach, becoming an object of humour for its well-heeled passengers. In a comic rewriting of the biblical parable of the Good Samaritan, the only character who aids Joseph is the postillion boy, who, the narrator informs us in a satiric aside on the class bias of the Bloody Code, was later transported for theft. Crime, then, is the raw material of comedy. Only once does it result in a trial, and there the criminal becomes the accuser, when Adams is accused of assaulting Fanny's would-be rapist. This trial displays the reliance on character evidence in criminal procedure of the time and allows a sustained exposure of the class bias in the system: when Adams is recognised as a gentleman he is released.

There are several episodes satirising ignorant and grasping lawyers and justices; but Fielding is most concerned to condemn misuses of the law, rather than law itself. Despite what Alexander Welsh calls his 'prosecutorial' mode, he notes the abuse possible under the Bloody Code.[28] He parodies a corrupt prosecution initiated by Lady Booby, who wishes to expel Joseph and Fanny from the district: Lawyer Scout obliges by swearing a complaint that he 'zede Joseph Andrews with a nife cut one hassel-twig, of the value, as he believes, of 3 half-pence, or thereabouts'. The spelling errors in this parodic deposition indicate the linguistic and legal barbarity of Lawyer Scout, for whom the law is an instrument of power. ' "Jesu!" said the squire, "would you commit two persons to Bridewell for a twig?" "Yes," said the lawyer, "and with great lenity too; for if we had called it a young tree they would have been both hanged." ' Fielding does not exaggerate: under one of the worst statutes of the Bloody Code, 31 George II c.42, it was a capital offence to cut down a cherry tree in an orchard.

Fielding's narrative technique offers an interesting variant of the writer-as-legislator ideology. As William Empson concludes in one of the classic essays on *Tom Jones*, 'he is always ready to consider what he would do if one of his characters came before him on the bench. He is quite ready to hang a man, but also to reject the technical reasons for doing so if he considers that the man's impulses are not hopelessly corrupted.'[29] Alexander Welsh has provided historical support for this conclusion by demonstrating the ubiquity of trial motifs in *Tom Jones*. As narrator, Fielding 'manages the evidence' that is presented to the reader.[30] That evidence consists not just of the personal testimony of a first-person narrator like Moll Flanders, but of circumstantial details, facts that exist independently of any individual's vision. As Barbara Shapiro has shown, the concept of 'fact' – a fundamental category in the mental world of Western modernity – was first recognised as a provable basis for knowledge in the field of law.[31] The probative value of circumstantial evidence was legally accepted during the eighteenth century, and Fielding transfers this habit of thought to his novels.

Yet the judicial urge and the comic urge do not easily harmonise in *Tom Jones*. While Joseph Andrews was an innocent, Tom is a miscreant, 'born to be hanged'. When he is accused of trespass, when he confesses to getting Molly Seagrim pregnant, when telling of his other misdeeds, the narrator always manages the evidence so as to acquit him, explaining the pressures of the situation, placing blame elsewhere, foregrounding Tom's good motives. As a result, readers are invited to enjoy his escapades, and to suspend or at least qualify judgment. Some readers both in the eighteenth century and more recently have found the novel's comic celebration of the illicit undermines its moral project, and have censured it. When Fielding was appointed magistrate in 1749, the year in which *Tom Jones* was published, the irony of this change of role did not escape his critics. His first publication after appointment, *A Charge to the Grand Jury*, was official and decidedly orthodox. It began with 'a kind of Rapture' about the jury as a cornerstone of freedom and included a condemnation of theatres, 'where the Exhibitions are not only contrary to Law, but contrary to Good-Manners'.[32] The altered tone and content of this work provoked charges of hypocrisy from Fielding's opponents, but the case is more interesting as evidence of an increasing differentiation between the discourses of literature and law.[33]

Fielding wrote one more novel, *Amelia*, but his later writings are polemical interventions in debates about crime and emerge directly from his work on the bench. Two pamphlets defend findings in controversial cases: *A True State of the Case of Bosavern Penlez* (1749), who was the only man convicted and executed after major rioting, and *A Clear State of the Case of Elizabeth Canning* (1753), who claimed to have been abducted by gypsies, but was later transported for perjury. Despite the doubts held over these cases, Fielding argued for a close relation between divine and human justice in

Examples of the Interposition of Providence in the Detection and Punishment of Murder (1752). His examples included ancient stories like Cain and Abel and contemporary *causes célèbres* such as Mary Blandy, who had poisoned her father that year.[34] The work is motivated by an apparent increase in the incidence of murder and aims to deter it through cautionary tales of detection.

A similar inspiration underlies Fielding's major contribution to the crime debate, *An Enquiry into the Causes of the Late Increase of Robbers* (1751). Its introduction affords a good example of the hyperbole characteristic of crime-wave rhetoric: 'I make no doubt, but that the Streets of this town, and the roads leading to it, will shortly be impassable without the utmost Hazard; nor are we threatned with seeing less dangerous gangs of Rogues among us, than those which the Italians call the Banditi.'[35] Perhaps because this is a work addressed to legislators, it lacks the broad vision of the novels and analyses property crime solely as a lower-class phenomenon. As Peter King has shown, this was not the case: 'A vast array of appropriational strategies was used by members of each social group. Rich officeholders frequently raided the state, for example. The trading classes used fraud, false weights, forestalling, food adulteration, etc.'[36] But apart from well-to-do forgers, practitioners of these dishonest arts tended not to attract the attention of the criminal law. Luxury, in the form of desirable consumer goods, proves an irresistible temptation to the poor in the new economy, Fielding argues, completely neglecting the smuggling of luxury goods practised in the governing class.

In *Tom Jones*, Fielding puts into the mouth of one of the characters an anecdote concerning the hanging judge, Baron Page, and a defendant charged with horse theft. To the prisoner's defence that he found the horse, the judge replied, ' "thou art a lucky Fellow; I have travelled the Circuit these forty Years, and never found a Horse in my Life; but I'll tell thee what, Friend, thou wast more lucky than thou didst know of; for thou didst not only find a Horse, but a Halter too." '[37] However, the novel uses this famous piece of legal wit to introduce another view of the situation in court. Partridge, the anecdotist, adds: ' "One thing I own I thought a little hard, that the Prisoner's Counsel was not suffered to speak for him, though he desired to be heard one very short Word; but my Lord would not hearken to him, though he suffered a Counsellor to speak against him for above half an Hour." ' Here Fielding realised the dialogical potential of the novel form to place trial procedure in dialogue with an external critique of justice, one that would take another century to be accepted into the law. In view of this critical representation of the death sentence, the *Enquiry* surprises by arguing for a more rigorous application of the death penalty in cases of theft.[38]

In this professional text, debate on the appropriateness of this penalty is not permitted in the public sphere but is interestingly carried on in the mind of the judge. Here a 'revealing dialogue' takes place between 'Reason' and 'Emotion' in which the former seeks reasons 'to reject the Arguments which a good Mind will officiously advance to itself; that violent temptations, Necessity, Youth, inadvertency have hurried him to the Commission of a Crime attended with no inhumanity'.[39] The elaboration of these claims, the recognition that they are the insights of a 'good Mind' suggests that Fielding was affected by the emerging movement of Sensibility. Nonetheless, he resists their appeal in the name of 'Reason', 'Law' and 'Rigour'.

Fielding's legal writings repress the critical debates that his novels promote. In doing so, they reveal traces of the new ideas and situations the law was facing. Hal Gladfelder, in the fullest reading of the *Enquiry*, notes that moral values, social observations and political anxieties infuse the writing and limit its diagnostic power: 'Even when he presents his account of the causes of crime in terms of moral denunciation, the burden of explanation rests on the material conditions of the poor and the ideological tensions fracturing the stable hierarchy of class relations.'[40] In the swiftly changing world of modernity, Fielding appears in these legal writings as a conservative, studying England's legal history for solutions to new problems, and lamenting the passing of the old stability.[41]

LAW AND REASON

Two major ways of speaking accreted round the Bloody Code: paeans of praise to the British constitution and the rule of law; and satiric condemnations of hanging judges, pettifogging lawyers and corrupt officials. A man like Fielding was ideally placed to offer powerful articulations of both, but his very location within the law muted his criticisms. Writers outside the law were deeply disturbed by the self-interest, formalism and complacency of its practitioners. A popular contemporary poem expressed some of the frustration felt by the public:

> Justice is as hard to gain
> As Nor-West Passage o'er the Main.
> Instead of which (O dire Disgrace!)
> A fiend call'd Mammon takes his place.[42]

The fact that officials at every level charged fees to perform their services contributed to this situation. Even Fielding was criticised as a 'trading justice'. Another factor was the decline of the Inns of Court as institutes of legal education in this century. No serious intellectual preparation for practice was offered, fostering a mechanical approach to the law. Lord Bolingbroke, a Tory historian who had made contacts among European philosophers while in exile, noted the effects of this diminished professional culture:

There have been lawyers that were orators, philosophers, historians: there have been Bacons and Clarendons ... There will be none such any more, till in some better age, true ambition or the love of fame prevails over avarice; and till men find leisure and encouragement to prepare themselves for the exercise of this profession, by climbing up to the *vantage ground*, so my Lord Bacon calls it, of science.[43]

Bolingbroke urges lawyers to pursue law as a rational and systematic study, including its philosophy and history, 'that they may discover the abstract reason of the law', and be able to analyse 'all the effects good and bad' of the English legal system. He contrasts his enlightened 'vantage ground' with base 'grovelling ... in a mean but gainful application to all the arts of chicane'. David Lemmings adduces Bolingbroke's views as evidence of an Enlightenment critique of common-law traditionalism, a wish to bring both Voltaire and Montesquieu to the Inns of Court, but they also suggest an attenuation of the bonds between law, literature and other cultural discourses. Was Fielding's secret fiction-writing on Circuit symptomatic of a narrower legal culture?

On leaving university to commence law in London, William Blackstone wrote a poem, 'The Lawyer's Farewell to his Muse'. In the polished couplets of Pope, he contrasted the pastoral scene of his youth spent in the company 'of Fancy and of Art' with the urban nightmare ahead:

> Me wrangling courts, and stubborn law,
> To smoke, and crowds, and cities draw:
> There selfish faction rules the day,
> And pride and avarice throng the way.[44]

This poem is often cited as evidence that law and literature had become strangers to each other. B. M. Jones suggests that Blackstone 'thought it necessary to signalise his abandonment of literature'.[45] The poem proceeds, however, to find another muse, Justice, 'in a winding close retreat', and the idealistic young aspirant dedicates himself to 'unfold[ing] with joy her sacred page'. Drawing on classical myth, he pictures Justice as residing like an oracle behind a veil or in a 'pure spring', which he desires to penetrate. A distrust of self produces an attachment to the law, and an unquestioning faith in its integrity:

> And other doctrines thence imbibe
> Than lurk within the sordid scribe;

> Observe how parts with parts unite
> In one harmonious rule of right.

The interest of this poem lies in its accidental discovery through 'Fancy' and 'Art', that is, through imagination and poetic technique, of Blackstone's *métier*, the exposition through writing of the common law as 'one harmonious rule of right'. In these lines, law becomes a subject worthy of poetry, and the common law's greatest ideologue finds literature a way of ennobling his professional life.

The eventual fruit of this hope, the *Commentaries on the Laws of England*, was published in four volumes between 1765 and 1769. Blackstone's ability to encompass within a single structure the entire common law made his work an instant classic of legal education. His search for the principles underlying rights and rules, and his references to a wide range of ancient and modern jurists led to the *Commentaries* being praised for their rhetorical skill and intellectual ambition. However, their very generality, so useful to students, was a limitation to professional lawyers. Sir William Jones described the book as 'the most correct and beautiful outline that was ever exhibited of any human science', but one that 'alone will no more form a lawyer, than a general map of the world, however accurately and elegantly soever it may be delineated, will make a geographer'.[46] Significantly, the map analogy builds on one of Blackstone's own metaphors.[47] Jones and the next generation of legal scholars followed Blackstone's example in producing textbooks that filled the gaps in his work. For these writers, and for his radical critic Bentham, the *Commentaries* lacked a consistent underlying theory of law as well as sustained reasoning on details of practice.[48] It is now possible to recognise the innovation of this text and its role in securing the ideological dominance of the common law in this century of change.[49] It is as a literary text, working to produce certain effects in its society, that the *Commentaries* merit our attention. In the best study from this perspective, Michael Meehan has concluded that it 'represents the furthest point of integration in a process of "twisting and interweaving" of aesthetic and legal discourse in the eighteenth century'.[50]

Despite his conservatism, his veneration for the common law as the blueprint of English society, Blackstone criticised the severity of the criminal law. More particularly, despite the almost mystical treatment of property in Volume II, he condemns the legislature's routine resort to capital punishment for minor offences in Volume IV.[51] In opening that volume on criminal law, he protests against the triviality of some capital crimes, such as breaking a fishpond, or cutting down a tree, echoing the example used by Fielding in *Joseph Andrews*.[52] In arguing thus, Blackstone endorses the principles of certainty and consistency that his European contemporary Beccaria had outlined as the basis of a rational theory of punishment.[53]

The integration of law, culture and reason promoted by Blackstone was by no means an agreed value among eighteenth-century English lawyers. In 1768, Edward Wynne's *Eunomus, or Dialogues Concerning the Law and Constitution of England* included a debate on whether an aspiring lawyer should give up reading non-legal texts. Employing the classical genre of dialogue for perhaps the last time in a legal treatise, Policritus uses the familiar terms of Blackstone's poem, declaring he is 'now obliged to quit those enchanting scenes of fancy for the dry and intricate paths of the law'.[54] Eunomus, his mentor, refutes this but acknowledges: 'You speak the sense of a large party, who have ever looked upon the black letter in the old reports and Statute Books as ... if lawyers had entered into a kind of recognizance to talk and think of nothing but law.'[55] Along with the supplementation of Blackstone's work by specialist treatises, and Fielding's secret continuance of fiction, *Eunomus* testifies to the increasing discursive separatism among lawyers. Writers, however, continued to be generalists.

SAMUEL JOHNSON, LL.D.

As the economy of literature shifted from one of patronage to a market-oriented mode of production, one of the major participants in the resultant public sphere was Samuel Johnson. Johnson was a prolific and versatile writer, who published poetry and literary criticism, edited journals such as the *Rambler* and the *Idler* and drafted speeches and pamphlets for others intervening in public and political debates. Late in life he devised legal arguments for his young friend and eventual biographer, the reluctant barrister James Boswell. As we shall see, Johnson was on friendly terms with many lawyers and participated as both writer and citizen in legal controversies. More than this, the discourse of law provided him with an analogy for the cultural responsibility of the writer.

In the spirit of the Enlightenment project of systematically advancing knowledge, Johnson compiled the first authoritative dictionary of the English language. In his *Plan of an English Dictionary* (1747) he offered a judicial approach to the work: 'I shall, therefore, since the rules of style, like those of law, arise from precedents often repeated, collect the testimonies on both sides, and endeavour to discover and promulgate the decrees of custom, who has so long possessed, whether by right or usurpation, the sovereignty of words.'[56] This analogy between the English language and the common law gives the lexicographer a power of authoritative declaration, and the *Dictionary* a prescriptive function. The experience of working on the *Dictionary* over seven years led him to a more descriptive practice, but in the preface to the completed work legal metaphors still shape his understanding of the project: 'when I took the first survey of my undertaking, I found our speech copious without order, and energetick without rules: wherever I turned my view, there was perplexity to be disentangled, and confusion to be regulated'.[57] One area of successful regulation was spelling: Johnson's deliberations effected an unprecedented standardisation of English orthography. His work contributed to 'the rise of prescriptive grammar', and a normative approach to pronunciation.[58] Even when counselling restraint in linguistic punctiliousness, and 'respect for antiquity', Johnson found the law a model: 'It has been asserted that for law to be *known* is of more importance than to be *right*. "Change," says Hooker, "is not made without inconvenience, even from worse to better." There is in constancy and stability a general and lasting advantage, which will always overbalance the slow improvements of gradual correction.'[59] Johnson's natural conservatism, his honouring the claims of legal and linguistic tradition, is revealed here. Pat Rogers's modern description of the *Dictionary* as a 'codifying and synthesising masterpiece' comparable to Blackstone's *Commentaries on the Laws of England* reflects its reception in his own age: for his achievement Johnson was awarded the honorary degree of Doctor of Laws by Trinity College, Dublin.[60]

Writing was for Johnson a deeply social activity, an aspect of civil society and a contribution to the public good. He numbered many lawyers among his friends, both contemporaries such as Lords Hardwicke and Mansfield and younger men like Boswell, Sir Robert Chambers and William Scott, later Lord Stowell. Chambers, Scott and Sir William Jones were elected as members of Johnson's Literary Club, along with Oliver Goldsmith, Edmund Burke, the actor David Garrick, the painter Sir Joshua Reynolds and the botanist Sir Joseph Banks. This intellectual and social network enabled conversations between disciplines and facilitated the diffusion of general knowledge. Such links entailed a respect for lawyers and law, as Johnson noted in a conversation with the solicitor Oliver Edwards: ' "You are a lawyer, Mr Edwards. Lawyers know life practically. A bookish man should always have them to converse with. They have what he wants." '[61] In this statement the word 'wants' is used in its eighteenth-century sense of 'lacks', rather than in our modern sense of 'wishes for'.

Johnson valorises the practical reason of the lawyer, which enables him to view law itself in an equally positive light. As he said in another conversation recorded for posterity, 'Law is the last result of human wisdom acting upon human experience for the benefit of the public.'[62] Given these normative predilections, Johnson has been something of a cultural hero for English lawyers. There is a building in the Temple, London's legal precinct, named in his honour, and lawyers have written about him.[63]

Although a conservative in temperament and principle, and an upholder of traditions in many facets of life, Johnson's views on the criminal law were reformist. He accepted the need for law and its sanctions, including capital punishment; however, he considered that the policy underlying the Bloody Code was misguided and wrote an essay in *The Rambler* explaining why. In this essay he offers a psychological acute view of the legislator's motives for seeking the capital sanction, including the temptations of power. He criticises the way that the wholesale use of the death penalty has obscured the varied degrees of seriousness among different offences. He advocates a new approach, namely a 'relaxation of the law, and a more rational and equitable adaptation of penalties to offences'. Written in 1751, the essay anticipates some of the new ideas of penal philosophy which came into practice later in the century:

> If those whom the wisdom of our laws has condemned to die had been detected in their rudiments of robbery, they might *by proper discipline and useful labour* have been disentangled from their habits, they might have escaped all the temptations to subsequent crimes, and passed their days in reparation and penitence; and detected they might have been, had the prosecutors been certain that their lives would have been spared [Italics added].[64]

Johnson's alternative to capital punishment, 'discipline and useful labour', is cast in the discourse of the emergent regime of penitence, personal reform and training identified by historians of the prison such as Michel Foucault.[65]

As might be expected given these views, Johnson intervened in cases where the threat of the death penalty existed. Two cases are particularly notable. In 1769 he gave character evidence for his friend Joseph Baretti, at the latter's trial for murder. Baretti, an Italian *émigré* writer, had stabbed a man during an altercation in the street. He pleaded self-defence, arguing that he was accosted by a prostitute and a crowd of men, and that he acted in fear and confusion. In a statement read to the court, he argued that 'a man of my age, character and way of life would not spontaneously quit my pen, to engage in an outrageous tumult', and that he carried a knife not as a weapon, but from habit gained in Europe where only forks were laid on the meal table, and everyone carried their own knife.[66] Witnesses confirmed this custom. Others testified to seeing his bruised face and body. The final aspect of the defence case was character evidence given by Reynolds, Johnson, Burke, Garrick, Goldsmith and others. Johnson told the court that Baretti was 'a man of literature, a very studious man, . . . A man that I never knew to be otherwise than peaceable, and a man that I take to be rather timorous.'[67] Boswell's comment, 'Never did such a constellation of genius enlighten the aweful Session-House', reflects his own capacity for hero-worship, and undervalues the coherence of the defence case.[68] We should beware of accepting this romantic hyperbole as evidence that writers and artists possessed cultural authority, for sprinkled among the *literati* were a couple of character witnesses from the aristocracy. It was the social standing, or class position, of the witnesses and accused that carried most weight when eighteenth-century judges and juries entertained character evidence. Through the combined agency of literary, legal and political figures, Baretti was acquitted.

The second case involved a guilty man, Dr William Dodd, who was convicted for forgery in 1777. Dodd, a celebrated preacher, forged Lord Chesterfield's signature to obtain £4,300. Johnson minimised the gravity of this offence and led an unsuccessful campaign for the remission of his death sentence. A petition containing 23,000 signatures was presented to the government, but unavailingly. While some historians have viewed this campaign as evidence of a new sensibility, and so an important step in the evolution of the new philosophy, V. A. C. Gatrell has noted how the outpouring of sympathy for Dodd did not extend to a boy hanged alongside him. This fifteen-year-old had robbed the passengers in a stagecoach of two half-guineas and a few shillings, but neither his youth nor the amount involved unsettled the onlookers at his execution. The supposedly universal and natural language of feelings depended in fact upon a selective and class-based perception.[69]

Johnson's major literary engagement with legal ideas occurred when he gave his talents to help his friend Robert Chambers devise a series of lectures on English law at Oxford University. Chambers was Blackstone's successor in the new Vinerian Professorship, but he suffered from an inability to write quickly and from a fear of comparisons with his predecessor, and was unable to deliver the contracted course of lectures until Johnson assisted him. Their collaboration, which lasted from 1764 to 1770, remained a secret until the twentieth century. Johnson's influence on the lectures is apparent in the opening definition of law, '*any kind of rule or canon whereby actions are directed*', which expands on the primary sense given in the *Dictionary*, 'A rule of action'.[70] It is difficult to separate Johnson's and Chambers's writings, but the more philosophical and less technical lectures are believed to be most heavily shaped, if not actually written, by Johnson. Part II of the *Course* deals with criminal law, and its opening lecture, having surveyed the emergence of criminal punishment from private revenge as an aspect of the civilising process, concludes with a view of eighteenth-century England as a society of Augustan stability:

> We who have always lived under the shelter of legal protection and in the safe calm of a settled society, are perhaps not sufficiently grateful to the care of legislators. Those who have never been sick have little sense of the comfort of health; and those feel not their obligation to the vigilance of law who have never been under any necessity of watching for themselves.[71]

Despite Johnson's long residence in London, there is little sense here of the perceived crime waves that prompted the harsh remedies of the Bloody Code. After a discussion of the history of punishments in the second lecture, the remainder of the course describes the current laws and penalties in 'complacent rather than condemnatory' terms. According to Thomas Curley, its treatment of the Code 'seems surprisingly contrary to the views expressed elsewhere by both Johnson and Chambers'.[72] In this institutional context, the close collaboration between writer and lawyer did not produce an enlightened or critical approach to criminal jurisprudence.

ROMANTICISM AND THE NEW PRISON

Thus far in this chapter, literature and law have been aligned in the quest for social order. Perceptions of disorder produced by rapid social change call forth a vision of the writer as legislator, monitor or judge. Under these legal metaphors, claims of individual rights take second place to those of social authority. Even the novel of criminal adventure concludes with repentance and a reaffirmation of community norms.

However, in the second half of the century, major ideological shifts were set in motion in the cultural and political spheres. In reaction to the stern justice and rigid rationalism of the Augustan age, a new emphasis on feeling and sentiment emerged. In spreading this cult of sensibility, novels – the most popular cultural innovation of the age – were crucial. In addition to narrating adventure and incident, this new form was capable of exploring emotion, conscience and other psychological states. In the sentimental novel the protagonist is typically a young woman who is the intended victim of a seduction plot. The narrative unfolds in the utmost detail her distress and strategies of resistance. This foregrounding of feeling is not gratuitous but draws from a belief that the development of emotion may provide humans with an ethical guide. The cult of sensibility's basic assumption about the goodness of human beings challenged the Christian tradition of original sin, which underlay the criminal law. This progressive morality was especially important in representations of crimes of sex and power, but it was not easily transferrable from the literary to the legal realm. In Samuel Richardson's *Clarissa* (1747–8), the rape of the heroine is the shocking culmination of the rake's will to power. The reader's empathy with her and condemnation of her attacker is not supplemented by legal punishment, for Clarissa has no faith in its justice: 'I would sooner suffer every evil (the repetition of the capital one excepted), than appear publicly in a court.'[73] Richardson presents the law as incapable of justly representing women's experience of rape.[74] Historical confirmation of his perception occurred in 1764 with the acquittal of Lord Baltimore in a case hauntingly similar to that in *Clarissa*.[75]

Another literary manifestation of this cultural shift was the gothic romance. Female gothic writers like Ann Radcliffe used the heroine's imprisonment by an evil guardian as a major convention in tales of terror that excite sympathy for the victim.[76] The cultivation of pathos in the literature of sentimentality served a political purpose, in that it dwelt on stories of violation of the powerless by their class or gender superiors, and so promoted through the moral economy of sympathy the idea of natural rights. These cultural phenomena provided a fertile ground for the positive reception of the philosophical critiques of absolute rule mounted by Voltaire and Rousseau and aided the revolutionary cry of 'Liberty, Equality and Fraternity'. In this context Romanticism emerged as a fully-fledged and radical alternative to the old order of terror symbolised in France by the Bastille and in England by the 'hanging tree'.

In this altered climate, criticisms of the Bloody Code began to grow in volume and conviction. The philosophy of punishment underwent a complete transformation. Michel Foucault has described how 'the great spectacle of physical punishment disappeared', to be replaced by the prison with its promise of the cure of the criminal through a regime of work, separation and routine.[77] Even so notable a defender of the old system as Henry Fielding contributed to this shift, recommending the abolition of the procession to Tyburn in favour of hangings at Newgate, and designing a Workhouse that separated the poor from the criminal inmates.[78] Beccaria argued forcefully against capital punishment and in favour of imprisonment, and his ideas appealed not only to Enlightenment radicals, but to acolytes of sensibility. Within two years, they were disseminated in the sentimental novel by Oliver Goldsmith.

A member of Johnson's circle, Goldsmith wrote on every conceivable subject in his career as a Grub Street hack, but in the 1760s he was particularly concerned to 'monitor' abuses in the criminal law. His novel *The Vicar of Wakefield* sees its hero-narrator imprisoned for debt. In chapter 27, he introduces a disquisition on punishments which is quite at odds with the kindly tone of the narrative up to that point:

Penal laws, which are in the hands of the rich are laid upon the poor . . . and as if our possessions were become dearer in proportion as they increased, as if the more enormous our wealth, the more extensive our fears, our possessions are paled up with more edicts every day, and hung around with gibbets to scare every invader.[79]

His critique of the Bloody Code, and his alternative scheme, 'that legislative power would thus direct the law rather to reformation than severity' by promoting industry and education in prison, are informed by the ideas of Johnson and Beccaria.[80] His explicit appeals to European practice and thought identify Goldsmith as an Enlightenment thinker. The passage quoted above offers an astute socioeconomic speculation on the link between the expanding criminal law and the rise of consumer society and is clearly indebted to Montesquieu's sociological approach to law. Goldsmith's startling image of 'our possessions . . . paled up with more edicts every day, and hung around with gibbets to scare every invader' is a powerful variation on the metaphor of law as a wall, here working as a 'reproof' of the class bias and the terror at the heart of the system.

The new theory of the prison was not easily implemented. The physical conditions and the financial administration of existing prisons undermined the idealism of the reformers. In the 1770s the Sheriff of Bedford, John Howard, inspected all the prisons of Britain and Ireland, and many in Europe, compiling data on the conditions in which prisoners were held. His report, *The State of the Prisons*, was published in 1777. It included statistics, descriptions of accommodation, work routines and rules, and brief histories of each property. His gathering of empirical detail was motivated by a humanitarian concern for the welfare of prisoners. In introducing his 'General View of Distress in Prisons', he abjures utterance 'of the declamatory kind' for a plain style, but nonetheless (mis)quotes an unnamed 'celebrated author' (Johnson): 'In a prison the check of the public eye is removed; and the power of the law is spent.'[81] Howard proposed improvements of a practical kind, using the mechanism of regulation to ensure that 'the power of the law' was effective. His evidence led to the passing of the 1779 Penitentiary Act, which allowed confinement in prison to replace transportation.[82] Despite this innovation in sentencing, it was not until the 1820s that law reformers were able to begin repealing the capital statutes.

Howard saw the 'check of the public eye' as a means of supervising the gaolers, however the real use of the power of vision within the new prisons lay in the observation of prisoners. Jeremy Bentham identified total surveillance as the key to the effectiveness of reformatory imprisonment. It is reflected in the name he gave to his draft model prison, the *Panopticon, or Inspection-House*. A central tower within a circular building ensured the guards saw into every cell, without being seen themselves.[83] Although the Panopticon prison was never built, the principle of controlling behaviour through surveillance and discipline informed the design and management not just of prisons, but of many modern institutions, such as workhouses, hospitals, schools and factories.[84]

This insight involves a critique of the idealism of the reformers, and their Enlightenment assumption that the shift to imprisonment was part of the progress of liberty in the criminal law. In the literature of the 1790s, prison and prisoners are major figures, but the poets and novelists of this generation do not subscribe to the Benthamite plan. For them, prisons remain places of tyranny and are typified by the Bastille. Their radical commitment to individual liberty as a human, not a civil, right led them to take an oppositional stance with respect to the laws of the state. In Romantic poetry it is the political prisoner, the revolutionary, who is extolled: contemporary heroes like Toussaint L'Ouverture, La Fayette, Kosciusko in sonnets by Wordsworth and Coleridge, or historical precursors like François de Bonnivard in Byron's 'Sonnet on Chillon':

> Eternal spirit of the chainless mind!
>> Brightest in dungeons, Liberty! thou art
>> For there thy habitation is the heart –
> The heart which love of thee alone can bind;
> And when thy sons to fetters are consigned –
>> To fetters, and the damp vault's dayless gloom,
>> Their country conquers with their martyrdom,
> And Freedom's fame finds wings on every wind.
> Chillon! thy prison is a holy place,
>> And thy sad floor an altar – for 'twas trod
> Until his very feet have left a trace
>> Worn, as if thy cold pavement were a sod,
> By Bonnivard! – May none those marks efface!
>> For they appeal from tyranny to God.[85]

In this sonnet and its longer companion, 'The Prisoner of Chillon', the realities of incarceration are transcended by the prisoner's intellectual and political conviction. Monika Fludernik has shown how the 'dungeon' persists as a literary trope long into the era of the new penitentiary.[86] The period under review here, however, was a transitional one, in which the old buildings and the old laws were still a vital, though contested, presence.

In reaction to the French Revolution, the English government cracked down on political expression, suspended Habeas Corpus and invoked the medieval law of treason. The Treason Trials of 1794, against Thomas Hardy, John Horne Tooke, John Thelwall and Thomas Holcroft, were a defining event in the emergence of the new order. The four were charged with constructive treason, with 'imagining the king's death', under 25 Edward III. The charge was based on their published political ideas, not on actions taken. The imagination, a key faculty in the new Romantic aesthetics, was suddenly the subject of a political trial. Defended by Thomas Erskine, the accused replied that their speech-acts did not fall within the Act as traditionally interpreted, and that any conspiracies existed only within the imaginations of the prosecutors.[87] A brave jury defied the government and acquitted them. While in Newgate on remand and trial, they exhibited in poems and journals the same firmness that Byron attributes to Bonnivard. In Tooke's diary he writes, 'I shall certainly dye With the principles I have always professed; and I am very willing to dye For them.'[88] Thelwall produced a volume of poetry, in which he scorned 'the stern Bastille – / Its bars, its iron doors, and caves forlorn.'[89]

The opportunistic and oppressive use of law by the authorities in the Treason Trials is identified as a recurrent problem in the radical (or Jacobin) novels of the 1790s. In the fictions of William Godwin, Mary Wollstonecraft, Mary Hays and Elizabeth Inchbald, the rural gentry harbours vicious despots who manipulate the law, twist public opinion and secure the imprisonment of the young man or woman who opposes his wishes. Where earlier in the century the squire's family and friends were the centre of Fielding's conservative comedy, their misdeeds always rectified or forgiven, now the focus of the novelist is on the victims, on the persistent campaigns of abuse they endure, on their unavailing 'appeal to the tribunal of [their] country', on their unrelieved suffering.[90] Godwin's *Caleb Williams* is subtitled *Things As They Are*, and though they draw on gothic and sentimental conventions, these novels use their very fictiveness to embody the systemic biases of the law. Moreover, in these novels, 'crimes are traced not to a sinful nature but to the corrupting power of institutions'.[91] The upshot of the long engagement with crime and punishment was a new framework, which later writers, lawyers and social theorists would take up: crime is a social and political phenomenon, not just an individual and moral one.

A generation later, in 1816, William Hazlitt recalled the example of the writers of the 1790s, and struggled to maintain their idealism: 'The spirit of poetry is in itself favourable to humanity and liberty: but not, we suspect, in times like these.'[92] Noting the defection of Wordsworth and Coleridge from the radical cause, he juxtaposed lawyers and poets among his 'modern apostates'. This led him to reverse the terms of an old analogy: 'Poetry, like the law, is a fiction; only a more agreeable one.' With this challenging insight, the terms for the modern engagement between law and literature had been set.

CHAPTER 5

The woman question in Victorian England

For the common law of England, the Victorian period was at once an age of reform and an age of ideological consolidation. Faced with the unprecedented social problems created by the Industrial Revolution and the unplanned expansion of factory towns and cities, the inherited institutions of law, government and social order could not cope with the demands placed upon them. Seeking to avoid a political revolution, English legislators, writers and intellectuals endeavoured to create new concepts in and through the law – new legal entities, new rights and duties, new forms of identity – whilst conserving the major institutions of the state. Animated by a liberal ideology of freedom and a belief in evolutionary, organic modes of social development, they drew on a positivist theory of law as the command of a sovereign authority to implement a gradual programme of change through Parliamentary statute.[1] To achieve this outcome they engaged in a series of remarkable struggles over words, fighting either to bring new words and hence new realities into the law, or to extend and adapt existing legal terms. In conducting their 'symbolic revolution' they developed a theory of reform, whereby established or traditional mechanisms were not overthrown but subjected to a test of their utility and efficiency. Under the inspiration of Jeremy Bentham, early Victorian reformers inaugurated the mechanistic reviews of social institutions that we now know as 'cost-benefit analysis' or more euphemistically, 'quality assurance'. In this spirit, the old Poor Law gave place to the new workhouse, the medieval officers of the watch were replaced by a professionalised and specially empowered Metropolitan Police and the right to vote in Parliamentary elections was gradually ceded to all adult males. Throughout the law, fundamental concepts and beliefs retained their authority, but Parliament recognised that new structures and procedures were needed to prevent injustice. Accordingly, many areas of the common law were amended by statute during the century of reform.

Advocates of reform acknowledged and exploited the power of literature to influence public awareness of social ills, and to contribute to the discourse of reform.² Rather than attempt to cover the spectrum of reforms, this chapter will focus on one area of symbolic conflict where the power of tradition proved especially resistant to the movement for change, namely the legal position of women. Controversy over the laws relating to women was part of a larger debate as to the status, social role and freedom of action of women which contemporary commentators summarised as 'the Woman Question'. The debate was carried on in courts, in the Houses of Parliament, in journals and in books, ensuring a significant cross-over between the languages of law and of literature.

The situation of married women under the common law was set out in Blackstone's *Commentaries on the Laws of England*:

By marriage the husband and wife are one person in law: that is, the very being or legal existence of the woman is suspended during the marriage, or at least is incorporated and consolidated into that of the husband: under whose wing, protection, and *cover*, she performs every thing; and is therefore called in our law-french a *feme-covert*; is said to be *covert-baron*, or under the protection or influence of her husband, her *baron*, or lord; and her condition during marriage is called her *coverture*. Upon this principle, of an union in person of husband and wife, depend almost all of the legal rights, duties, and disabilities that either of them acquire by the marriage . . . For this reason, a man cannot grant any thing to his wife, or enter in to covenant with her: for the grant would be to suppose her separate existence; and to covenant with her, would be only to covenant with himself.³

The doctrine of coverture rests on a legal fiction, that is a counterfactual assertion which the law accepts as true, and upon which it acts. This trope of idealised union did not describe the reality of marriage. Nonetheless, it had very real effects, despite its fictional basis. In an essay to be discussed more fully below, the Victorian feminist and anti-vivisectionist Frances Power Cobbe wrote with incisive realism, 'The husband and wife are assumed to be one person and that person is the husband.'⁴ In her recent study of adultery narratives in literature and law, Laura Hanft Korobkin shows that this legal fiction was a linguistic performative, in that it created what it said, and its terms structured the reality of marriage for all husbands and wives. The submergence of the wife's will in the husband's was justified in many idealisations of marriage and female nature in Victorian literature. The classic text for this ideological smokescreen was Coventry Patmore's poem, 'The Angel in the House':

> Man must be pleased; but him to please
> Is woman's pleasure; down the gulf
> Of his condoled necessities
> She casts her best, she flings herself . . .

> She loves with love that cannot tire;
> And when, ah woe, she loves alone,
> Through passionate duty love springs higher,
> As grass grows taller round a stone.[5]

Long after the eclipse of feudal society, the common law preserved through its resort to the language of *baron* and *feme* a view of marriage as a relationship of lord and vassal. Korobkin notes the cultural effect of this legal fiction: 'the law's extinguishing of married women's legal existence operate[d] over hundreds of years to reinforce in women a sense of incompetence, marginality and worthlessness'.[6]

The legal non-existence of married women was for Blackstone a cause for pride. He concludes his chapter, 'Of Husband and Wife', by remarking complacently, 'So great a favourite is the female sex of the laws of England.'[7] Strict enforcement of the principle of coverture in the courts led in the nineteenth century to manifestly unjust results. 'Married women were unable to control their own property, administer their own earnings, or even, on separation, retain control of them. Even more harshly, estranged wives were not permitted to keep custody of their children.'[8] The conservative jurist Henry Sumner Maine noted in his *Ancient Law* 'the rigorous consistency with which the view of a complete legal subjection on the part of a wife is carried by [the English common law], where it is untouched by equity or statutes'.[9] Reformers responded to this rigorous enforcement of ancient legal rules by campaigning to have the common law amended by parliamentary statutes. Throughout society, women and men used the written word to bring about what Karen Chase and Michael Levenson call 'the legal reform of the family'.[10] This campaign will be traced initially through a study of the case of Caroline Norton. Norton was a professional writer, a poet, novelist and editor, and her polemical writings on the laws relating to women derived from her own bitter experience of their inadequacy. Her pamphlets are among the most urgent and persuasive writings on law in the Victorian period, and they helped reform the laws relating to custody, divorce and the rights of separated women to their earnings. As such they represent a major point of convergence between legal and literary discourse.

CAROLINE NORTON, VICTIM AND CAMPAIGNER

Caroline Norton was the granddaughter of the playwright and Whig MP Richard Brinsley Sheridan, whose daring wit she inherited. Economic necessity and family pressure led her to accept the marriage proposal of

George Norton, a barrister and Tory MP. His financial position was less secure than the Sheridans had been led to expect. Caroline's sentimental verse was one of the staples of the annual keepsake books, and she was soon a highly regarded poet. After some successful volumes of poetry, she was offered the editorship of a fashionable annual. When George lost his seat in the House of Commons, Caroline pulled strings among her Whig connections. Through Lord Melbourne, he was appointed a magistrate, which required him to attend court three afternoons a week. His lazy and bullying temperament soon showed through, as he found the midday start too early, and he reacted boorishly to criticism.[11]

The marriage was not happy. George was outshone by his wife and resented it. She soon lost respect for him and would not bow to his narrow expectations for her. In narrating the history of the marriage, biographers have not noticed that literary responsibility conflicted with wifely submission: on one occasion after a quarrel at dinner, she went to the drawing room to write, and, locking the door, desired him to leave her in peace. He followed her, broke down the door, scattered the furniture and her papers and tried to force her from the room. To teach her not to 'brave' him, he used physical violence on several occasions. Eventually, she left him and sought protection among her family. After a contrite request for reconciliation, she returned to him. His brutal and exploitative treatment continued, however. When she refused to consent to his mortgaging her trust fund, they quarrelled, and to punish her, he removed the children from their home.

He then commenced proceedings in criminal conversation, alleging that his wife had committed adultery with Lord Melbourne. To this form of action, the prelude to divorce, the wife was not a party. Nor could she appear and give evidence on her own behalf, though it was her reputation that was at stake. The evidence was paltry. When it was proved that the witnesses had been paid and housed by Norton's brother, the jury returned a verdict for Lord Melbourne without the defence calling evidence. This result vindicated Melbourne, but it did not restore Caroline's reputation. About her the scandal continued to linger, assisted by the continuing marital discord.

After the trial, Caroline sought advice whether she had grounds for a divorce due to George's violence, but her lawyers advised that with her temporary reconciliation, she had 'condoned' his matrimonial offences, and lost any chance of divorcing him. In this situation, separation from her children was hardest to bear, and Caroline sought their return. Once again seeking legal advice, she learnt that the husband's right was absolute, even though one was still a baby.

In a decisive response to this third disappointment, Caroline lobbied among her parliamentary acquaintances to change the law and wrote her first pamphlets, *The Separation of Mother and Child by the Law of Custody of Infants, Considered* (1838) and, under the pseudonym Pearce Stevenson, *A Plain Letter to the Lord Chancellor on the Infant Custody Bill* (1839). Thomas Talfourd, who had been junior counsel in the Melbourne case, promoted a bill in the Commons, quoting from Norton's *Plain Letter*. The successful passage of the Infant Custody Act enabled separated mothers to obtain custody of children under the age of seven and access to children under sixteen. Chase and Levenson praise the 'deft rhetoric of motherhood' deployed in the pamphlets and in Norton's subsequent poems and argue that she exploited the symbolic capital of the discourse of maternity to become 'a Whig poetic mother, a public mother resolved to teach the lessons of reform'.[12]

As a result of one scurrilous review of her pamphlet, Norton sought to sue the *British and Foreign Review* for libel. Her lawyers informed her that because her legal identity was merged with that of her husband, Mr Norton would have to sue on her behalf. Reflecting back on her legal history in her 1855 pamphlet *Letter to the Queen*, she expostulated: 'I was left to study the grotesque anomaly in law of having my defence made *necessary* – and made *impossible* – by the same person.'[13]

During their separation, Caroline supported herself by writing. She edited several annuals, reviewed books and wrote more ambitious poetry on reformist topics, such as *A Voice from the Factories*. In a bid to increase her income, she began to write fiction, often using stories of marriages that drew on her own experience and wishes. Throughout this time, her situation was precarious because Norton broke agreements he had made, including with regard to money. His final demonstration of the law's inequity occurred when they signed a contract granting Caroline an annuity. Finding that she received money from her late mother's estate, he arbitrarily reduced the annuity. She pleaded the contract, and he replied that because man and wife were one in law, he could not contract with himself. This issue finally brought them to court, because Caroline then referred her creditors to George, who refused to pay them. George subpoenaed Caroline, and her banker's and publisher's accounts, making a claim to all her literary earnings. Using her finances as a pretext, he raked over her literary career, revived the Melbourne scandal and impugned her care of her sons. He won the case against the creditor on a technicality and was deemed bound in honour though not in law by the contract. Though widely deplored, the trial was a *cause célèbre*.

Unable to contract, unable to sue, deprived of the right to her own earnings and unable to divorce, Norton was clearly 'excluded from [legal] discourse and imprisoned within it'.[14] It is little wonder that she concluded in her *Letter to the Queen*, 'I have learned the law respecting women, piecemeal, by suffering from every one of its defects of protection.'[15] However, as Mary Poovey points out, this and the earlier pamphlet, *English Laws for Women in the Nineteenth Century* (1854) depend on Norton transforming herself from a 'long-suffering victim of injustice [into a] vindicating polemical writer'.[16] In the pamphlets she claims a right to speak the discourse. In *English Laws for Women*, Norton dramatically locates her conversion at that moment in the witness box, when her husband questioned her relations with Lord Melbourne:

But on that day, when in cold blood for the sake of money, Mr Norton repeated that which he knew to be false, the waters of Marah, by which he sought to whelm my soul, made the great gulf that shall divide us forever! In that day, when he met me face to face, shivering with the frenzy of mingled anger, shame, and fear ... – in that little court, where I stood apparently helpless, mortified and degraded – in that bitterest of many bitter hours in my life, I judged and sentenced him ... I sentenced Mr Norton to be KNOWN.[17]

Representing herself as the vulnerable heroine of sentimental literature Norton switches from moral to legal discourse. Her sentence, unrecognised by law, will be pronounced in the forum generated by the literary marketplace, public opinion. Accordingly she wrote to *The Times* and published *English Laws for Women* and *Letter to the Queen*, all against the advice of her family and lawyers.

Lord Cranworth's Matrimonial Causes Bill had been introduced into Parliament, but left undebated. This provided an immediate political focus for the discussion of her own treatment under the existing law. Norton was right: the pamphlets created much sympathy for her, and debate about the legal position of women. By representing herself in print as a 'case' of legalised injustice, Caroline Norton propelled the reform of the divorce laws. Lord Lyndhurst quoted from *Letter to the Queen* in his speeches to the Lords, and Norton's points were incorporated in the 1857 Act. The new law reduced the complexity and cost of the divorce procedure and secured the earnings of separated wives, but it kept the sexual double standard in place. A husband could divorce his wife on the ground of her adultery, but a wife had to prove adultery and another offence, such as bigamy or cruelty, in order to divorce her husband. This inequity did not trouble Caroline Norton, who despite her sense of justice, accepted the inferiority of women and only desired a law that really protected the underdog.

In 1847 Caroline Norton accepted an invitation from the Irish painter Daniel Maclise to model the Spirit of Justice for a fresco in the chamber of the House of Lords. It is a nice irony that a woman who had experienced the defects of the law should become the central figure in an allegory of Justice set before a legislature composed of men. However, while the choice of Norton was provocative, it was also entirely justified, for she was a liberal reformer who used the established channels of power, namely Parliament and the written word, to improve the law for women.[18]

LITERARY WOMEN AND LAW REFORM

Among the immediate effects of Norton's case was a campaign to reform the laws relating to married women's property. While Norton herself was a suspect figure, the cause of law reform became vital for young feminists like Barbara Leigh Smith, who saw that their attempts to expand women's work and public roles needed to be backed up by a just and equitable set of laws. Accordingly women writers began to follow Norton in writing about the law. In 1854 Leigh Smith wrote a highly successful pamphlet, *A Brief Summary, in Plain Language, of the Most Important Laws Concerning Women: Together with a Few Observations Thereon*. The exactness of the title is important, particularly the insistence on 'Plain Language', for it highlights a commitment to clarity over technicality and imagines an audience of legal subjects not legal practitioners. The *Brief Summary* takes women out of the obscurity of coverture and sets out in specific terms the extent of their freedom to act. It is practical and clear, and forceful: 'A woman's body belongs to her husband; she is in his custody, and he can enforce his right by a writ of *habeas corpus*.'[19] Leigh Smith displaces coverture by starting with the property rights and liabilities of single women. 'A single woman has the same rights to property, to protection from the law, and has to pay the same taxes to the State as a man' (23). Having noted this fundamental equality, Leigh Smith creates a powerful sense of discrimination as she proceeds to enumerate the limitations which the law imposes on women. She strikes a prophetically modern note when she observes that the law is gendered masculine in its very language: 'the law speaks of men only, but women are affected by all the laws and incur the same responsibilities in all their contracts and doings as men' (24). Leigh Smith remedies this silence by making women, married and single, middle- and working-class, the subjects of the legal sentence. Having concluded her comprehensive factual summary, she appends an argument for reform, introducing specific suggestions with an appeal to the period's critical attitude to law: 'It is not now as it once was, when all existing institutions were considered sacred and unalterable; and the spirit which made Blackstone an admirer of, rather than a critic on, every law because it was *law*, is exchanged for a bolder and more discriminating spirit, which is to judge calmly what is good and to amend what is bad' (30).

However, this reformist mentality and critical temper were not universally shared. The Scottish novelist and reviewer Margaret Oliphant took issue with Leigh Smith's analysis in an article, 'The Laws Concerning Women'. Oliphant restated the fundamental unity of husband and wife as a 'fact' in 'truth and in nature', and on this Blackstonian basis justified the common law: 'The laws which govern human intercourse are for the most part only fixed and arbitrary demonstrations of natural rights and necessities.'[20] Whilst claiming to avoid either 'the authoritative hardness of legal phraseology or the sweet jargon of poetic nonsense', she adopted an idealistic view of marriage as a mutual influencing in which each party is changed by joining its life with the other (307). Faults, animosities and practical disputes about rights, such as those which overtook the Norton marriage, are dismissed in favour of a sentimental vision: 'For it is not the question of the wife's earnings or the wife's property which lies nearest the heart of this controversy: there are the children – living witnesses of the undividableness of the parents' (309). Concerning herself with the spirit of marriage, Oliphant ignored the content and the operation of the law.

Not surprisingly, feminist reformers continued the debate in the periodical press.[21] Writing in the radical *Westminster Review*, Caroline Cornwallis, a respected author on scientific and philosophical subjects, identified the Utopian element in Oliphant's argument: 'we might deem it the gentle dream of some Utopian legislator, who in his primitive innocence, had never heard of extravagant wives or brutal husbands'.[22] Cornwallis has a sociologist's interest in how the law affects social conduct: 'The effect of a law', she argues, 'can rarely be measured by its active interference in the affairs of life; its influence is spread over a much wider area; for custom assimilates itself to the law when it has existed unchanged for any long time' (310). This insight into the cultural consequences of law enables her to discern how the law governing married women's property has 'influenced the position of *all* females', for it has justified a limited education and so narrowed the scope of women's work and social role. Where Oliphant is sentimental, Cornwallis observes with epigrammatic wit how the property laws distort the feelings of the parties. For example, in accepting a marriage settlement, the device invented by Chancery to protect the property of wives, an engaged woman was acting as if she distrusted her *fiancé*. Thus, Cornwallis writes, 'the first flow of generous affection is dammed up by legal instruments' (312). Apart from its effects on women, the law promotes fortune-hunting and so 'acts as a direct tempter to man'.

Amid this discursive pressure Leigh Smith's pamphlet attracted the attention of the Law Amendment Society, which sponsored a bill to reform the married women's property laws. To indicate the extent of public support for this reform, Leigh Smith and her colleagues circulated a petition which was presented to Parliament in 1856. It drew some 76,000 women as signatories. Literature had a prominent part in the petition: not only was it a carefully composed document, which comprehended the needs of all classes and both sexes, but many of the names who headed the petition were well-known writers. This was a conscious strategy, for Elizabeth Barrett Browning, Harriet Martineau, Anna Jameson, Elizabeth Gaskell, Mary Howitt, Jane Carlyle were at once famous and respectable. Literature was one of the only acceptable professions in the public sphere for women at the time. Moreover, the numbers of women successfully taking up the profession of writing conferred urgency on the petition. While Caroline Norton was not approached to sign the document (her damaged reputation may have been a liability rather than an asset to the cause), her case lay behind the wording of its first paragraph:

> That the manifold evils occasioned by the present law, by which the property and earnings of the wife are thrown into the absolute power of the husband, become daily more apparent. That the sufferings thereupon ensuing extend over all classes of society. That it might once have been deemed for the middle and upper ranks a comparatively theoretical question, but is so no longer, since married women of education are entering on every side the field of literature and art, in order to increase the family income by such exertions.[23]

Lord Brougham presented the petition to the House of Lords, as Sir Erskine Perry did to the House of Commons. However, the Married Women's Property Bill was perceived as a radical restructuring of relations between the sexes, whereas the Matrimonial Causes Bill promoted by Norton was less far-reaching in its effects on the existing gender order. It was preferred by the politicians, and the Married Women's Property Act was not to be passed for another fourteen years.

In the late 1860s, women again began to agitate for property rights not to be lost upon marriage. John Stuart Mill's *Subjection of Women* and his adoptive daughter Helen Taylor's 'Women and Criticism' were important texts in the renewed campaign for legal and political equality between the sexes. Less well known, but more specifically directed to the law are the writings of Frances Power Cobbe. As we have seen, Cobbe acerbically critiqued the reality of coverture in 'Criminals, Idiots, Women and Minors: Is the Classification Sound?' (1868). She also diagnosed the fictive basis of the law:

Where women are concerned, English law ceases to be a dry system, regardful of only abstract justice and policy. Themis, when she presides at the domestic hearth, doffs her wig and allows herself to be swayed by poetical, not to say, romantic considerations. We are rarely allowed in debating it to examine accurately the theory of conjugal justice. We are called upon rather to contemplate the beautiful ideal of absolute union of heart, life and purse which the law has provided for and which it alone deigns to recognise.[24]

Cobbe proves an adept student of law and literature with this insight into the sentimental basis of the law. The legal fiction of coverture is at base a 'poetical' ideal, but more importantly in Cobbe's view, this sentiment is the emotional basis of Englishmen's attitudes to marriage, and hence the real stumbling-block to reform of the law. Cobbe is a resourceful polemicist, and she attacks the ideal in several ways. Throughout the text she alternates between a rigorous practical analysis of the law in operation, what she calls here an accurate examination, and a series of imaginary scenarios, fictions that bring the law's absurdities into high relief: the goddess of justice off-duty and off-guard; or a visitor from Mars who, noticing the husband's vow in the marriage ceremony, 'With all my worldly goods I thee endow', asks naively, '"Does that mean that she henceforth will have the control of his money altogether, or only that he takes her into partnership?"' His English guide blandly replies that neither of these alternatives is correct: '"By our law it is *her* goods and earnings, present and future, which belong to him from this moment."' The incredulous Martian strives to understand the contradiction between word and deed: '"the man who promises giving nothing, and the woman who is silent giving all?"' (109)

Above all, Cobbe's strategy was to build on the empiricist and realist biases of her culture. To readers who valued facts as truth she offered details of actual cases; her arguments were models of practical reasoning, inquiring into real causes and consequences, rather than elaborating general principles; and she wrote in a plain style, that implied eloquence was the tool of mystification.

When the Married Women's Property Act (1870) 'put an end to the chartered robbery by husbands of their wives' earnings', Cobbe turned her attention to other abuses within marriage, and in a later article, 'Wife-Torture in England' (1878), took up the cause of battered wives, making a case for reform through narratives drawn from newspaper and parliamentary reports.[25] Unlike the earlier essay, this one assembles statistics on the prevalence of domestic violence, names judges and lawyers who have supported law reform and summarises reports presented to the Congress of the Social Science Association. It is therefore an exemplary text of the Victorian reform movement, making its case for social improvement by drawing on the specialist discourses of the institutions to be repaired, in this case the legal profession. Her article includes the complete draft of a new law to prevent domestic violence. However, while Cobbe had a speaking position within the journalistic and feminist public spheres, she could do no more than critique the discourse of the law: her Bill was drafted by Alfred D. Hill, a Justice of the Peace from Birmingham. Despite the expertise evident in the writings of Cobbe, Leigh Smith and Norton, women were not admitted as legal practitioners in England until the Sex Disqualification (Removal) Act was passed in 1919.

THE NORTON CASE IN FICTION

Like many another *cause célèbre* before and since, the Norton story proved irresistible to writers, especially to young men serving a dual apprenticeship in the Inns of Court and Grub Street. First to appropriate an aspect of the case was Charles Dickens, whose long engagement with legal questions will be discussed below. As a journalist, Dickens reported on the criminal conversation trial for the *Morning Chronicle*. George Norton's reliance on Melbourne's brief letters to Caroline, for example, 'How are you? I shall not be able to call today but probably will tomorrow', to establish their adultery provoked laughter in court. Dickens parodied this scene in the trial in *The Pickwick Papers*, when Serjeant Buzfuz solemnly reads Pickwick's notes to Mrs Bardell as declarations of love: 'Dear Mrs B., I shall not be at home till to-morrow. Slow coach ... Don't trouble yourself about the warming-pan.'[26]

One of the most extensive fictional treatments of the experience of Caroline Norton is Thackeray's *The Newcomes* (1853–5). A panoramic study of the mores of high society, it undertakes a sustained examination of money and class as motives for aristocratic marriage. Thackeray, who qualified as a barrister at the Middle Temple but did not practise law, met Norton through writing for *Fraser's Magazine*, and they became friends. Micael M. Clarke suggests that Norton exercised a powerful influence on Thackeray's novels, and that she is 'a probable "original" for Lady Lyndon, Becky Sharp and Clara Pulleyn Newcome.'[27] In *The Newcomes*, Thackeray divides the traits of Caroline Norton between two characters, Clara, whose marriage to Barnes Newcome resembles that of Norton in her experience of violence and bullying, and Ethel Newcome, Barnes's sister, who is given Caroline's wit, determination and beauty. Ethel is groomed by her worldly grandmother for a socially advantageous marriage, but breaks off her engagement to the rich but empty-headed Marquess of Farintosh after seeing Clara's fate. Clara's impoverished aristocratic family reject her first love, Jack Belsize, and insist that she marry Barnes Newcome, whose family are wealthy bankers. His abuse drives her to seek help from Belsize. The narrative exposes the double standard or moral contradiction of society's response, at once appalled by Barnes's conduct and requiring Clara to maintain the façade of a happy marriage. Belsize's rescue of Clara mobilises the legal fictions underlying criminal conversation and divorce, drawing forth the narrator's ironic condemnation: 'quick, let us hire an advocate to roar out to a British jury the wrongs of her injured husband, to paint the agonies of his bleeding heart . . . and to show Society injured through him. Let us console that martyr, I say, with thumping damages; and as for the woman – the guilty wretch! – let us lead her out and stone her.'[28]

Counterpointed with its attack on the 'marriage market', the novel represents the happiness of those who marry for love, especially Laura Pendennis, wife of the narrator, confidant and friend to other women, and upholder of 'the Sacred Law' of worship, love and duty (666). Though insightful and assertive, Laura stands for the womanly vocations of wife and mother. While Thackeray foregrounds the nexus of gender and class ideology which sees young women valued and offered for sale like paintings in a gallery (362), he yet retains the angelic wife and mother as his heroine.

The major fictional exploration of Caroline Norton, as a personality and as the subject of harsh legal and historical forces, is George Meredith's *Diana of the Crossways* (1885). Published shortly after her death, this work enjoyed great success. Norton's family objected to some aspects of her representation, perhaps prevented from detecting the sympathetic understanding in the portrait by Meredith's notoriously indirect and elliptical narrative voice. Sir Frederick Pollock, the eminent legal scholar to whom the novel is dedicated, said that Meredith 'drilled [his words] like an ingenious ballet master in fantastic groups and poses'.[29]

Norton's career is simplified and reshaped by Meredith in his creation of Diana Merion Warwick. Diana has her own home, the Crossways, and no children. An Irishwoman in England, beautiful and articulate, she suffers from the scandal of a false allegation of adultery that is unsuccessfully aired in court. With the failure of this action, she is 'exonerated . . . [b]ut not free'.[30] Though she lives apart from her spouse, the unhappy marriage remains in existence, and open to legal enforcement at his instigation.

She flees to Italy 'to escape the meshes of the terrific net of the marital law brutally whirled to capture her by the man her husband' (161). Meredith rejects the moralistic and omniscient narrator used by Thackeray and Dickens, confining criticisms of the law to the minds of characters. Thomas Redworth, Diana's faithful lover, is a solid British man of business, but 'compensatingly heterodox in his view of the Law's persecution of women' (311). Diana herself declares to Percy Dacier, the politician with whom she falls in love after the trial, '"only gruesome German stories will fetch comparisons for the yoke of this Law of yours. It seems the nightmare dream following an ogre's supper"' (346). Her Gothic vision of Law as personified cruelty breaks through the narrator's reserve and transforms him briefly into a reformist advocate:[31]

the world of the Laws overloading her is pitiless to women, deaf past ear-trumpets, past intercession; detesting and reviling them for a feeble human cry, and for one apparent step of revolt piling the pelted stones on them. It will not discriminate shades of hue, it massacres all the shadowed. They are honoured, after a fashion, at a certain elevation. Descending from it, and purely to breathe common air (thus in her mind) they are scourged and outcast. And alas! the very pleading for them excites a sort of ridicule in their advocate. (347)

Whereas Thackeray invoked the biblical type of the woman taken in adultery with grim irony, Meredith presents the comparison with detachment, and for once, directness. His reference to scourging and outcasting, ancient punishments directed at the body, lends weight to Diana's perception of law as a regime of violence and horror.

Uncomfortable with the role of advocate, as the last sentence quoted above shows, the Meredithian narrator soon reverts to drama and implication, and mounts through these means a broad-based critique of power relations in Victorian England. Unhappy marriage regulated by unjust law is a realist subject in *Diana of the Crossways*, but it also functions as a poetic figure, as the metonymic reference to another site of oppression. The subjugation of Diana, an Irish woman, by her English husband and his nation's law, is linked to the enforced union of England and Ireland. Diana urges Dacier to '"give some thoughts to Ireland – and the cause of women"', and not just devote his energy to 'these Corn Law agitations' (186). The yoking together of these three issues indicates the general reformist project of the novel. That it is Diana who takes up the cause of the oppressed is part of the novel's radicalism. Dacier has love on his mind and wants to keep politics and romance as separate spheres, but Diana refuses to adopt the conventional feminine role or to accept that love is apolitical: '"Politics everywhere! – in the Courts of Faery! They are not discord to me."' Meredith underlines the power relations that inform even loving marriages when Diana signifies her acceptance of Redworth's proposal with a telling substitution, '"Here goes old Ireland!"' (478). Diana's willingness to submit to the yoke of marriage, to give up her long-desired independence with this resigned irony, suggests a final tension in this novel. Having told a story of the structural flaws of the marriage law, Meredith cannot resist the power of the love plot. Yet the ending of the novel is open rather than closed, and romantic desire is made the vehicle of hope for a better world: Diana's friend remarks, '"Old Ireland won't repent it!"' and her rejoinder, '"A singular transformation of Old England!"' (493), adds a reformist note to the implications of harmony and continuity traditionally symbolised by the marriage ending of romantic comedy.

Although written in the 1880s, *Diana of the Crossways* is set during the 1830s and 1840s. Early readers were encouraged to reflect on the transformations that had or had not taken place in Old England and Ireland in the interim. The forward-looking orientation of the text is not visible only in its ending, but in an earlier statement of Diana's: '"I should like to write a sketch of the woman of the future ... What a different earth you will see!"' (328).[32]

CHARLES DICKENS, REFORMIST WRITER

In the epigraph to her *English Laws for Women* Caroline Norton quotes from Charles Dickens's *Bleak House*: 'It won't do to have Truth and Justice on our side. We must have Law and Lawyers.' Her invocation of Dickens is entirely appropriate because a commitment to social reform was an integral part of his immense literary reputation. While Norton's reformism was pursued through personal contacts with the Whig party, Dickens's career as a writer advocating social change was founded on his early association with radical journals, like the *Morning Chronicle*, the *Examiner* and the *Daily News*. Like Meredith after him, Dickens was originally employed in a lawyer's office but found the work uncongenial, and went into journalism through Parliamentary and court reporting.

One of his early pieces for the *Morning Chronicle*, 'Doctors' Commons', later reprinted in *Sketches by Boz*, encapsulates his attitude to the law. Boz presents himself as a kind of accidental tourist in his own city. He stumbles upon this precinct of ecclesiastical law and claims a 'curiousity' to examine 'the Court, whose decrees can even unloose the bonds of matrimony'.[33] He observes minutely the archaic dress of the judge, lawyers and court officials, then tells the story of an equally anachronistic trial that he witnesses. He blends a reformist critique with an ironic mimicry of legal language:

under a half obsolete statute of one of the Edwards, the Court was empowered to visit with the penalty of excommunication, any person who should be proved guilty of the crime of 'brawling,' or 'smiting,' in any church, or vestry adjoining thereto; and it appeared by some eight-and-twenty affidavits, which were duly referred to, that on a certain night, at a certain vestry meeting, in a certain parish particularly set forth, Thomas Sludberry ... had made use of, and applied to Michael Bumple ... the words 'You be blowed'. (91)

Leaving the Court, Boz ironically praises 'the beautiful spirit of these ancient laws, the kind and neighbourly feelings they are calculated to awaken' (92). The core elements – the characters, the plots, the musty milieu of futility and formality, the narrator's brusque dismissal of legal tradition – of his later fictional representations of law are all registered in this early sketch.

As a journalist in the radical press, Dickens also reported gleefully on the caprices of the judges and the abuses of the law. There is no better illustration of this than the short lampoon, 'A Truly British Judge', published in the *Examiner* in the revolutionary year, 1848. The judge in question, Baron Platt, presided at the trial of a ten-year-old boy for stealing a purse. Upon the verdict of 'Guilty', Platt ordered one month's gaol and a flogging. On learning from his clerk that flogging was not allowed, he imposed a sentence of seven years' transportation to Australia. On the following day, he revoked that sentence and ordered the boy to serve two years' imprisonment instead. Dickens exposes 'the vacillating conduct of the serio-comic functionary' by presenting the Court record in the form of a play script in which the judge responds to his Clerk of Arraigns' corrections by pronouncing ever more arbitrary sentences. 'It *was* a maxim of English jurisprudence that punishment should be proportioned to the crime', he writes, openly criticising the judge's harshness and ignorance.[34]

In addition to criticising reactionary judges, Dickens showed a reformist concern to ensure that the doctrines and processes of the law were well adapted to the goals of public and private justice. In an item in his own journal, *Household Words*, he adopted the voice of a working-man to tell 'A Poor Man's Tale of a Patent', revealing the cost and duplication of his attempt to patent his invention. Six years later, in 1856, again in *Household Words*, Dickens addressed the tendency of public institutions to overlook the victim. 'The Murdered Person' of his title was, he argued, completely forgotten in publicity about prison philanthropists who claimed to secure the repentance of criminals. Believing this instance to be symptomatic of a pervasive attitude, he suggests some other situations in which victims are overlooked by the self-interested defence of tradition. The divorce law provides another example. With a passion that may have proceeded from personal unhappiness, he complains that 'from the tie of marriage there is no escape to be had, no absolution to be got, except under certain proved circumstances ... and then only on payment of an enormous sum of money. Ferocity, flight, drunkenness, felony, madness, none will break the chain without an enormous sum of money.'[35] When reform is proposed, 'panegyrics on Marriage as an Institution' are offered, and the 'tortures and wrongs of the sufferer' are disregarded. While Dickens probably had parliamentarians like Gladstone and Bishop Wilberforce in mind, the contributions of writers like Margaret Oliphant also forget the 'murdered' person.[36] To counter the vision of marriage as a sacred and therefore indissoluble bond, Dickens invokes the reality of physical abuse, though he locates it in the working class. Defenders of the status quo contribute to this violence, 'they mount upon the mangled creature to deliver their orations', he argues with extreme emotion. This is the key Dickensian strategy. Like Caroline Norton, he uses the body of the victim as a sentimental spectacle, mobilising reform through the cultivation of pity.

Dickens recognised the importance of the Norton case, and the contribution Norton made by writing about it, in exposing the defects of the law and activating its reform. He published several articles on the matter in *Household Words*, including Eliza Lynn's 'The Rights and Wrongs of Women' and 'One of Our Legal Fictions' in 1854, W. H. Wills's 'A Legal Fiction' in 1855, and Lynn's 'Marriage Gaolers' in 1856. The first two appeared alongside instalments of Dickens's novel, *Hard Times*. Lynn's engagement with these issues is historically interesting because she is best known to students of literary history as the notorious anti-feminist, Eliza Lynn Linton.

Hard Times shows yet another example of border-crossing by the languages of law and fiction. Legal historians believe that the law of divorce was brought to public attention in 1844 by Mr Justice Maule, in the unlikely forum of a criminal court. In a rare display of sustained judicial irony, he sentenced a bigamist as follows:

Prisoner at the bar, you have been convicted of the offence of bigamy, that is to say of marrying a woman while you have a wife still alive, though it is true she has deserted you, and is still living in adultery with another man. You have, therefore, committed a crime against the laws of your country, and you have also acted under a very serious apprehension of the course which you ought to have pursued. You should have gone to the ecclesiastical court and there obtained against your wife a decree *a mensa et thoro*. You should then have brought an action in the courts of common law and recovered, as no doubt you would have recovered, damages

against your wife's paramour. Armed with these decrees you should have
approached the legislature, and obtained an Act of Parliament, which would
have rendered you free, and legally competent to marry the person whom you
have taken on yourself to marry with no such sanction. It is quite true that these
proceedings would have cost you many hundreds of pounds, whereas you probably have not as many pence. But the law knows no distinction between rich and
poor. The sentence of the court upon you therefore is that you be imprisoned for
one day, which period has already been exceeded, as you have been in custody
since the commencement of the assizes.[37]

So unusual and so resonant was this speech that it circulated widely in
several versions.[38] One of the subplots of *Hard Times* concerns Stephen
Blackpool, a factory hand whose estranged, alcoholic wife has returned
home. Stephen is a conscientious man, but the marriage has long been a
source of misery to him. He asks his employer, the pompous and hypo-
critical Bounderby, if there is any lawful way he can be released from the
marriage. As K. J. A. Asche and John D. Baird have noted, Bounderby's
reply clearly echoes Maule's utterance:[39]

'Why you'd have to go to Doctors' Commons with a suit, and you'd have to go to
a Court of Common Law with a suit, and you'd have to go to the House of Lords
with a suit, and you'd have to get an Act of Parliament to enable you to marry
again, and it would cost you (if it was a case of very plain sailing) I suppose from a
thousand to fifteen hundred pound.'[40]

However, the irony that Maule deliberately marshalled to indict a defective
law is here directed against Bounderby, as part of its critique of the 'self-
made man' as well as against the law. Bounderby's own marriage will later
founder for lack of sympathy, and his insistence on Stephen's fulfilling the
letter of the wedding vow, 'for better, for worse', rebounds against himself,
as he sloughs off the obligations, though not the legal tie, of marriage
without a second thought (185). All the marriages in *Hard Times* are
characterised by a lack of intimacy, and it can be read as a timely intervention in the debate about marriage law reform.[41]

Hard Times is best known as an industrial novel, with its portrait of the
blackened landscape, the degraded lives of the workers, and their union-
isation and strike action. Yet for the Victorians the obverse of this public
and masculine world of work was the female space of the home. One of the
achievements of this novel is its recognition that the so-called 'separate
spheres' are interconnected. The alienated and hierarchical relationships
demanded by the factory system are paralleled in the domestic realm. The
severely rationalist ethic enforced by Thomas Gradgrind upon his children
and students marginalises his wife in her own home. Her querulous

invalidism is a predictable response to the emotional repression and the intellectual and economic dominance cultivated by her husband. Marriage is reduced to a matter of rational calculation, in a caricature of Benthamite analysis, when Gradgrind advises his daughter, Louisa, about accepting Bounderby's proposal. His confident predictions are disproved, and his philosophy discredited, through a plot which exposes the Gradgrind children to irrational desires and resentments. In a wide-ranging critique of programmatic social policies, Dickens presents sentimental narratives of individual hardship or rebellion, cases that show the return of the repressed in both marriage and industry.

The depth of Dickens's interest in law is illustrated by its ubiquitous appearance in his fiction, from the comedy and pathos of *Pickwick Papers* (1836–7) to the verbal portraiture of the aggressively professional lawyer, Jaggers, in *Great Expectations* (1861). This chapter has focused on the involvement of literature in the campaign to reform the legal disabilities of married women, but Dickens's broader literary activism must be noticed, if only briefly. The use of imprisonment as a remedy for debt was a recurrent target of his journalism and novels, spurred undoubtedly by the painful childhood memory of his father's incarceration. His primary interest always lay in the human consequences of the law, rather than in the content or rationale of legal rules. This emphasis is most clearly demonstrated in *Bleak House* (1852–3).

Here the action centres on a long-running and labyrinthine Chancery suit, *Jarndyce and Jarndyce*. Far from being a plot that issues in the discovery of truth and the resolution of conflict, the story of the *Jarndyce* case is one in which substantive questions of equity and justice are endlessly deferred by technical disputes about procedure and costs. Progress in this narrative can only take place outside the case; inside all is fog and deadlock. As a result, Dickens represents the Court of Chancery and its lawyers as a self-serving bureaucracy, causing public harm through wasteful and rigid formalism. Eschewing the dramatic trials of much literature on law, *Bleak House* opens with a satiric prose-poem that identifies legal London as 'the heart of the fog', but it lingers in the purlieus of the law only to identify the evils produced by the system, the disappointed litigants, rapacious lawyers and underpaid copyists. While the narrative of the case is stalled, the novel takes up the many stories of the victims. Through these, the novel offers new insights into law, particularly into its operation as a system and into the experience of litigation.[42]

As in *Hard Times*, Dickens builds his novel around a contemporary social abuse and adds to the existing rhetoric of reform by making the deficient institution the symbol of a larger social disorder. With *Bleak House* he draws on the campaign to reform the Chancery Court, gathering many well-publicised proofs of its deficiency into a single 'monument of Chancery practice'.[43] However, Dickens's treatment of the lawsuit stresses that it has a representative significance. The issues and problems raised by *Jarndyce and Jarndyce* are not peculiar to that family or to Chancery but are symptomatic of what Dickens sees as the condition of England. The disease of jaundice is aurally suggested in the name Jarndyce, and the obstruction of bile and the discoloration associated with this disease are the vital signs in Dickens's diagnosis of the body politic. In his representation of characters and places, fog, cotton wool, disfigured bodies, and waste paper collections abound, serving as metaphors of class bias, blind traditionalism, acquisitiveness, sexual repression and other obstructions to personal and social development. Through *Jarndyce and Jarndyce*, Dickens pioneered the legal trial as an allegory of modern society, a possibility exploited by Kafka, William Gaddis and others.

To the defenders of this jaundiced social order, *Bleak House* threatens a semi-apocalyptic death by Spontaneous Combustion, rather than the mundanely probable reform by parliamentary legislation. This fantasy of institutional self-destructiveness is not really an insurrectionary 'bonfire of the equities', as Antony Julius argues, but a warning of the urgent need for systemic reform. Moreover, the inaction of the Lord Chancellors, the failures of the law, are redressed in the novel by the practical guardianship of John Jarndyce and the maternal care given by Esther Summerson. Dickens draws from equity and Christianity a traditional ethic of assistance to the weak, substantive justice ahead of legal form and the fulfilling of trust. His decided preference is for individual, rather than institutional, remedies to the social ills he catalogues so convincingly. In this too, he draws on the traditions of equity, which in its original jurisdiction was a personal appeal to the King or his Chancellor.[44]

The national allegory of *Bleak House* is accompanied by a domestic plot told in the autobiographical voice of Esther Summerson. Esther's progress from abandoned child to paid companion to model wife and mother shows Dickens's investment in the traditional angelic heroine of Victorian gender ideology. In this novel, the 'reform of the family' takes place along class and moral lines, but while the order of gender is destabilised by weak men, the women must still conform to the underlying ideologies of gender and sexuality. The limits of Dickens's reformism are exposed in the story of Lady Dedlock. Her sexual history and her maternity are the true secrets of this narrative. Their gradual discovery is the occasion for a conflict of values, as the agents of law, first the family solicitor and then the detective, pursue her, one to bring punishment and the other to offer forgiveness. The novel's commitment to sentimental romance through its domestic plot creates a measure of sympathy for Lady Dedlock as she discovers her daughter, but this sympathy is contained by the detective plot, in which she figures as the criminal. The detective plot is the engine of public morality, and while this capacious novel raises a challenge to some punitive ideas, such as the shame of illegitimacy, it cannot leave unpunished the past sexual transgressions of a woman. Her husband may forgive her, but Lady Dedlock must die.

Her death, like the exhaustion of the Chancery case, enables the future-oriented narrative of Esther's marriage to take centre stage, to provide a happy ending. Dickens was an important propagator of the domestic ideal through his novels and journalism. His magazine, *Household Words*, in its title and in its statement of editorship, 'conducted by Charles Dickens', suggests how he placed himself before his audience in the role of *paterfamilias*. That self-construction was disturbed in 1858, the year after the passage of the Matrimonial Causes Act, when Dickens separated from his wife, Catherine. His marital breakdown has a particular bearing on the present discussion because he sought to control public reception of the fact by making a personal statement in *Household Words* and other journals:

Some domestic troubles of mine, of long-standing, on which I will make no further remark than that it claims to be respected, as being of a sacredly private nature, has lately been brought to an arrangement, which involves no anger or ill-will of any kind . . .

By some means . . . this trouble has been made the occasion of misrepresentations, most grossly false, most monstrous and most cruel – involving not only me, but innocent persons dear to my heart, and innocent persons of whom I have no knowledge, if indeed they have any existence . . .

I most solemnly declare then – and this I do, both in my own name and my wife's name – that all the lately whispered rumours touching the trouble at which I have glanced, are abominably false.

Not the least remarkable feature of this quasi-legal document was its evasiveness, as Dickens tried to squash rumours of sexual misconduct whilst retaining his reputation as the high priest of home and hearth. Dickens could not bring himself to remain silent, but nor could he write openly, like Caroline Norton, about his marriage. As a result his 'solemn declaration' is deeply contradictory: it claims to respect the sanctity of the private sphere yet it violates that sanctity through its very publication; it is circuitous and illogical, invoking the feelings of third parties, presumably

Ellen Ternan and Georgina Hogarth, whilst denying their existence; and it claims to speak on behalf of the wife from whom he has separated. Dickens did obtain Catherine's consent before using her name, but the published statement reinforced his authority to speak and her silence. Under the terms of the separation agreement, he profited from the law, retaining custody of his children and granting Catherine access. While the separation was amicable enough, it was secured at Dickens's instigation and on terms reflective of his economic power. The ill-judged letter shocked his readership and cost him the friendship of Bradbury and Evans, his publishers, who refused to carry the statement in *Punch*. As a result, *Household Words* shut down, and Dickens opened a new journal, which on advice he decided not to call *Household Harmony*!

CONCLUSION: BREAKING THE SEAL

Although Dickens exploited the sanctity of private life in order to curtail public discussion of his marriage breakdown, the exposure of marital unhappiness, and its consequences, is a major concern of Victorian literature and law. In an era when cases like Caroline Norton's brought publicity to the unjust fiction of coverture, the need for law reform was advanced both directly and indirectly through the medium of print. In addition to the polemical writings, the legal documents and the reformist utterances in fiction, poetic and prose narratives broke the seal of oppressive confidentiality by revealing the emotional costs of gender inequality in marriage.

The common law allowed and even fostered the domination of wives by husbands, causing Eliza Lynn to reach for Gothic analogies in her article for *Household Words*, 'Marriage Gaolers'. She describes marriage as a prison with the husband as gaoler and the wife as his prisoner. This figuration represents a confluence of literary convention and legal case studies. The Brontë novels are a probable literary source, especially the literal imprisonment of Bertha Mason by her husband Rochester in *Jane Eyre* and the exploitation of Isabella by Heathcliff in *Wuthering Heights*. However, the violation of women sanctioned by law in the three cases Lynn cites is comparable with these extreme representations. The clearest examples of the marriage-as-prison trope occur in the 'sensation novels' of the 1860s. According to Henry James, these stories 'introduced into fiction those most mysterious of mysteries, the mysteries which are at our own doors'.[45] Wilkie Collins and Mary Elizabeth Braddon were for James the inaugurators of the 'novel of domestic mystery' as surely as Austen and Richardson

were of the 'novel of domestic tranquillity'.[46] They located their sensational plots of bigamy, murder, arson and insanity within modern English
marriages, ensuring readerly recognition by adapting the details of well-
known contemporary crimes to the scenes of ordinary life. The Norton
marriage with its multiple scandals was ripe for treatment as a sensation
novel, and Caroline Norton herself wrote it, in *Lost and Saved* (1864).[47]

Collins's *The Woman in White* (1860) presents itself as an evidentiary
narrative, a collection of witness statements, which expose the plot of a
marriage-gaoler, Sir Percival Glyde. This detective novel solves a criminal
enterprise made possible by the legal disabilities of coverture. Braddon's
Lady Audley's Secret (1862) is based on the Yelverton bigamy trial but
reverses the gender roles, exposing an English wife as a perpetrator of
murder and other crimes.[48] In this text the crime is solved and justice
enforced by a lawyer, but the plot is equally important for its registration of
female desire. Patrick Brantlinger has suggested that 'rather than striking
forthright blows in favour of divorce law reform, sensation novels usually
tend merely to exploit public interest in these issues'.[49] However, their
exploitations pushed the boundaries of representation and brought into
fiction a new, decisive, even subversive heroine. Wilkie Collins, who
studied law at Lincoln's Inn, was exceptional in his blending of reformist
and sensational elements. His *No Name* (1862) centres its plot around
deficiencies in the law of illegitimacy. Two daughters left illegitimate by
their father's untimely death take contrasting steps in response – one
accepts her fate, and becomes a governess, the other determines by fair
means or foul to regain her inheritance. The novel shows women's precarious relation to law as the Vanstone daughters lose their legal identity
along with their (father's) name.[50] *Man and Wife* (1870) sought reform of
the marriage laws through a marriage-gaoler tale, while *The Law and the
Lady* (1874) showed a determined wife taking on the masculine discourse of
the law to clear her husband's name of a murder accusation left open by the
Scottish verdict of 'Not Proven'.[51]

These texts observe the ambivalence towards tradition and change
characteristic of the reformist mentality. They juxtapose a story of abuse
within marriage with a love plot, and a story of rebellious acts with one of
punishment. Thus they give heart to both reformers and defenders of
marriage. In their private lives, Braddon and Collins chose to cohabit
with their respective partners without entering the contract of marriage.
These unorthodox relationships were not representable under the informal
censorship which governed the treatment of sexuality in novels during the
nineteenth century. The de facto marriage of the Vanstones in *No Name* is

the shameful secret which precipitates the novel's crisis. Although the sensation novelists tested the boundaries of propriety in their exploration of domestic crime, they shared their society's view of the public function of literature, to teach and to delight. Accordingly, they balanced their undoubted pleasure in illicit passions with more normative stories of conventional marriage.

Immensely popular on publication, the Victorian domestic mysteries retain their narrative power today. Although the common-law fiction of coverture has long been reformed, marriage and crime continue to exercise our culture, both separately and together. In combining family law and criminal law, the sensation novel was a significant vehicle for a society which was redefining the rights of husbands and wives, and newly applying criminal sanctions to conduct previously accepted as private. One effect of this combination is to subvert the boundary between public and private spheres, and to imagine new spaces for women, new constraints on men. Another, probably more powerful effect is to police the family and set limits to the movement of those boundaries. As we face the challenge of equality in relationships, our search for practices that fulfil our ideals may be assisted by reading the cross-currents of reform in Victorian law and literature.

CHAPTER 6

The common law and the ache of modernism

> Modern times find themselves with an immense system of institutions, established facts, accredited dogmas, customs, rules, which have come to them from times not modern. In this system their life has to be carried forward, yet they have a sense that this system is not of their own creation, that it by no means corresponds exactly with the wants of their actual life, that for them, it is customary, not rational. The awakening of this sense is the awakening of the modern spirit.[1]

This chapter is concerned with 'the awakening of the modern spirit' in the late nineteenth and early twentieth centuries. It explores the response of lawyers and writers to the growing gap between the traditional normative world of custom and rules on the one hand, and 'the wants of their actual life' on the other. Matthew Arnold registered 'this strange disease of modern life', in poems like 'The Scholar-Gypsy':

> 'Tis that from change to change their being rolls;
> 'Tis that repeated shocks, again, again,
> Exhaust the energy of strongest souls
> And numb the elastic powers.[2]

Arnold saw the rapid changes of modernity as traumatic. Marshall Berman, writing one hundred years later, shared Arnold's sense of 'the maelstrom of modern life', but viewed it more ambivalently as 'an environment that promises us adventure, power, joy, growth, transformation of ourselves and the world – and, at the same time, that threatens to destroy everything we have, everything we know, everything we are'.[3] Capitalism and industrialism are the material forces that bring modernity and its ceaseless changes into being. Modernism, by contrast, is a cultural movement critical of modernity. From the 1890s, Thomas Hardy and others gave voice to 'the ache of modernism', expressing both their disbelief in inherited ideas and their alternative hypotheses with a candour that shocked the public.[4] Hardy, Oscar Wilde and the New Woman novelists engaged with the evolutionary theories of Charles Darwin, the new psycho-analysis of Sigmund Freud and Friedrich Nietzsche's call for a revaluation of moral values. These ideas threw into doubt long-held beliefs concerning the creation of the world and the central place of human beings in it, the unified rationality of the human mind and the universal basis of moral values. This context of philosophical revisionism provided modernist literature not only with new vocabularies, but with the means to shape new forms, such as stream of consciousness.

The common law, with its medieval roots, its reverence for precedent and its piecemeal reform, was a major bulwark of the system of inherited custom. How would it respond to the ceaseless changes wrought by modernity? And in its relations with literature, how would it respond to 'the repeated shocks' of the new? These are the questions for this chapter, not only in relation to England, but America and other jurisdictions as well, for the period under review, from 1890 to 1940, saw waves of migration and imperialism that demand an international perspective.

In answering these questions, we might begin with a statement penned by a critical legal scholar and a feminist art historian working in collaboration:

> Lawyers live by the text, and love the past, they hate novelty and misunderstand new languages. The law is able to appreciate new art only after it becomes a matter of convention, use and habit, in other words, when art becomes like law. Great art, on the other hand, precisely because it breaks away from conventions and rules and expresses creative freedom and imagination, is the antithesis of law.[5]

While it may be an overstatement to propound a general rule that 'great art . . . is the antithesis of law', the experience of modernist writers provides ample evidence of law's suspicion of cultural novelty. As I argued in chapter 2, modernism was a 'revolution of the word', and the committed experiments with form, language and representation carried out by writers such as James Joyce, D. H. Lawrence, Radclyffe Hall, Theodore Dreiser and many others led to prosecutions under the law of obscenity. While some books were banned, Joyce's *Ulysses* was freed with the aid of a judge happy to learn its new fictional language. Law and literature both depend on a verbal medium, so any opposition between them might well be less than that between law and the visual arts. One of the tasks of this chapter is to show whether lawyers felt 'the ache of modernism', what literary conventions they invoked in their writings, and whether when the shocks of modernity were brought to the courtroom they called forth any legal creativity.

In a number of other famous cases of the period, modernism was virtually placed on trial. Among these *causes célèbres* was the 'Scopes Monkey Trial' held in Dayton, Tennessee, in 1925. This was a test case brought to challenge a law forbidding the teaching of the evolutionary theory of biology 'or any theory that denies the story of the Divine Creation of man as taught in the Bible' in Tennessee's public education system.[6] Testimony concerning Darwin's theory or challenging the Bible was not allowed to be given in the courtroom, but the case (and with it the conflict) made news across the world. Scopes was convicted and fined, and the statute was not repealed until 1967. Another case in which law categorically rejected the modern spirit of criticism was that of Oscar Wilde in 1895. After unsuccessfully bringing a libel case against the Marquess of Queensberry over allegations of sodomy, Wilde was arrested on charges of homosexual conduct under the Criminal Law Amendment Act (1885). His first trial resulted in a hung jury, but he was convicted on the retrial and imprisoned for two years with hard labour. Wilde lived out the aesthetic creed he expounded in his writings, and so in his person he combined offences to prevailing norms of sexuality and to Victorian notions of literature as a vehicle of morality. He seemed the very symbol of a new order of gender and sexuality, of political and aesthetic radicalism, and thus his trial was not a private but a social drama, a battle between dominant ideologies and the modern spirit. The clash was most visible in the cross-examination of Wilde by Edward Carson, where passages from his books were put to him and to the jury as evidence of criminal tendencies:

CARSON: 'Your slim gilt soul walks between passion and poetry.'
WILDE: Yes.
CARSON: Is that a beautiful phrase?
WILDE: Not as you read it, Mr Carson. When I wrote it, it was beautiful. You read it very badly.
CARSON: I do not profess to be an artist, Mr Wilde.
WILDE: Then don't read it to me.
CARSON: And if you will allow me to say so, sometimes, when I hear you give evidence, I am glad I am not –[7]

Wilde's eloquent defence of 'the love that dare not speak its name' was confronted with a determined campaign to stigmatise homosexuality as deviance; his belief in equality and socialism was unavailing in a court that was routinely biased against working-class people, and favoured the upper classes; his cultivation of the beautiful met with Philistine contempt; and his assertion of a larger sphere of personal freedom induced a redoubling of the exercise of social power.[8]

While the law reinforced boundaries between citizen and criminal, human and animal, truth and error, Wilde made a career as a writer by confounding them. Modernist literature is a space in which traditional boundaries and categories are questioned, and for this reason its representations of the law tend to be deeply critical. In some of Joseph Conrad's works, such as 'The Secret Sharer' and *Lord Jim*, the distinction between the criminal and the hero, and the capacity of law for just adjudication are doubted.[9] Yet, as Richard Weisberg has shown, lawyers and legalistic protagonists abound in the fiction of the period, from Melville to Dostoevsky to Faulkner to Camus, and their constructions of reality implicitly invite comparison with literary ones.[10] One of the leading modernist poets, Wallace Stevens, was a lawyer.[11] A number of significant judges and jurists interested themselves in literature, yet one literary lawyer reflected the passing of his order in the title of his autobiography, *Confessions of an Un-Common Attorney*.[12] The question to be asked of all participants in this legal-cultural formation, however, is how did they engage with the new experiences presented by modernity?

MODERN LAW'S MEDIEVALIST ROMANCE

Sir Frederick Pollock (1845–1937), whom we last met as a friend of George Meredith, was the doyen of Victorian jurists. He was Corpus Professor of Jurisprudence at Oxford, author of leading textbooks on torts, contract and land law, founder of the *Law Quarterly Review*, editor-in-chief of the Law Reports and a notable legal historian. He was also 'a very good classic and philosopher, a mathematician of considerable ability, a versist in English, French, Italian, German, Latin and Greek, an Orientalist, a public servant, a competent fencer and mountaineer'.[13] The breadth of his interests and the distinction of his reputation led Gareth H. Jones to call him 'one of the last representatives of the old broad culture'.[14] In his legal writings, he 'sought the principles underlying the morass of case law', and he firmly believed that law was 'neither a trade nor a solemn jugglery, but a science'.[15] Pollock was one of the 'conceptive ideologists' of the common law as a system of justice in late nineteenth- and early twentieth-century England,[16] and his commitment to it was fervent. His pride in this system included a nurturing interest in its expansion, as a consequence of British imperialism, into other countries, especially America. He made several visits to America, lecturing at various law schools and developing a network of friendships with like-minded scholars, lawyers and judges, the most notable of whom was Justice Oliver Wendell Holmes.

On his first visit, in lectures later published as *The Expansion of the Common Law*, he revealed that the law was for him not simply an intellectual or professional commitment, but an emotional attachment: 'our lady the Common Law is not a task-mistress but a bountiful sovereign whose service is freedom'.[17]

This feudal and chivalric rhetoric was expanded in a later series of lectures, *The Genius of the Common Law*, delivered at Columbia University and published in 1912. Here Pollock distils what he sees as the distinctive features of the common law from its infancy to its modernity. However, *The Genius of the Common Law* is chiefly remarkable as an instance of the 'old broad culture', for Pollock's enunciation of legal principle is infused with literary and cultural references in a tour de force of humanistic jurisprudence. The governing trope of this apologia of the common law is that of the medieval quest romance, but its range is eclectic:

We are here to do homage to our lady the Common Law; we are her men of life and limb and earthly worship. But we do not worship her as a goddess exempt from human judgment or above human sympathy. She is no placid Madonna sitting in a rose garden; rather she is like the Fortitude of the Florentine master, armed and expectant, her battle-mace lightly poised in fingers ready to close, at one swift motion, to the fighting grip. Neither is she a cold minister of the Fates. Her soul is founded in an order older than the gods themselves, yet the joy of strife is not strange to her, nor yet the humours of the crowd. She belongs to the kindred of Homer's gods, more powerful than men, but not passionless or infallible. She can be jealous with Hera, merciless with Artemis, and astute with Athena.[18]

As with Caroline Norton modelling Justice in the 1840s, the common law is here allegorically represented as a woman attended by a group of select male subjects who faithfully fight on her behalf. In representing legal history as a romance narrative, Pollock is committed to an anachronistic gender politics in which woman is passive muse, not active subject.[19] Moreover, Pollock transforms the adversary system of the common law trial: the ultimate loyalty of these knights is not to their clients, but to law. The knightly 'worship' of the goddess Law is demonstrated through the 'perpetual quest' against a range of enemies, such as formalism and special pleading, in the common law's history, rendered aptly as 'Surrebutter Castle'.

Yet Pollock's narrative does not solely present the common law on the defensive. In a chapter entitled 'Alliance and Conquest' he explores relationships with other legal systems. In the eighteenth century, with the growth of modern commerce, Lord Mansfield incorporated the Law Merchant into the common law, a development Pollock calls 'the greatest of our lady's acquisitions, the more remarkable because it was made in a generation not otherwise distinguished for creative power or large enterprise' (82). One 'large enterprise' that began around this time, the British empire, is viewed by Pollock with modest pride: 'wherever the British flag has gone, much of the spirit of the Common Law has gone with it, if not of the letter also' (85). He reads the legal aspect of the ensuing cross-cultural encounter as a juristic competition in which the common law prevails because of its superiority. Writing from the centre of the empire, Pollock obscures the military, economic and political dominance which underwrote this jurisprudential triumph. In the case of India, he criticises the wholesale enforcement of common-law precedents: for example, 'technical rules of English real property law have been relied on in Indian courts without considering whether they had any reasonable application to the facts and usage of the country' (92). Yet this critique does not expose a failing of the system, merely over-zealous knights: 'Still all this homage is done to the Common Law, whether with the best of discretion or not.' Pollock, then, was a man of his time, patriotically supportive of Britain and its empire, but professionally committed to a rational system of law. His jurisprudential romance is a myth that conceals these contradictions.

The chapter on 'Conquest' makes clear the idealised and abstract quality of Pollock's account of the common law. Personified as 'our lady', an inspiration and object of service, the law is beautiful and beyond reproach. The encounters that form her quest are not battles with living people or monsters, but debates between different value systems, allegorically embodied as competing powers. In keeping with the discourse of medieval romance, an ultimate order underlies this imagined world, according to which the common law is a good power and its opponents are evil.

Such medievalism was not peculiar to Pollock but was a broad cultural movement that reclaimed the medieval past as a nostalgic corrective to the alienation of modernity. In the second half of the nineteenth century, the period of Pollock's maturity, the most influential propagator of medievalist values was Alfred Tennyson. His complete cycle of poems on the legend of King Arthur and the Round Table, *The Idylls of the King*, was hugely popular. These poems refine and allegorise the raw material of the original stories, turning physical action into moral exemplum:

> To reverence the King, as if he were
> Their conscience, and their conscience as their King,
> To break the heathen and uphold the Christ,
> To ride abroad redressing human wrongs, . . .
> To love one maiden only, cleave to her,

And worship her by years of noble deeds,
Until they won her.[20]

With their moral idealism, their support for imperial conquest ('to break the heathen'), and their belief in the sublimating force of a pure love in noble deeds, these lines can be seen as a likely inspiration for Pollock. The figure of the knight errant was transmuted into the gentleman and the imperial hero. With these cultural appropriations around him, his own engagement with medieval legal history and an ascendant ideology of the rule of law, Pollock was able to metamorphose the original circuit judges of Edward II, and their successors, into knights errant of the common law.

Ironically, political developments in England at the time Pollock was writing were rendering his medievalism anachronistic: the suffragettes were demanding a more active role for women in law-making than that of muse; the political power of the hereditary aristocracy in the House of Lords to withhold approval of the elected government's Budget was ended; labour was enforcing recognition of its political rights through a crippling coal strike; and the debate over Irish Home Rule was challenging England's first colonial conquest. In this light, the high romance of *The Genius of the Common Law* can be interpreted as the dream of a legal traditionalist facing the crises of modernity.

OLIVER WENDELL HOLMES

Among Pollock's legal community, perhaps the most revered champion of the common law was his friend and long-time correspondent, Oliver Wendell Holmes. Holmes became a legend in his thirty years on the Supreme Court of the United States, renowned for his Olympian detachment from partisan causes and his commitment to the development and exposition of legal principle. As the 'great dissenter' he was the model of the heroic judge for legalists from Pollock to Ronald Dworkin.[21] Yet in their responses to the challenges of modernity, Holmes and Pollock afford a signal contrast with each other. Despite admiring *The Genius of the Common Law*, Holmes was a realist by temperament, and his writings self-consciously apply the fruits of modern thought to the inherited legal system. In the oft-quoted opening of his own treatise, *The Common Law* (1881), he placed legal history and theory at the service of present needs:

The life of the law has not been logic: it has been experience. The felt necessities of the time, the prevalent political and moral theories, intuitions of public policy, avowed or unconscious, even the prejudices which judges share with their fellow-men, have had a good deal more to do than the syllogism in determining the rules by which men should be governed. The law embodies the story of a nation's development through the centuries, and it cannot be dealt with as if it contained only the axioms and corollaries of a book of mathematics. In order to know what it is, we must know what it has been and what it tends to become. We must alternately consult history and existing theories of legislation. But the most difficult labour will be to understand the combination of the two into new products at every stage.[22]

In recognising 'the felt necessities of the time' and stressing the importance of 'new products', Holmes evinces a preference for contemporary need over tradition. In this respect his enterprise is consistent with that of the writers and artists of the time, who sought to register the pressure of modern experience.

As this passage shows, Holmes was an accomplished rhetorician. His essays, judicial opinions and speeches were regarded by his contemporaries as possessing literary merit, and were frequently collected and published. Like Pollock, Holmes had been influenced by Victorian medievalism in his youth.[23] In an after-dinner speech to the Suffolk Bar Association in 1913, he appears to draw on Pollock's notion of the law as a mistress, but a remote and demanding one, 'only to be wooed by a sustained and lonely passion, – only to be won by straining all the faculties by which man is likest to a god'.[24] Holmes's legal romance is an exercise in heroic rationality, ascetic where Pollock's is aesthetic. Despite being an avid reader he dismisses the pleasures of literature: 'To the lover of the law how small a thing seem the novelist's tales of the loves and fates of Daphnis and Chloe! . . . For him no less a history will suffice than that of the moral life of his race.' And yet, as William Moddelmog shows, these very terms view law as 'a kind of master narrative of a community's history, values and beliefs'.[25] In an interesting variation on the female personification of law, Holmes envisions her as a woman artist, 'a princess mightier than she who once wrought at Bayeux, eternally weaving into her web dim figures of the ever-lengthening past, – figures too dim to be noticed by the idle, too symbolic to be interpreted except by her pupils, but to the discerning eye disclosing every painful step and every world-shaking contest by which mankind has worked and fought its way from savage isolation to organic social life'.[26] In this analogy law is a creative endeavour. Like all arts it involves a symbolic representation of human history. In its obscurity to the mass of the people, and its ambitious attempt to forge an image for the whole age, it bears a surprising resemblance to the modernist epics of James Joyce and T. S. Eliot. These writers eschewed conventional narrative forms for montages and mythic parallels between ancient and modern worlds, as a way of 'giving shape and significance to the immense panorama of futility and anarchy which is contemporary history'.[27] Yet while Eliot presented a world in ruins in *The Waste Land*, Holmes's account draws on a different aspect of modern thought, the Darwinian theory of evolution. In his representation of a movement 'from savage isolation to organic social life', a Social Darwinist belief in the struggle for survival, and in the emergence of higher from lower forms of life is evident. As Benjamin Kaplan has written, 'Accepting Darwin and Malthus, Holmes saw out his window a Darwinian wild, an endless struggle of groups and classes as well as individuals . . . Might made right, or nearly so.'[28]

The extent to which modern ideas impacted on his philosophy of law can be seen in an address to the Boston University Law School in 1897, 'The Path of the Law'. Holmes begins by distinguishing between law and moral ideas, and thence offers a decidedly unsentimental definition of law: 'The prophecies of what the courts will do in fact, and nothing more pretentious, are what I mean by the law.'[29] With its emphasis on fact, its focus on practice and outcomes and its displacement of 'pretentious' ideals, this famous sentence demonstrates the realist and pragmatic bases of Holmes's approach to law. Pragmatism is an American school of philosophy that developed in the 1880s, founded by Charles Sanders Peirce, William James and John Dewey. Pragmatists hold to a relativistic and experiential idea of truth and stress the importance of results over general theories. Holmes was acquainted with some of these men and with contemporary debates in philosophy through his reading of their works and his early membership of the Metaphysicals Club at Harvard. Although he never declared himself a pragmatist thinker, there are strong affinities between his approach to law and pragmatist tenets, as Thomas C. Grey has shown: 'When Holmes defined law as the prediction of judicial action, he was theorising in the pragmatist way, contextually and instrumentally.'[30] Holmes reveals the consequences of pragmatism in a later passage in 'The Path of the Law':

an evolutionist will hesitate to affirm universal validity for his social ideals, or for the principles which he thinks should be embodied in legislation. He is content if he can prove them best for here and now. He may be ready to admit that he knows nothing about an absolute best for the cosmos, and even that he knows nothing about a permanent best for men. Still it is true that a body of law is more rational and more civilized when every rule it contains is referred articulately to an end which it subserves, and when the grounds for desiring that end are stated or are ready to be stated in words. (49)

Holmes's modernism stresses the need for a rational system of law, one which can be analysed in terms of its ends and means.

As a young man, Holmes was wounded three times during his service on the Union side in the American Civil War. The experience of war proved a formative influence on his later outlook, convincing him of the emptiness of all ideals except duty, and of the inescapability of struggle and pain in life.[31] This experience, confirmed by his later Darwinian reading, led him to reprobate some aspects of modernity, especially what he saw as its anodyne preference for and expectation of comfort. He protested in 'The Soldier's Faith' against the modern 'revolt against pain':

From societies for the prevention of cruelty to animals up to socialism, we express in numberless ways the notion that suffering is a wrong which can and ought to be prevented, and a whole literature of sympathy has sprung into being which points out in story and in verse how hard it is to be wounded in the battle of life, how terrible, how unjust that anyone should fail.[32]

One consequence of Holmes's rationalism and disillusionment is a harshness and antipathy that can be traced in some judgments and in the ceremonial writings studied here. Thomas Grey has noted that these writings demonstrate the danger of addressing an audience of initiates: in inspiring fellow lawyers with a heroic vision of their profession, they ignore 'the immediate and material external consequences of their work on others'.[33] The lack of any attention to the perspective of the litigant is a limitation of these writings.[34] Holmes's engagement with modernity was complex and contradictory. While dismissing 'the literature of sympathy', Holmes was a lifelong reader of novels! In addition, as part of his scientific approach to law he sought to rationalise the law of negligence for modern needs. It is to the question of suffering, its literary representation and legal redress that we now turn.

THE LITERATURE OF SYMPATHY AND THE TORT OF NEGLIGENCE

Holmes was not unique in registering the challenges posed by pain and suffering in modern society. Law, medicine, economics and literature were all exercised by the apparent prevalence of pain, its causes and costs. Noting its 'new visibility' and urgency across these disciplines, Wai Chee Dimock has argued that 'pain might well be the key word of the nineteenth [century]'.[35] Besides war and illness, 'a whole new arena of suffering' was opened up by the industrial revolution, and especially by 'the rate of industrial accidents'.[36] These accidents and the injuries they caused led to claims for compensation, bringing unprecedented stories of loss and suffering before courts and legislators. Narratives without precedent place new demands on legal reasoning, just as new experiences do on literary conventions. Injury and pain form part of the 'ache of modernism', then, and both writers and lawyers sought what Virginia Woolf called 'new forms for our new sensations'.[37]

In the first decade of the twentieth century, as Holmes observed with anxiety, literature addressed itself to law-makers, appealing on behalf of the poor or the outcast, using sympathy as a vehicle for possible reform. Although 'novels with a purpose' had been influential in the middle of the nineteenth century, through Dickens, Gaskell and Harriet Beecher Stowe, the literature of sympathy gathered new momentum under the twin influences of socialism and naturalism. As its name implies, socialism was a collectivist response to the hardships visited upon workers by laissez-faire economics in the industrial age. Naturalism was a literary movement which told stories of the most extreme poverty and degradation in society, based on a quasi-scientific model of empirical research and narrative detachment. Although its originator, Emile Zola, eschewed the sentimentality of the earlier reforming novelists by stressing biological and economic determinism, his aesthetic creed attracted social reformers as a way of drawing attention to social exploitation. For writers like Jack London and Upton Sinclair, scientific objectivity was a strategy that needed to be supplemented by a recognition that social and economic forces could and should be changed. The combination of naturalism and socialism produced a literature of sympathy that relied on detailed documentation rather than sentimental rhetoric to promote institutional change. These protest novels were published in popular journals such as *McClure's Magazine* and the *American Magazine*, alongside the newly developing investigative journalism. Novelists and reporters were exposing abuses in industry and government.

Upton Sinclair's 1904 novel, *The Jungle*, was commissioned by the *American Socialist Monthly* to report on conditions in Chicago's meat-packing industry. *The Jungle* is really interesting for students of law and literature. Not only does it frankly take up Holmes's Darwinian metaphor of life as a battle for survival, but it questions the ideology of natural competition that capitalism promotes as a basis for social organisation. Centred round the appalling conditions in which the members of an immigrant family are required to live and work, their vulnerability to fraud, unsafe working conditions, and the betrayals of their equally desperate fellow-workers, the novel was a sensation. Originally rejected by publishers, it became a bestseller. As a novel, it is heavy-handedly didactic, and its cry of protest against the exploitation of workers in the abbatoirs is hard to miss. From a prison cell where he awaits trial for assaulting a corrupt foreman, the protagonist Jurgis muses, 'their justice – it was a lie, it was a lie, a hideous brutal lie, a thing too black and hateful for any world but a world of nightmares'.[38] The legal system, whether criminal or civil, is a tool of class oppression. Sinclair quotes Oscar Wilde's *Ballad of Reading Gaol*, which highlights the injustice of the criminal law.[39] On the civil side, when Jurgis is injured by a runaway steer on the killing floor, no legal redress or medical aid is offered him. However, despite its melodramatic starkness, his fate struck readers with less force than did the novel's exposure of the unhygienic procedures adopted by the industry in max-imising its profits. One notably influential reader who reacted to this was President Theodore Roosevelt. He read *The Jungle* in 1906 and ordered an immediate government inspection of the industry. That report confirmed Sinclair's claims, and by 30 June that same year, Congress had passed the Pure Food and Drug Act 1906 and the Meat Inspection Act 1906.[40] This legislative success was a measure of a broader shift in public opinion towards an acceptance of communal responsibility to protect citizens from harm, in which the literature of sympathy played an integral part. Yet this implementation of socially responsible laws was slow, and the success of *The Jungle* shows how readers' sympathy for the victims of laissez-faire individualism may be mobilised by self-interest as much as by altruism.

For all its contemporaneity of subject and its progressive politics, *The Jungle* is old-fashioned in its narrative form. With its omniscient narrator openly tugging at the reader's emotions through sentimental rhetoric, it owes more to Dickens than Zola. Many of Sinclair's younger contempo-raries rejected the convention of omniscient narration as incompatible with the relativistic theories of knowledge and ethics developed by modern philosophy. Joseph Conrad, Henry James, Virginia Woolf and F. Scott Fitzgerald all tended to use dramatic narrators, characters located in the action rather than above it, or when using impersonal narration to confine the narrative to the perspective of a particular character. With an increased attention to individual psychology, and a rejection of traditional discourses of morality and sentiment, the modernist novel adopted a more restrained and indirect approach to the representation of the pain and suffering occa-sioned by machine-related injuries. Poets, too, embraced the dramatic mono-logue or the concrete image over the oracular pronouncement of deep feeling or high philosophy. The Wordsworthian poet as seer gave way to a more ironic, colloquial and iconoclastic poet best exemplified by Ezra Pound. In this modernist writing the narrator is positioned as a witness, not as a judge.

The poet as witness was an important trope in twentieth-century literary history.[41] In the 1930s, this testimonial poetics engaged with industrial accidents. Charles Reznikoff, a lawyer, constructed a long poetic sequence entitled *Testimony* out of witness statements he found in the law reports while working on a digest of legal cases for a publisher.

Once in a while I could see in the facts of a case details of the time and place, and it seemed to me that out of such material the century and a half during which the US has been a nation could be written up, not from the standpoint of an individual, as in diaries, nor merely from the angle of the unusual, as in newspapers, but from every standpoint – as many standpoints as were provided by the witnesses themselves.[42]

From these witness statements and legal narratives Reznikoff distilled vignettes which, placed together, formed a montage representing the national experience. He deliberately drew his stories from every region, from all the law reports, and took particular note of cases of racial injustice, child abuse and industrial accidents. Reznikoff was a member of the Objectivist group, who believed that an incident or object sparely described could generate an emotional response in the reader. These poems are little known, so the following example is quoted in full:

Amelia was just fourteen and out of the orphan asylum; at her first job – in
the bindery, and yes sir, yes ma'am, oh, so anxious to please.
She stood at the table, her blonde hair hanging about her shoulders,
'knocking up' for Mary and Sadie, the stitchers
('knocking up' is counting books and stacking them in piles to be taken away).
    There were twenty wire-stitching machines on the floor, worked by a shaft that
ran under the table;
as each stitcher put her work through the machine,
she threw it on the table. The books were piling up fast
and some slid to the floor
(the forelady had said, Keep the work off the floor!);
and Amelia stooped to pick up the books –
three or four had fallen under the table
between the boards nailed against the legs.
She felt her hair caught gently;
put her hand up, and felt the shaft going round and round
and her hair caught on it, wound and winding around it,
until the scalp was jerked from her head,
and the blood was coming down all over her face and waist.[43]

This harrowing poem tells its story in plain language but catches the reader with the sudden shock of Amelia's entanglement. The modernist literature of sympathy is dramatic and undemonstrative but sharply evokes the experience of suffering through a commitment to documenting detail.

Throughout the modernist period, novels treat accidents involving machinery as a significant aspect of modernity. F. Scott Fitzgerald's tragic romance of the moneyed elites of the American 1920s, *The Great Gatsby*, finds the perfect metaphor for its vision of defeated idealism in a hit-and-run car accident. Shipping collisions and loss of life at sea are not only the interest of Joseph Conrad: they form part of the encyclopaedic range of James Joyce's *Ulysses*. In the 'Eumaeus' episode Bloom and his companions tell stories of ships lost off the Irish Coast. In British fiction dealing with the working class, industrial accident is a major theme. In D. H. Lawrence's *Sons and Lovers* (1911) the protagonist's father is always being injured at work in the coal mine, and one especially serious accident, causing a multiple fracture in his leg, contributes decisively to his bitterness, alienation and descent into alcoholism. Henry Green's *Living* (1929) is a brilliant depiction of factory life drawing on the perspectives of both management and workers. In this understated novel, accidents occur, but without causing injury, and suffering is traced to economic and psychological forces, not to sudden events. In this workplace, which is drawn from Green's family business, law is marginalised: only one character sees it as a way of solving problems.[44]

As with poetry, some historical accidents were so devastating that they inspired repeated literary treatment. On 3 November 1927, forty people died in Sydney Harbour when the ferry *Greycliffe* collided with the liner RMS *Tahiti*. Poignantly, their ages ranged from two to eighty-one. Despite three trials, key questions of causation and responsibility remained controversial. Christina Stead's story, 'Day of Wrath' (1934), places the quest for causes and reasons into a modernist philosophical context, casting doubt on Sydneysiders' attempts to moralise the event.[45] Eleanor Dark links the collision to the broader clash of political and economic forces in the 1930s in her social-realist novel *Waterway* (1938).[46] Adapting the modernist preference for synchronous plotting across a single day, Dark presents a cross-section of Sydney society and its quotidian journeys across the Harbour, culminating in the tragedy.

As the sources of some of these fictions show, workers and citizens injured by the new machinery actively sought redress from the courts, placing pressure on the common law to adjust its conception of torts or civil wrongs. Like other judges, Oliver Wendell Holmes saw the need to update this branch of law, and prominently addressed the subject in *The Common Law*. As legal historian David Rosenberg notes, 'Industrial production, as Holmes observed, generated systematic risks to person and property of such unprecedented volume and technological sophistication as to overwhelm the law of torts crafted from more prosaic and "ungeneralized" cases of assault, carriage collision, and slander.'[47] As the tenor of Holmes's comments in 'The Soldier's Faith' implies, nineteenth-century judges were not receptive to claimants injured by machinery, and in apportioning responsibility for accidents, tended to blame the victim. The common law was changed – in ways that favoured industry. Whereas traditionally the master–servant rule made an employer vicariously responsible for employees injured in the course of work, now a 'fellow-servant rule' was enunciated which limited the employer's liability and left the victim to bear the loss. Negligence emerged as a separate category within tort law in the nineteenth century, and it too was conceptualised in restrictive ways. Plaintiffs' injuries were only compensable if the defendant owed them a duty of care, and if the plaintiffs had not 'voluntarily assumed the risk' of a dangerous occupation. Courts also limited the scope of negligence by insisting that the defendants' actions must be the 'proximate' cause of the injury suffered, narrowing the 'radius of pertinence' when assessing causation.[48] In rationalising the law of torts, Holmes argued that moral concepts of blame had no place in the law, that judicial assessments of liability involved not assigning moral fault, but making social policy about where the loss should be borne. This pragmatic suggestion was, however, less influential than his serviceable division of torts into 'intentional wrongs, negligence, and strict liability'.[49]

Despite these inauspicious beginnings, negligence became a site of judicial creativity in the twentieth century. One of the key figures here is Holmes's judicial disciple, Benjamin Nathan Cardozo. Cardozo shared the broad cultural interests of Holmes, his commitment to an impersonal role of the judge, and his awareness of law's literary basis. His essay, 'Law and Literature', positions the judicial opinion as a rhetorical practice: 'The opinion will need persuasive force, or the impressive virtue of sincerity and fire, or the mnemonic power of alliteration and antithesis, or the terseness and tang of the proverb and the maxim. Neglect the help of these allies and it may never win its way.'[50] Though presented as literary commentary, these ideas have special force for a judge seeking to break new ground in the law.

Cardozo used the narrative techniques of the literature of sympathy in *Hynes* v. *New York Central Railroad*, describing the plaintiff as 'Harvey Hynes, a lad of sixteen', and his electrocution by the defendant's falling wire as 'this disaster'. In a fact-laden opinion, he deprecates the defendant's reliance on '"a jurisprudence of conceptions"', the extension of a maxim or definition with relentless disregard of consequences to a "dryly logical extreme"'.[51] Legal reasoning and narration are virtually interfused in this text, which yet cites no previous cases. By contrast, the abstract, depersonalised approach of the 'jurisprudence of conceptions' is clearly dominant in his decision against the plaintiff in the famous case of *Palsgraf* v. *Long Island Railroad*.[52] Another Cardozo judgment that did 'win its way' was *MacPherson* v. *Buick Motor Company*. In this case the car manufacturer was held liable to the ultimate purchaser who was injured when a defective wheel collapsed, and he was thrown out of the vehicle while driving. Cardozo found that like poisons and explosives, a car was a thing of danger if negligently made, extending the authorities to impose a duty of care on the manufacturer. This duty was owed not merely to the immediate purchaser, a car dealer, through their contract, but to the ultimate consumer under the law of tort. 'Precedents drawn from the days of travel by stage coach do not fit the conditions of travel today. The principle that the danger must be imminent does not change, but the things subject to the principle do change. They are whatever the developing civilization requires them to be.'[53]

This expansive approach to legal responsibility was cited with approval in the leading English case on negligence, *Donoghue* v. *Stevenson*, in 1932. In this case, another of the ordinary incidents of modern life went wrong. May Donoghue bought a bottle of Stevenson's ginger beer at a café. In pouring a second glass, she noticed the remains of a decomposed snail in the bottle. As a result, she was made physically sick, and eventually required hospital treatment. In a close 3:2 judgment in the House of Lords, it was held that Donoghue was owed a duty of care. Addressing this new situation, Lord Atkin penned an eloquent statement of the existence of a general duty of care in the common law:

In English law there must be, and is, some general conception of relations giving rise to a duty of care, of which the particular cases found in the books are but instances. The liability for negligence, whether you style it such or treat it as in other systems as a species of 'culpa', is no doubt based upon a general public sentiment of moral wrongdoing for which the offender must pay. But acts or omissions which any moral code would censure cannot in a practical world be treated so as to give a right to every person injured by them to demand relief. In this way rules of law arise which limit the range of complainants and the extent of their remedy. The rule that you are to love your neighbour becomes in law, you must not injure your neighbour; and the lawyer's question, Who is my neighbour? receives a restricted reply. You must take reasonable care to avoid acts or omissions which you can reasonably foresee would be likely to injure your neighbour. Who, then, in law is my neighbour? The answer seems to be – persons who are so closely and directly affected by my act that I ought reasonably to have them in contemplation as being so affected when I am directing my mind to the acts or omissions which are called in question.[54]

In this passage, Atkin practises a jurisprudence of relations, placing the conception of a duty of care into a social framework, and then personifying it by invoking the biblical parable of the Good Samaritan. He fuses moral obligation with the legal discourse of right and restriction by honouring the lawyer's question, 'who is my neighbour?' with a practical reply. The metaphor of the neighbour exhibits Cardozo's 'terseness and tang of the proverb', but it also prompts the law to an ethical concern, much like the literature of sympathy. And yet, as Atkin's biographer has pointed out, this declaration is followed by eleven pages of close analysis of existing cases, identifying the underlying principle running through the myriad of cases.[55] As a result, 'the revolution [in the law of negligence] was not destructive', but came to seem part of the organic growth of the common law.[56]

One of the judges who congratulated Atkin on 'the Snail Case' was the Australian Herbert Vere Evatt, who wrote in a letter: 'on all sides there is profound satisfaction that, in substance, your judgment and that of Justice Cardozo of the USA coincide, and that the common law is again shown to be capable of meeting modern conditions of industrialisation, and of striking through legal forms of separateness to reality'.[57] The enunciation of this general duty not only allowed May Donoghue to recover damages but opened up the law to a much wider range of stories of injury.[58] However, in accordance with the common law's practice, the ensuing cases proceeded cautiously in awarding damages for new classes of injury.

Among the new dangers created by industrial society were psychological and emotional damage. Ravit Reichman has pointed to intriguing parallels between the way a novelist, Virginia Woolf, struggled to represent the shellshock suffered by soldiers and the unresolved grief of their families in the First World War, and the difficulty within negligence law of acknowledging 'nervous shock' caused by negligent action. In 1901, Reichman notes, such 'invisible' damage was recognised, but only if accompanied by physical injury, and prompted by fear for one's own safety.[59] These provisos eventually gave way before advances in neurology and psychiatry and to the general principle outlined in *Donoghue* v. *Stevenson*, but courts exhibited 'pronounced caution' in their approach to such claims.[60] In *Chester* v. *Waverley Corporation*, the High Court of Australia found that the shock experienced by a mother on seeing the drowned body of her seven-year-old son lifted from a trench dug by council workers was not compensable. The majority made short work of her appeal, Rich J.

declaring the trend inaugurated by *Donoghue* 'unbelievable', and Starke J. finding 'the shock of the appellant ... not within the ordinary range of human experience'.[61] The sole dissent, by Justice Evatt, proceeds like the creative opinions of Atkin and Cardozo, in attending to the narrative and actively interpreting the cases to define the legal principle. More than this, it draws on the literature of sympathy, seeking to demonstrate the reasonableness of the mother's reaction by quoting from William Blake's 'The Little Girl Lost', and by allowing one of the recurrent horror stories of white Australian culture, the lost child, to inform its understanding.[62] By openly drawing on literary traditions of sympathetic identification, Evatt was able to place his view of the law in the avant-garde of negligence doctrine.

MODERNIST CRITIQUES OF LAW

Thus far we have identified two major instances of legal creativity in this period, the poetic and nostalgic 'lady of the Common Law', and the practical and legal creation of the tort of negligence. Taken together, they demonstrate that the 'creative verbalisation' shared by law and literature can be a constructive and socially committed force, albeit variously directed. Despite its Victorian provenance, 'Our Lady the Common Law' remained in the currency of legal discourse after the First World War. Cardozo employed it in a Graduation Address as late as 1939. However, it never crossed into literary discourse, despite the many traffickings between the two fields. A literature intent on 'making it new', on smashing and breaking the old idols, had no taste for veneration. A gap had opened up between the habitual ways of speaking of each discipline. Owen Barfield, an English solicitor and philologist, noted that personification was no longer a credible technique in modern poetry, whereas in law it seemed entirely apt, as the idea of corporate personality in modern company law showed.[63] When professional writers considered law in relation to women, they identified bias and injustice, not an abstract ideal. Susan Glaspell's play *Trifles* (1916), and her related short story 'A Jury of Her Peers' (1917), were inspired by the 1902 trial of Margaret Hossack for the murder of her husband. They rewrite the story so as to expose, and overturn, the gendered assumptions of the law.[64] F. Tennyson Jesse, a well-known playwright, novelist and criminologist in the interwar years, based her novel *A Pin to See the Peepshow* on the case of Edith Thompson, whose conviction for murdering her husband in 1923 was based on moral repugnance at her adultery, and not on any positive evidence.[65] Bernard Shaw's *Saint Joan* (1924), on the life, death and rehabilitation of Joan of Arc, might also figure in this list, including as it does her trial for heresy.

The example of another *cause célèbre*, the trial of Oscar Wilde, is invoked by implication in James Joyce's *Ulysses*. In the Night-town or 'Circe' episode, which takes the form of an Expressionist play, Bloom is brought before a court to answer a number of shifting charges. In one guise, he appears 'pleading not guilty and holding a fullblown waterlily'.[66] With the waterlily, an emblem of aestheticism, Bloom is an echo of his fellow-Irishman, Oscar Wilde.[67] Joyce's representation of the trial process is at one level a travesty, for Bloom is asked to 'provide a bogus statement'. The resulting parody of a plea for mercy is a good example of what Melanie Williams has called 'empty justice'. However, at another level, the trial works as an Expressionist text, to bring out Bloom's hidden sexual desires. By articulating these in the context of a mock trial, Joyce uncannily anticipated his book's own trial for obscenity. While Bloom is condemned, his accusers are shown to be equally depraved, and much more vengeful. The role accorded to unseemly desires in the behaviour of both accusers and defendant exemplifies the modernist critique of the individual as a 'free, thinking and responsible subject, the traditional model of legal subjectivity'.[68] Joyce underscores the provisional nature of identity when he has Bloom survive his execution and become a law-giver!

However, the most sustained representation of law in modernist literature was undertaken by Franz Kafka. A trained lawyer, Kafka worked principally in insurance corporations, experiencing at first-hand the bureaucratic-administrative forms of modern governance. Writing by night, he adopted the general modernist rejection of realism, specialising in the gnomic form of the parable, fusing fantasy, mystery and the grotesque in obviously symbolic narratives. The enigmatic quality of 'Before the Law', 'In the Penal Colony' and other parables mirrors the law's own obscurity of language and challenges its assumption of interpretative facility, its demand for decidability in all other utterances. Unlike Pollock or Holmes, Kafka did not write as an insider; rather he approached the culture of legality as a resident alien, stressing the law's remoteness from ordinary people. In 'Before the Law' and other parables, he focuses on the individual who is subject to the law, who obeys its call, but who is never admitted beyond its threshold and dies disappointed. Here the abstract regime is literalised as a place but is defamiliarised by the unexpected course of events. The law excludes its supplicants, prompting questions: how?

why?[69] In 'The Problem of Our Laws', Kafka propounds an informed sociocultural critique:

> Our laws are not generally known; they are kept secret by the small group of nobles who rule us. We are convinced that these ancient laws are scrupulously administered; nevertheless it is an extremely painful thing to be ruled by laws that one does not know ... The very existence of these laws, however, is at most a matter of presumption. There is a tradition that they exist, and that they are a mystery confided to the nobility, but it is not and cannot be more than a mere tradition sanctioned by age, for the essence of a secret code is that it should remain a mystery.[70]

The common law is such a 'tradition', but the order of knighthood lauded by Pollock is shown to perform an exclusory and mystifying function.

Kafka's full-length representation of law, *The Trial*, shows what happens to a person who somehow gets 'inside' the law. Caught in a system which is bewildering, evasive and endless, a criminal version of *Bleak House*'s Chancery, Joseph K. is as perplexed as his readers by the bizarre twists of legal process and the soul-destroying deferral of justice. Kafka draws on the criminal law and procedure then in force in the Austro-Hungarian empire but introduces several distortions to maximise its symbolic impact.[71] *The Trial* thus works on a number of levels: viewed metaphysically, it explores the human experience of guilt and meaninglessness; viewed sociologically, it is 'the alphabet of our totalitarian politics'.[72] From a law-and-literature perspective, it reveals through the conversation between Joseph K. and Titorelli, the court painter, the role of art within the domain of the law. Titorelli's portraits of judges are conventional and idealising yet also deconstruct these ennobling visions, as the figure of Justitia merges with the aggressively partial goddesses of Victory or the Hunt.[73]

One of Kafka's successors in the modernist debunking of legal ideology is Christina Stead in her *The Salzburg Tales* (1934). The first book Stead published after her arrival in Europe from Australia, it is a 'twentieth-century Decameron', a collection of stories told by a group of narrators who are cultural tourists assembled in Salzburg for the Mozart Festival, and in particular for a performance of Hofmannsthal's medievalist play, *Jedermann* (Everyman).[74] They are characterised by their occupations, nationalities and other indices of social identity, not by name. Through the range and sharpness of its portraits, this text offers a satiric typology of European culture in crisis.

The lawyer from Budapest parodies the English 'juridical nationalism' of Pollock and his forebears in opening his tale, 'Speculation in Lost Causes':

> One of my ancestors was sent to the colonies for an epigram; my great-grandfather was governor of a gaol, my grandfather, Speaker in a colonial legislative assembly

and my father a life member of the Selden Society: in my cradle my mother crooned me to sleep with the more lyric passages in Dicey, Maitland and Blackstone. Thus we have profited by poetic justice.[75]

This brief genealogy sketches a plot of fall and redemption that mirrors Australia's colonial history in terms of law's intersections with literature. From convict beginnings as a result of seditious libel, family and colony accept a place within the British legal order, rising from gaoler to legislator in the ambiguous system of colonial self-government, and thence not to the expected knighthood and elevation to the Privy Council, but rather bathetically to life membership of the Selden Society, joining Sir Frederick Pollock in the aesthetic and ideological work of preserving and publishing English legal heritage. In what might be a dig at the Anglophiliac tendencies of Australian lawyers, the narrator has been cleansed of any convict stain, and given an identity within the paradigmatic English ideology of the rule of law. However, this mildly satiric tale of reward for good behaviour – 'poetic justice' – is immediately supplemented by a darker vision of law.

One night in childhood the Lawyer dreamt of a grotesque allegorical representation of traditional Justice:

I saw lying asleep inside thorns, a woman with a heart-shaped bodice, a wig of steel shavings and a bicornuate headdress made of two ink-horns. Her eyeballs rolled and tears ran freely from the lids and watered the ground. Aconite grew round her bed, the legs of which had long sunk deep in the earth and been eaten by roots and lichens: her pillow was stuffed with nettles and her coverlet was made of leaves fallen through the years from overhanging plane-trees: but the leaves of the plane-trees were papers, signed, sealed, beribboned. In one hand hung a cat-o'-nine-tails: in the other was a leather purse with drawstrings, overflowing with money . . . By the bedside two lackeys in black clothes leaned on their staffs asleep, and each had a slave's collar in gold with his name on: one had the white, aristocratic, tarnished face of a Chief Justice grown old, and had on his collar the word 'Intention', and the other, with pince-nez, young, cunning, handsome, affected, bore the name 'Letter'. On the pillow sat, widawake, a monkey with a nimbus, looking at himself in a mirror and arranging the lady's curls in true lovers' knots, and above, hanging in the canopy was a bat, half-angel, half attorney-general, fast asleep, and from his mouth a scroll issued with the words, 'Ideal Justice'.

This Gothic representation of law as a struggling, weeping woman attended by animals rather than knights makes a striking contrast with the chivalric vision of 'Our Lady the Common Law' composed by Pollock.

Where Pollock envisions an emblem of grace and beauty, Stead refuses idealisation. The child's dream reveals what the chivalric romance of law represses. It draws on images that have been deployed by anti-legal satirists such as Hogarth and Dickens: the overflowing purse balanced by the cat-o'-nine-tails, a soporific body comforting itself with layers of legal paper. To this traditional imagery is added a peculiarly modernist recognition of the animal basis of human life, and the inevitable competition between cultural systems and forces of instinct sketched by Freud in *Civilisation and its Discontents*. As against the forward-moving quest for freedom of modernity's legal tradition, this tableau is full of portents of degeneracy, with its aged sleeping Chief Justice, its foundations being eaten away by roots and lichen, and the collapse of the scales of justice. In this expressionist nightmare of traditional Justice, a worthy successor to Joyce's Night-world, the professionals are enslaved to concepts that are either rigidly narrow (literalism or the 'Letter') or epistemologically unsound ('Intention'). In their effective absence, the law's real attendants are sensuality (the monkey) and irrationality (the bat). Ineffectual and corrupt, the law is situated in a poisoned landscape similar to T. S. Eliot's classic topography of modernity, *The Waste Land*.

The child's father interprets the monkey in the dream not as a Darwinian symbol, but as 'poetic justice' (313). When asked to explain this concept, he replies mischievously,

'The hand of heaven making an apple-pie bed for the man who cooked the accounts for the sleeping partner; ... nonagenarian Dives who stole oranges when a guttersnipe of ten, dying of the pip ...: so with a quip-pro-quo tickle the ribs of the superannuated saints and stuff with prunes and prisms the last yawn of the third act.'

With its crazy reversals, its puns, and its mockery, this explanation stresses the arbitrariness of the idea of poetic justice, echoing Oscar Wilde's ironising of the sententious Miss Prism in the third act of *The Importance of Being Earnest*, '"The good end happily and the bad unhappily. That is what fiction means."' To the traditional distribution of rewards and punishments to the good and evil characters respectively, this commentary adds a sense of ironic appropriateness in the kinds of punishment meted out to the latter. Poetic justice was part of a normative and didactic view of literature when originally formulated in the Renaissance, betokening a belief in a natural order of right and wrong. 'We are glad when we behold his crimes are punished, and that Poetical Justice is done upon him', wrote Dryden in his 1679 preface to *Troilus and Cressida*.[76] With the onset of modernity such narratives of justice came increasingly to seem too simple and improbable in ordinary experience to be anything but the wish-fulfilments of fiction.

While the philosophical basis of this critique is evidently powerful, the culture of justice in England was deep and pervasive throughout the eighteenth and nineteenth centuries, and both fictional and legal narratives reinforced it. So it is not surprising that the actual tale told by the Lawyer is a story of injustice redressed! A young woman and her lover are gaoled for the murder of her elderly husband and for a fraud concerning his will. Her evidence that she was innocent, and that the real villains were her stepsons is ignored. The Lawyer takes up her case, gradually assembles the facts and successfully petitions the court for a retrial. Unlike such contemporary *causes célèbres* as *Sacco and Vanzetti* or *Thompson and Bywaters*, in this story the prisoners had escaped the death penalty, and so 'remedial justice' was open to them through a second trial (324). In concluding his story the Lawyer performs the traditional task of pointing out its meaning. Dismissing poetic justice, he first stresses his faith in his own powers and the integrity of the legal system by insisting that that 'all was possible in remedial justice'. Finally, however, he avers that the case is not about law, but about the destructive power of *eros*, 'the horrors and death-heads that let themselves into civilised households under the cloak of romantic love'. With this statement he aligns himself against his clients, opening up a gap between law and justice. What had been a tale of justice through law turns out to reveal the uncivilised desires that shadow civilised law.

Like Joyce and Kafka, Stead's modernism exposes 'the Problem of Our Laws'. Their stories of anguished suffering and their new symbols of the attenuated hopes of modern humanity provide a challenging counterpoint to the antique formalities of the jurists. Their work 'breaks away from conventions and rules'.[77] By contrast, legal creativity exhibits a more cautious process of adaptation and updating of existing rules in its endeavour to minimise what Evatt called its 'separateness to reality'. Alongside literature's revolution went law's evolution of the word.

CHAPTER 7

Rumpole in Africa: law and literature in post-colonial society

The colonisation of other lands by European nations must rank among the most significant movements of world history during the last 500 years. Few if any of the indigenous peoples of America, Asia, Africa or Oceania escaped the vast disruptions of imperialism. The empires of Spain, Britain, Holland and the rest, once so extensive and powerful, have now been dismantled, but the effects of this long domination may be seen in impoverished and unstable post-colonial societies across the globe. Law was obviously an indispensable resource in the maintenance and the justification of the empires, 'a tool of colonialism, aesthetically representing Western rationality to native disorder and pragmatically overriding local understandings to suit the needs of the conqueror'.[1] Literature too played an important role in inculcating the ideology of imperialism.[2] However, literature and law could be tools of resistance as well as tools of oppression in the colonial context. Mahatma Gandhi and Nelson Mandela were lawyers who used the legal process to protest against the racially discriminatory laws of the colonisers. And for the newly independent nations and the anti-colonial movements of Africa and Asia in the 1950s and 1960s, literature assumed a special importance. It affirmed the identity of indigenous peoples through images of traditional society; it challenged the legitimacy of Western imperialism by telling stories of oppressive power; it portrayed the conditions and hopes of the emergent nations through national allegories. The post-colonial context therefore provides a key perspective for the study of law and literature in contemporary society, for post-colonial theory is 'the main mode in which the West's relation to its "other" is critically explored'.[3]

However, in recognition of the breadth of this topic and the worldwide spread of colonial and post-colonial experience, the present chapter is focused on a single nation, Nigeria, and structured around a particular case study, the radio-station case of 1965 involving Wole Soyinka as defendant and John Mortimer as counsel. That case provides a fertile starting point for a more general study because its several retellings explore the relations between law, language and power from the perspective of both the metropolitan centre and the former colony.

RUMPOLE AND MORTIMER FOR THE DEFENCE

Language and politics lie at the centre of the radio-station incident which led to Soyinka's trial in November 1965. At that time, a deliberate campaign of electoral malpractice and political intimidation by the ruling party in the then Western Region culminated in the broadcasting of fictional election results of victories for government candidates. In response to this, Soyinka designed and effected a stunning *coup de théâtre* on the political stage. The Prime Minister, Chief Akintola, had recorded a victory speech to be transmitted over the government radio station. Just as this recording was due to be broadcast, Soyinka held up the studio operatives and forced them to hand over the tape and in its stead to play an alternative recording: 'This is the Voice of the people, the true people of the nation. And they are telling you, Akintola, get out! Get out and take with you your renegades who have lost all sense of shame.'[4] He successfully escaped the building and went briefly into hiding from the police, then delivered himself into their custody, with a view to obtaining more publicity for the resistance cause through standing trial. Soyinka was not immediately charged, and began a hunger strike. Mortimer was briefed by Amnesty International, and was admitted to practice in Nigeria for the eventual trial. Together with distinguished Nigerian defence lawyers, he succeeded in obtaining an acquittal at a well-conducted trial. The different meanings attributed to these legal proceedings in subsequent writings by Soyinka and Mortimer will now be addressed.

In *Clinging to the Wreckage* Mortimer remembers the Soyinka defence as a personal revelation of the integrity of the legal system. The case was won by casting doubt on the evidence of identification, but he was most deeply impressed by the fairness and thoroughness of the trial, while all around, the country was in political turmoil. By seeming to symbolise the rule of law, it renewed his commitment to common-law advocacy:

as I drove away from Ibadan I thought of the law as something other than a maze of absurdities from which people had to be rescued. We had been stopped for a long time at a level crossing the night before and seen the flash of knives and machetes in the bush, and heard the cries of the wounded; and yet, wearing their absurd version of eighteenth-century English legal costume, barristers had been arguing reasonably and a Judge had been determined to convict no one unless he was satisfied beyond reasonable doubt. Perhaps you have to go a long way to appreciate the virtues of our legal system, up the long road into a rain forest, or even to South Africa where, with the politicians daily violating natural justice, a fearless barrister can still set an example by asking all the wrong questions at the inquest of a political prisoner unaccountably dead in the alleged safety of a cell. Since then I have stood in a Far-Eastern country and cross-examined its Prime Minister according to our procedure, before the inscrutable figure of a wigged and gowned Chinese Judge. In the countries which have received our law it often proves a most durable commodity, keeping a flicker of freedom alive when all else has broken down. Driving away from Ibadan that night I had the unoriginal thought that British law might, together with Shakespeare, Wordsworth, Lord Byron and the herbaceous border, be one of our great contributions to the world.[5]

Against the tide of specialisation, Mortimer links English law and English literature as cultural phenomena. His formulation distantly echoes Matthew Arnold's definition of culture as 'the best that is known and thought in the world'.[6] Their survival is presented as a function of innate, universal value, a view which ignores the imperial context, the forcible imposition of alien systems of law, language and other aspects of culture upon indigenous populations, and the displacement of local cultures.

Mortimer's claims for the civilising power of these achievements in the modern world are less expansive than Arnold's: the law does not guarantee freedom, but keeps the 'flicker' alive; and a note of self-deprecatory irony is heard in the references to 'unoriginal thought' and 'the herbaceous border'. This text gets close to acknowledging the law as a specifically colonial legacy but evades the fact of past domination by using the technical, indeed fictional, language of the doctrine of legal reception: '[i]n countries which have received our law'. The categories and concepts of English law structure Mortimer's perceptions, so that the point of view given is an English rather than a local one. The 'inscrutable Chinese Judge' and the warring factions in Ibadan would represent themselves differently from their portraits here. Reportage is inseparable from judgment and the judgments offered are indeed 'unoriginal', often to the point of cliché (e.g. 'when all else has broken down'). To a post-colonial critic, such unoriginality is crucially interesting, because it reveals the operation of inherited ways of speaking in English about other cultures, utterances which express one culture's 'truth' about another, statements in which dogmatism and insight stand in inverse proportion. Taken together they form a discourse of imperialism, a body of knowledge which served, through justification and explanation, the expansion of British power. Mortimer draws automatically on some of its traditional formulations: the racial stereotype of the Chinese Judge, the juxtaposition of law and violence in Africa and the 'great contribution' of English law to the world.

This belief, that 'the legacy of legality, the rule of law, and equal and uncorrupt justice was an important benefit conferred by colonisation' is evaluated by Martin Chanock, in his anthropological study *Law, Custom and Social Change*, as 'one of the most stubborn fantasies about British colonialism'.[7] He locates the mythology in the writings of Baron Hailey and other defenders of empire, for whom the British brought to Africa their law, as light to darkness. Chanock's study refutes the two assumptions of this belief system, that there was no system of effective social regulation before their arrival, and that the imported legal system worked as an instrument of justice for indigenes as well as colonisers. Across Africa, the machinery and principles of European legal systems function alongside indigenous customary law.[8] State law recognises this pluralism, according to Jennifer A. Widner: 'most African constitutions made family life, personal status, succession and inheritance the domain of the customary'.[9] The experience of this legal pluralism, the relations between the various systems, and especially their jurisdictional conflicts, are vital to the post-colonial engagement with law and literature. By focusing explicitly on the perspectives of the subordinated other, the colonised people, post-colonialism brings into view the 'multicentric legal orders' of Nigeria and the other African nations.[10]

In adopting the language of imperialist mythology, Mortimer is perpetuating it, even though he is not seeking to defend the empire. Furthermore, his conjunction of literature and law in this context cannot be detached from the colonial past. His praise is juxtaposed against the image of a night of knives: English law is still represented as the light in the darkness of African savagery. The persistence of this valorisation recalls the confidence of the nineteenth-century legislator and historian Thomas Babington Macaulay, on the enduring aspects of Britain's Indian empire:

The sceptre may pass away from us . . . But there are triumphs which are followed by no reverse. There is an empire exempt from all natural causes of decay. Those triumphs are the pacific triumphs of reason over barbarism; that empire is the imperishable empire of our arts and our morals, our literature and our laws.[11]

The coupling of literature and law by Mortimer repeats, in the post-colonial age, one of the central devices of the imperialist project. It implies a continuing local need for the civilising functions of European culture. By constructing the colonised peoples as barbaric, it affirms the self-identification of the English as rational.

If the noises in the bush remain a distant background to the radio station case in *Clinging to the Wreckage*, they become an integral part of the action in Mortimer's fictional reworking of his African brief in 'Rumpole and the Golden Thread'. As a result, the connection between politics and law, minimised in the memoir, is reasserted. The story is principally set in a fictional Central African state, Neranga, formerly called New Somerset. Rumpole's narration is both conscious and critical of the colonial heritage: the colony of New Somerset ignored local culture and incorporated under British rule two tribes with a tradition of enmity which persists and which provides both the initial impetus and the resolution of the plot. Neranga is 'a lump of land carved out by the British'.[12] Likewise, Nigeria has been described as 'an "arbitrary block" carved out of Africa by the British'.[13] Rumpole condemns the authoritarian practices of imperialism: the British suspended trial by jury and their example is followed in independent Neranga; David Mazenze, the accused, had 'that essential training for all successful African politicians – a fairly long term of imprisonment by the British' (p. 244). Rumpole's anti-imperialist irony is shared by his creator. Mortimer creates his High Commissioner, Arthur Remnant, as a satiric figure: "'I'm Mr Old England'" (p. 259).

Various remnants of colonialism figure in the action: fragments of English literature and history are sprinkled in the speeches of Mazenze, the Chief Justice and the Attorney-General, as well as Rumpole; the High Court is 'British-built' with a 'white-pillared portico'; and the law administered there is the 'common law'. Taken together, these suggest that a large portion of the imperial fabric woven in England and exported to Africa last century, and not just a remnant, remains. How that fabric is regarded and used by Rumpole and by the Nerangans, whether cherished, manipulated or challenged, is the central thread of my text. First I wish to examine how Rumpole, despite his criticism of the imperial past, celebrates one aspect of the fabric, the common law and its 'golden thread', the presumption of innocence.

All the lawyers in the story – Rumpole, Mazenze, Taboro, Banzana – pay eloquent tribute to the common law and conduct themselves in elaborate conformity to its traditions. A complex affiliation of pupil with teacher and of colonial lawyer with imperial law is traceable in David Mazenze's rhapsodic instruction to Rumpole to rely on "'the Common Law of England! The Presumption of Innocence, you know what you taught me: the Golden Thread which goes through the history of the law. I like that phrase so very much'" (p. 254). Rumpole is moved by the rhetorical power of this language of legal ideals and duly constructs his final address around the 'golden thread', but in conjunction with English literature:

when London is but a memory and the Old Bailey has sunk back into the primeval mud, my country will be remembered for three things: the British Breakfast, *The Oxford Book of English Verse* and the Presumption of Innocence! That presumption is the Golden Thread which runs through the whole history of our Criminal Law – so whether a murder has been committed in the Old Kent Road or on the way to Nova Lombaro, no man shall be convicted if there is a reasonable doubt as to his guilt. (p. 274)

Rumpole is conscious of the decline of Britain, of the depreciated value of British civilisation, but minimises his post-colonial anxiety through a longer, apocalyptic perspective on history. Echoing his creator, he saves from the wreckage of historical change a secular trinity of cultural monuments: the British Breakfast, *The Oxford Book of English Verse* and the Presumption of Innocence. Though partly comic, this list juxtaposes law and literature as related cultural discourses and sites of social solidarity. The burden of the story is to test the value of this universalist rhetoric in the polyglot world of post-colonial Africa.

THE GOLDEN THREAD OF INTERTEXTUALITY

The golden thread of Mortimer's title is taken from the leading English case on the burden of proof, *Woolmington* v. *DPP*: 'Throughout the web of English Criminal Law one golden thread is always to be seen, that it is the duty of the prosecution to prove the prisoner's guilt.'[14] Rumpole's great speech, remembered and quoted by Mazenze, interweaves this phrase with another well-known legal maxim, 'Better that ten guilty men should go free than one who is not guilty should be convicted.' This thread runs back through Blackstone's *Commentaries on the Laws of England* to Sir Edward Seymour in the *State Trials* from 1696, who cites as his precedent the ancient Roman trial of Catiline.[15]

Viscount Sankey's image of the law as a web composed of various threads suggests a complex and harmonious structure of rules. Repeated in this fictional context, however, the material from which this gossamer is formed – language (some of it golden, much of it leaden) – and its workings, are highlighted. The web of law, the language of law, exists in time as well as space, and although changes occur in response to altered conditions, a sense of continuity is preserved through the doctrine of precedent, which keeps inherited formulae in circulation. This analogy applies almost as strongly to literary texts, though the canon of great works here is not entrenched by binding precedent but is an orthodoxy open to challenge and debate. As the related word 'texture' shows, 'text' ultimately derives from the Latin verb *texere*, to weave. An individual literary text, as much as a legal one, is a web or fabric woven out of the available languages. To regard it in this light is to downplay its capacity to reflect the world and to stress by contrast its composition out of fragments of other texts, its relationship with those others. This process has come to be called 'intertextuality'.

Judith Still and Michael Worton outline a broad theory of intertextuality, arguing that 'the writer is a reader ... before s/he is a creator of texts, and therefore the work of art is inevitably shot through with references, quotations and influences of every kind'.[16] The individual text ceases to be viewed as an autonomous whole. Rather, Still and Worton quote Julia Kristeva's argument that 'every text is under the jurisdiction of other discourses'. They pursue the implications of her legal metaphor, suggesting that this 'jurisdiction' may be accepted or contested in varying degrees, that the quotation and adaptation of other texts operate as 'textual modalities of recognition and transgression of the Law'.[17] Rumpole's invocation of the presumption of innocence appears to function straightforwardly as seeking 'recognition' for this law, but in this post-colonial context the issue is complicated by the question, whose law? England's or Neranga's? Before exploring this example, it is worth noting the general point that all the Rumpole stories flaunt their intertextuality through the barrister's oratorical and conversational quotation of poetry. Rumpole's entire understanding of the trip to Neranga is structured around a poem, James Elroy Flecker's 'The Golden Journey to Samarkand'. Through this work, desires unfulfillable at home, desires for beauty, glory, wisdom, may be played out in a timeless, romanticised and entirely imaginary otherworld called, in a long-standing Western tradition, the 'Orient'.[18]

> We are pilgrims, master; we shall go
>   Always a little farther; it may be
> Beyond that last blue mountain barred with snow
>   Across that angry or that glimmering sea
>
> White on a throne or guarded in a cave
>   There lives a prophet who can understand
> Why men were born; but surely we are brave
>   Who make the Golden Journey to Samarkand.[19]

That an African nation may so readily substitute for this dream-world indicates how imaginary this geography is.

English literature is perhaps the most significant intertextual resource in this story. Through its many references we may explore the extent and limits of hegemony. Not only does Rumpole quote Wordsworth's 'Immortality Ode' (p. 268): David Mazenze effortlessly adapts Rupert Brooke's lines,

> If I should die, think only this of me:
> That there's some corner of a foreign field
> That is forever England,

into, "'If I'm hanged, think of this, Horace, that there's some corner of a Nerangan jail house that is forever Moreton-in-Marsh'" (p. 253). The case against Mazenze rests on another quotation, which, unrecognised by his secretary, is taken for a real threat to murder: 'Who can rid me of this turbulent priest?' Literary works also furnish parts of Mortimer's plot. Mazenze's secret marriage to a Matatu woman and the tragic outcome of its revelation is a type of *Romeo and Juliet* plot. In this post-colonial text intertextuality itself becomes a site of political contest, of writing back to the centre. The Chief Justice, in his summing up, treats Rumpole's great speech on the golden thread as a commonplace. In intertextual terms this is what it is, a thoroughly known – but still authoritative – legal utterance. The conflict here is not the usual one between Rumpole and his judge, but between representatives of 'the New Neranga' and 'Old England'. When Sir Worthington Banzana pronounces the law, he rewrites the words of Viscount Sankey, and 're-places' the primary source of the presumption of innocence: "'We know that a man is innocent until proved guilty. That is the golden thread which runs through the law of Neranga. This law is also followed in Britain, I believe'" (p. 275).

From a post-colonial perspective another important function of intertextuality is that it draws critical attention to the presence within the text of language drawn from imperialist discourses. Rumpole clearly adopts the language of colonial administration and law, albeit with mock seriousness, before his departure: 'Hilda! Africa is waiting. The smoke signals are drifting up from the hills, and in the jungle the tom-toms are beating. The message is, "Rumpole is coming, the Great Man of Law"' (p. 247). That this is ironically spoken does not detract from it as a display of clichés drawn from Tarzan and other popular cultural representations of Africa. Such texts drew on imperial ideology and helped to propagate it by constructing stories of British heroism in the 'dark continent'. A set of reductive binary oppositions was developed around the traditional Western colour symbolism whereby white signifies good and black evil. Applied in the African context by slave traders and then explorers, white/black ramified into a 'Manichaean allegory' of Europe/Africa, civilisation/barbarism, enlightenment/superstition, reason/passion, and law/violence.[20] Rumpole's self-description as 'the Great Man of Law' draws on the intertext of imperial adventure stories such as Edgar Wallace's *Sanders of the River* (1911), which culminates in this apologia from the District Commissioner:

'I am your father and mother . . . I carry you in my arms; when the rains came and destroyed your garden, I came with manioc and salt and saved you; when the sickness came I brought white men who scraped your arms and put magic in your blood; I have made peace and your wives are safe from M'gombi and Isisi folk, yet you are for killing me.'[21]

Although Rumpole's mockery is directed partly against the primitiveness of this *vision* of Africans, the cultural stereotypes propagated by Wallace can survive the irony of modern authors and the dismantling of the empire. The tribes of Mortimer's Neranga are as simplistically rendered as the M'Gombi and Isisi: sunk in immemorial violence and hatred. This is not to deny such phenomena, but as a representation of indigenous society it is manifestly inadequate. Nor can it be defended as mere background: the cause, the climax and the denouement of 'Rumpole and the Golden Thread' all depend on this conventionalised enmity. Rumpole's role, like Sanders's, is precisely to intervene in this darkness with the light of law. Hence his outburst on winning the trial: '"We did it, Freddy . . . we brought the Golden Thread to Samarkand!"' (p. 276). Interweaving literary and legal texts Rumpole describes the win in the Macaulayan language of the civilising mission, with himself as the law-giver.

Rumpole's delight in the victory is not shared by his client. For the Apu People's Party, it destroys both the grounds for their projected uprising and the credibility of their leader. The political undercurrents of the trial are finally comprehended by Rumpole. Far from being a bringer of peace and justice in the mythical mould of Sanders, he becomes an unwitting instrument of his client's enemy and hastens Mazenze's death. Mortimer's story refashions the triumphalism of the imperial hero as a fantasy imposed through ignorance of the complexities of post-colonial politics. With the murder of David Mazenze, the story closes where it began. The mood of the ending is disillusioned and anti-romantic: '"Samarkand is definitely off"' (p. 280). If the aim of trial procedure is to find the truth, as Rumpole believes (p. 258), then this case is a double failure: who killed the Bishop, and who killed Mazenze remain mysteries. In this negative resolution of the plot we can trace the influence of other texts of Europeans in Africa. Christopher L. Miller surveys this body of writing and concludes, 'Even in the presence of empirical knowledge, Africa and things African remain a privileged locus of lags, breaches, delays and failures of understanding in knowledge. The perception of the continent remains "dark".[22] Edgar Wallace's *Sanders* typically projects this lack of knowledge onto Africa: 'There are many things in the heart of Africa that no man can explain; . . . a story of Africa must be a mystery story.'[23] In this story, then, Mortimer moves beyond the praise of English cultural institutions proffered in *Clinging to the Wreckage* by incorporating the intimations of violence glimpsed at the railway crossing into a story about the workings of the law. The court is no longer a privileged site of rationality in a riotous jungle, but the arena of a struggle for power as well as for justice. The intertexts provided by English literature and law do not afford Rumpole an adequate interpretation of the post-colonial court.

BLACK FACES, WHITE WIGS

In *Clinging to the Wreckage* Mortimer self-consciously employs a cinematic montage to move from his humdrum English divorce practice to the inspiriting defence of Soyinka in Nigeria. A similar structure underlines Rumpole's entry into the Nerangan High Court, as he moves from unpaid VAT cases to capital murder, from home to Samarkand. This opposition-ality is limited, however, by the surprising sameness of the courtroom: 'Apart from the fact that all the faces under the white wigs, except for mine, were black, the Court was set out exactly as it is in the Old Bailey' (p. 262). The common law appears to Rumpole not a mere remnant of colonialism, but a still-complete structure. 'Imperialist law', Gary Boire suggests, 'is perhaps the quintessential signature of colonial authority.'[24] The survival of the English system in post-independence society raises questions of continuing dependency.

What is signified by these black faces in white wigs? The continued imitation of European cultural traditions has led a number of post-colonial writers to theorise the significance of 'colonial mimicry'. The expatriate West Indian novelist V. S. Naipaul construes such mimicry as a sign of the derivativeness and inauthenticity of ex-colonial societies: 'There [in Europe] was the true, pure world. We, here on our island, handling books printed in this world, . . . pretended to be real, to be learning, to be preparing ourselves for life, we mimic men of the New World.'[25] For Naipaul, mimicry is the fate of the ex-colony. Others see it differently. It is startling to contrast both Naipaul and Mortimer with Frantz Fanon's exhortation to his Third World comrades to reject the idealist humanism of the imperial powers: 'Let us waste no time in sterile litanies and

nauseating mimicry. Leave this Europe where they are never done talking
of Man, yet murder men everywhere they find them.'[26] Fanon accuses
the elites of the new African nations of creating mere caricatures of
European ideas and urges them to reintegrate with their own peoples
and to find alternative models of human development. Homi Bhabha
adapts Fanon's critique in 'Of Mimicry and Man: The Ambivalence of
Colonial Discourse'.[27] Bhabha examines mimicry from both a historical
and a psychoanalytic viewpoint. In his complex argument the difference
in skin colour is crucial, for it marks the limit of success for English
attempts to create a class of imitation whites among colonised races: the
barristers are Anglicised but not English, 'not white/not quite'; and that
margin of difference leaves open a space for doubt as to whether the
black's mimicry of white ways betokens complete acceptance or parodic
pretence.

Rumpole assumes that in court he is on utterly familiar territory, but this
assumption proves fatal for his client. The forms of English criminal
procedure are followed minutely, but the process is viewed by the other
participants not as an end in itself, but as an instrument of the will to
power. These issues are focused in the exchange when prosecutor Taboro
lends Rumpole some collar studs:

'That's remarkably civil of you' [said Rumpole].
'Merely in accordance with the best traditions of the Bar. I see young
Jonathan Mazenze had his friends from Rent-an-Apu out there to greet you.'
'Yes. I found it rather encouraging,' I told him. 'The people cheering on my
victory.'
'Your victory?' Taboro smiled tolerantly at me. 'Do you really think that's
what they want?'
And, before I could ask him what the hell he meant, he had glided away about
his business. (pp. 261–2)

What Rumpole reads as remarkable civility, Taboro dismisses as acting
'merely in . . . the best traditions of the Bar'. Yet, this trial is being conducted
under the watchful gaze of Justitia International and the Western press.
Nerangan justice has reason to present itself in conformity to those traditions. This does not mean that the trial is a sham, but Bhabha's theory of
mimicry enables us to see how the imported forms can be used for a number
of indigenous political ends, as well as the manifest legal one: to advance
Apu or Matatu goals; to confuse the London expert; to impress the international agencies. To revert to the intertextual terms proposed by Still and
Worton, this trial both recognises and transgresses the discourse of the
(imported) Law.

This section examines how the disconcerting phenomenon of 'black faces, white wigs', of legal mimicry of the kind represented by Taboro and Banzana, has been repeatedly treated by African writers. Such mimicry, that is to say, forms for the post-colonial reader of contemporary African legal and literary texts a zone of intertextuality. To facilitate the discussion my account of these texts is structured as a dialogue between one written from within the law and several viewing it from outside.

Mr Justice C. A. Oputa's *Conduct at the Bar and the Unwritten Laws of the Legal Profession* (1976) warmly recognises the authority of English law. There is no post-colonial re-placement of the centre in this textbook for practitioners. On the contrary, it unequivocally claims 'the British tradition' of justice as 'our common inheritance, our heritage':

> In our Courts we have all the external paraphenelia [sic], all the external trappings quite clearly visible. We have, and retain the lawyers' wig and gown. We have the Judges' red robes, buckled shoes, and even ceremonial breaches [sic] and stockings. But we need to copy and apply, not only the outward signs of British justice, but what is more, we have also to inculcate and nurture that inward strength, which had all along, through many turbulent years, preserved the sanctity of that justice and made it the envy of the world, and a model for other countries to copy or admire.[28]

The Arnoldian idealism of this vision of the common law as 'the best that is known' obscures the historical reality that in Africa this system was imposed before it was admired.

By contrast, Chinua Achebe's classic novel *Things Fall Apart* (1958) portrays Ibo society at the dawn of colonisation.[29] As a result it displaces English mores from the centre of the fictional world, depicting the colonial law and religion as invasive and destructive of an effective, though not perfect, indigenous culture. A traditional Ibo justice ceremony is represented. Nine leading men of the clan don masks as *egwugwu*, or ancestral spirits, and give the clan's judgment on an offender. Achebe demonstrates the workings of a system of law which has as much claim as Oputa's to the title of 'our heritage'. Late in the novel, resisting tribal leaders attend the courthouse, having been promised mediation of a dispute between their village and some members who have converted to Christianity. They are captured. Through this betrayal Achebe unmasks English law as an instrument of imperial power. Whilst taking his title from W. B. Yeats's poem, 'The Second Coming' ('Things fall apart, the centre cannot hold'), Achebe reinstated a traditional Nigerian culture at the centre of his fictional world, offering his colonised compatriots a compelling vision of their indigenous civilisation and so bolstering through literature their political campaign for independence.[30]

A principal site for mimicry in the law is dress. Mr Justice Oputa's concern with judicial costume is extended when the dress standards of barristers is treated first among his 'unwritten laws' of the Bar. 'The tradition of the profession demands that the lawyer appears in a **dark suit** ... – a dark suit, clean, white bibs, ironed out and not neglected and rumpled ... Clean dress habits underline and underlie clean and clear pleadings and clean legal battles.'[31] One can imagine his approving the sartorial elegance of Taboro and censuring the 'rumpled' look of the visiting barrister.

In Anglophone African fiction court dress is an oddity, persistently, even obsessively, mimicked in a second level of fictional imitation, and yet contained or distanced by various narrative strategies. The most literal containment occurs in Chinua Achebe's *A Man of the People*. The hero finds his barrister friend at breakfast, 'already dressed for Court (striped trousers and black coat)'.[32] The uniform is worthy of annotation, but only in passing. The parenthesis functions to reduce and to contain the phenomenon of legal formalism as an irrelevance in a political context of corruption and coercion.

Wole Soyinka's novel of 1965, *The Interpreters*, is a linguistically rich and sharply satiric representation of the new, hybridised culture of post-colonial Nigeria. Traditional beliefs compete with modern values such as individual fulfilment and material success as a group of alienated young professional men search unavailingly for meaning and direction. This polyphonic novel juxtaposes existentialist philosophy and indigenous myths, following its protagonists as they interpret their new society. In this world mimicry is both a social phenomenon and a literary-political tactic. Sagoe, one of the interpreters, gatecrashes a party hosted by the new Professor, Oguazor, who sports a tuxedo and a mannered accent which the narrator parodies: '"Ceroline, der, the ledies herv been wetting fer you."'[33] Soyinka's comment on this mimicry ('From the marionette pages of Victoriana') echoes the condemnations of Fanon and Naipaul.

This critique takes aim at the law when Sagoe joins the funeral procession of a judge, Sir Derinola. It crosses a bridge, which Sagoe interprets as leading from the living to the dead. Among the dead are 'the suburban settlements of Ikoye where both the white remnants and the new black oyinbos [white men] lived in colonial vacuity' (p. 111). Sir Derinola is the principal target of a wide-ranging satire on legal and political corruption. Sagoe, recovering from a hangover, converses with the dead judge. In this satiric fantasy Sir Derinola is first contained in a hatbox, the repository of the top hat and wig which symbolise his knighthood and his judicial office.

His corpse then emerges from a wardrobe, not wigged and gowned, but 'naked except for a pair of [Sagoe's girlfriend] Dehinwa's brassieres over his chest' (p. 64). This ribald apparition serves as a travesty of the model common-law judge. A bribe-taker and party-servant when in office, Sir Derinola appears as an honest realist in his nakedness: "'I cannot change my principles. The cloth does not make the man. Do you realize the newspapers still quote me on that?'" (p. 65). The robes of office do not guarantee an upright judge. In disgrace and even in death he clings to his knighthood: the medals of his order of chivalry are to be pinned on the brassiere. Soyinka here combines pathos and mockery, to register both the social and psychological rewards of colonial mimicry and the absurdity of chivalric honour in the post-colonial context.

The Interpreters, then, unmasks the superficial and self-serving heritage of English law in the immediate post-colonial period in Nigeria, the dispensability of its values and concepts from ordinary understandings of reality. The shade of Sir Derinola haunts Mr Justice Oputa's textbook. In his conclusion he contextualises the rules of conduct as part of a commitment to the rule of law. Barristers and judges regulate power in the service of a feminine icon of Justice:

The Bench and the Bar form the greatest gulf between the citizen and all forms of totalitarian rule ... It needs a strong, courageous and fearless but responsible Bar and a free, indomitable and impartial Bench to enthrone Justice on her proud and lofty Seat and keep her there, visibly elegant and dignified, a comfort and an asylum to the oppressed, a sure and guaranteed hope for the innocent, and a chilling terror to the malignant and the vile. (p. 46)

Perhaps the key word in this otherwise unrestrained paean to Justitia is 'need'. That courage, fidelity and impartiality are needed throughout the legal system implies that to some extent they have been lacking. These fervent, rhythmic and superabundant words (proud and lofty, sure and guaranteed, malignant and vile) reveal a sense of anxiety or urgency about the present state of legal institutions in his country. For at the time this book was written, Nigeria had been under military rule for ten years, and the courts had been criticised for their acquiescence to the illegal directives of those in power.

One accuser was Wole Soyinka, who was again in prison, this time detained without trial, between August 1967 and October 1969.[34] In his prison writings, *The Man Died*, Soyinka takes the murder of an Ibo photographer, Emmanuel Ogbona, for which two soldiers were charged, but released without trial, as indicative of the collapse of law before a policy of genocide of the Ibo. He demands, like Mr Justice Oputa, a renewed commitment to judicial independence:

I only demand that one way or the other, the Western [Region] Judiciary place itself in such a position that no power within or without the region can ever again interfere with its judicial processes and render it, as it is today, accomplices by default in the doctrine of justifiable genocide.[35]

During his detention Soyinka draws on the 'golden thread' of Nigerian law to resist his interrogators: 'are you admitting that you presume me guilty already?' (p. 44) and 'you have accused me of nothing' (p. 51). These intertexts enable justice to be sought through a specific and answerable demand, not allegorised on a pedestal. Soyinka invokes the fruits of colonial law, however poor the crop, as one element of his post-colonial struggle for justice.

Indigenous culture also sustains Soyinka in prison. There are 'many ghosts that haunt me here, ... grandfather especially, and ... Adekunle Fajuyi' (p. 154). In conversation with Fajuyi, who was murdered in June 1966, Soyinka appraises the Nigerian courts much less grandiloquently than Mortimer does. When asked about the radio-station case, he cites his acquittal by the court. After laughing, Fajuyi acknowledges the integrity "'of *that* court, of *that* judge"' and asks Soyinka his opinion of Western Nigerian courts generally. "'Subverted. No-one believes in the courts any more"' (p. 156).

In retrospect, the radio-station trial remains an isolated, even exceptional, occurrence. For Soyinka and Mortimer, it can no longer signify a general level of justice, only a potential one. In 1993 the Nigerian government withheld the results of the country's general election. In the context of this repetition of the events of 1965, Soyinka penned his memoir, *Ibadan: The Penkelemes Years*.[36] In this text the trial is further marginalised, figuring not in direct representation, but in a passing comment between the accused in custody and a visiting friend. This minimal, indirect reference on the evening before the verdict, "'I only know that the judge will administer justice"',[37] is a confident statement of faith, and a firm espousal of an absolute standard. Though his faith was vindicated by the subsequent acquittal, the memoir stops short of that event, leaving the reader uncertain of the hero's future. This inconclusiveness may also have reflected Soyinka's political anxieties at the time of writing, his sense that the time of the '*penkelemes*', the 'peculiar mess' of flagrant corruption and bravado, had returned. Subsequent events bore out this interpretation, as Soyinka's passport was seized in September 1994, and he subsequently fled the country.

In *Ibadan* Soyinka offers a long-awaited and comprehensive account of his hijacking of the airwaves. In doing so, he keeps the courtroom off-stage, concentrating on the political rather than the legal action. That episode and his subsequent writings show how activism and writing are intertwined. He returns to this theme in a 1996 jeremiad written from exile: 'our function is primarily to project those voices that, despite massive repression, continue to place their governments on notice'.[38] In the context of contemporary Africa, law and literature are not monuments for patriotic affirmation, but spaces for advocacy in which truth may be spoken to power, and justice sought not only for one individual or one party in the state, but for all. This belief of Soyinka's is most directly expressed in *The Man Died*: 'for me, justice is the first condition of humanity'.[39] The golden thread of Western law is only one element in this evolving struggle to rid the post-colonial nation of the 'totalitarianism and violence of colonial governments'.[40]

CHAPTER 8

Race and representation in contemporary America

I want to end this historical overview of relations between law and literature by focusing on the United States of America in the mid- to late twentieth century. It was here that 'Law and Literature' emerged as a field of study, and that the conscious dialogue between lawyers, writers and critics began to take place across the wall erected in modernity by both disciplines. The ensuing conversation has ramified into the many debates discussed in this book (and others), and has sponsored new knowledges capable of transforming the practice of law and the humanities.

As a movement combining theoretical analysis and practical application, Law and Literature has had a particular commitment to equal justice in American society. What Brook Thomas calls 'literature's ability to produce alternative narratives to the dominant ones of a culture' has made Law and Literature the site of an invaluable critique of the stories and ideologies upheld by America's legal system.[1] As a result, the law's treatment of women, people of colour, the disabled, children and many other marginalised groups has been an integral concern of this interdisciplinary field. Yet this respect for minority rights has been sustained not only by the possibilities of literature, but by a cultural commitment enshrined in the law. The nation's basic legal framework includes the Fourteenth Amendment to the Constitution:

All persons born or naturalised in the United States, and subject to the jurisdiction thereof, are citizens of the United States and the State in which they reside. No State shall make or enforce any law which shall abridge the privileges or immunities of citizens of the United States; nor shall any State deprive any person of life, liberty or property without due process of law; nor deny to any person within its jurisdiction the equal protection of the laws.

The ideal of equality under the law has sanctioned the hopes of, and provided the juristic grounds of appeal for, reformers attempting to relieve the oppressions suffered by minorities. Nowhere has this reformist zeal been more necessary or more intense than in the realm of race relations. Equally, the nexus of race, law and justice has rarely been far from the surface of Law and Literature scholarship. From Richard Weisberg's study of the French reception of Nazi laws against Jews to the stories of institutional racism in the law analysed by Patricia J. Williams, Richard Delgado and other Critical Race theorists, the long quest for racial justice has been advanced by the foregrounding of stories about the experience of racism, and the analysis of the unconscious perpetuation of racist ideologies in law's ways of speaking.[2] Race and law has proved a controversial, even violent, conjunction in recent American history, a site of immense ethical and political energy. In this context memorable utterances have been produced in courtrooms and prisons, on the streets and airwaves, in books and learned journals.

BROWN V. BOARD OF EDUCATION OF TOPEKA

Although the words of the Fourteenth Amendment, as enacted in 1868, promised equality before the law to all American citizens, the experience of non-whites up to the first half of the twentieth century was of a racially biased law. In the 1896 case of *Plessy* v. *Ferguson*, the Supreme Court held that 'separate but equal' facilities for different races did not violate the Fourteenth Amendment and so justified the regime of racial segregation maintained through law and custom throughout the southern states with a view to ensuring continued white supremacy.[3] Segregation was total, and it ensured that the great majority of African-Americans remained poor, ill educated, dependent on whites for employment and stripped of their civil rights. The *Plessy* doctrine remained in force for over fifty years. A new era was inaugurated in 1954, when the Supreme Court in *Brown* v. *Board of Education* ordered that segregation in public schooling contravened the equal protection clause. According to the constitutional scholar Bruce Ackerman, *Brown* was 'the single most important decision of the modern era'.[4]

The theoretical claim of equality made by the 'separate but equal' doctrine was a sham, and in the educational field, the facilities afforded to white children greatly outstripped those provided for African-Americans. From the 1930s onwards, the National Association for the Advancement of Colored People (NAACP) challenged inequities in the courts, chipping away at the system of segregation. In the post-war period, the NAACP strategically targeted regions such as South Carolina, where Negro school conditions of the most basic and underfunded quality existed, or where a local community with educational aspirations, as in

Topeka, Kansas, was demanding comparable facilities to whites. Sites of manifest inequity were identified, and claims made to local school boards for specific redress, whether in the form of a school bus or a new building. These claims were routinely and sometimes violently rejected. Refusal became the trigger for legal proceedings in this co-ordinated campaign. As a result, a group of challenges to the *Plessy* doctrine came before the Supreme Court in 1952. Thurgood Marshall argued the case for the petitioners. At the conclusion of the initial argument, the members of the court were split, with judges from southern states favouring the retention of segregated schools, and other judges in favour of overruling *Plessy*, or wary of the juristic or political consequences of doing so. The decision was stalled, and the deadlock was only broken by the sudden death of the Chief Justice, Fred Vinson. The case was re-argued, with the new Chief Justice, Earl Warren, showing an immediate capacity for leadership and consensus-building.[5]

Warren delivered the unanimous judgment of the Court outlawing segregation on 17 May 1954. His opinion was notable for eschewing the technical discourse of the law in favour of plain language. Aware of the broad community interest in the case, Warren was brief and direct and highlighted psychological and other social science research concerning the effects of segregation upon children's development, to conclude that 'in the field of public education the doctrine of "separate but equal" has no place. Separate educational facilities are inherently unequal.' His invocation of empirical data reflects the prestige of science in this period, as advances in knowledge and their practical application in medicine and industry were transforming everyday life. A scientific truth about the effects of racial separation carried the possibility of universal acceptance, whereas the conflict over legal doctrine exposed deep divisions in American society. In addition, Warren's projections of full or arrested development for black children imply a notional biography of the good citizen, which, as Carol J. Greenhouse has shown, derives from literature.[6] Drawing on these discourses, the judgment was written and spoken in a low-key voice and a conciliatory tone that sought to avoid condemnation, or the exposure of ideological conflicts.

However, the attempt to invoke an 'end-of-ideology' consensus failed. The ruling was widely resisted by politicians and white communities throughout the southern states, and by legal academics critical of its failure to engage closely with previous doctrine. In the second *Brown* case, called to determine how the epoch-making judgment was to be implemented, Warren continued his conciliatory strategy, acknowledging that local authorities had the best grip on local needs, and so should set the pace of implementation. He simply ordered that desegregation proceed 'with all deliberate speed' – an equivocal if not oxymoronic ruling that left open the possibility of endless delay.[7] While some boards of education worked through their opposition, including that in Richmond, Virginia, where the future Supreme Court Justice Lewis F. Powell was chair, many obstructed and even sought to evade the new law.

WRITING CIVIL RIGHTS

The implications of the *Brown* judgment for the legal and social tradition of Jim Crow were patent and profound: desegregation could not be confined to the schools. For African-Americans it raised new hopes of equality and social transformation. However, many whites determined to resist this encroachment on their historical privilege. The ensuing two decades were a period of action and reaction, of great energy for change and scarifying violence. Literature proved once more to be a significant weapon for advancing progressive opinion, as explorations of race-based injustice became the subject of significant writing in all genres.

In Little Rock, Arkansas, one of the most infamous attempts to sabotage desegregation was masterminded by the state governor, Orval Faubus. In 1957 he overrode the plans by the local Board of Education to enrol six African-American students in the city's Central High School. He ordered the National Guard to prevent the new students from entering the premises on the first day of the new school year. Faced with this violation of a Federal court order by a State authority, President Eisenhower dispatched Federal troops to Little Rock. In the unseemly mêlée that followed, Elizabeth Eckford and the other new pupils were subjected to spitting, verbal abuse and physical attack.

One of the most significant literary explorations of this reaction was a poem by Gwendolyn Brooks, 'The Chicago *Defender* Sends a Man to Little Rock'. Brooks, who became the first African-American poet to win the Pulitzer Prize in 1950 with her sharply focused images of black life in Chicago's south side, begins this poem not with reportage of the events, but with an evocation of the culture of Little Rock. In this account it is the ordinariness of the town that is striking:

> In Little Rock the people bear
> Babes, and comb and part their hair
> And watch the want ads, put repair
> To roof and thatch. While wheat toast burns
> A woman waters multiferns.[8]

Hardship and violence are displaced from this picture. The deftly accumulated images of fifties suburbia with its 'many tight and small concerns' encapsulate the conformity and polite evasions of middle-class America in the Eisenhower era. As the poem proceeds, the lines lengthen to explore some typical events, the baseball game and the Open Air Concert. Brutality and gentility coexist in this society, kept in gendered compartments: the men 'raw and implacable / And not intellectual', and the women 'wash away old semi-discomfitures'. In this repressive context, the latent violence erupts in racial terror, 'a scythe / Of men harassing brownish girls'. As a parting image, Brooks offers her reader the simple picture of a victim, 'a bleeding brownish boy', and invokes the Christian beliefs of mainstream America by juxtaposing this portrait with that of another sacrificial victim: 'The loveliest lynchee was our Lord.'

Brooks continued her poetic witness to racist violence against African-Americans with two poems on the lynching of Emmett Till in August 1955. Emmett Till was a fourteen-year-old Chicago boy, who on a visit to Mississippi allegedly insulted a local white woman. Three nights later, her husband and his stepbrother took him from his bed and brutally murdered him. National outrage followed the discovery of his body, but at the ensuing murder trial, the all-white jury acquitted both defendants after only sixty-seven minutes. Emmett's corpse was returned to Chicago, where his mother held an open-casket funeral. The pitiful spectacle of his young body produced an immediate sense of injustice. As a Chicago poet, Brooks was moved to a deep cultural meditation by the mother's grief. In 'A Bronzeville Mother Loiters in Mississippi. Meanwhile, a Mississippi Mother Burns Bacon', she enters the consciousness of the white woman who claimed to have been insulted by Emmett. She locates this woman's experience of the event and the ensuing vengeance in terms of the romantic ballad tradition:

> Herself the milk-white maid, the 'maid mild'
> Of the ballad. Pursued
> By the Dark Villain. Rescued by the Fine Prince.
> The Happiness-Ever-After.[9]

Gradually, the woman realises the discrepancies between this ideology and the facts of the case: the 'infant softness' around the mouth incompatible with a Dark Villain; the violence of her own Fine Prince. Brooks posits a connection between racial terror and sexuality in this poem, and as her character experiences a revulsion at this 'love' she also remembers the eyes of her opposite number, Emmett's mother, from the courtroom:

'decapitated exclamation points in that Other Woman's eyes'. This moment of haunting leads into the accompanying poem, 'The Last Quatrain of the Ballad of Emmett Till', and it is the other half of this poetic diptych, an imagistic exploration of Emmett's mother's bereavement: 'She kisses her killed boy / and she is sorry. / Chaos in windy grays / through a red prairie'. In Brooks's powerful images, the landscape of loss is suffused with blood.

The NAACP and other organisations followed up on the gains of *Brown* by launching campaigns to desegregate many other public facilities. Meeting intransigence from local government officials, they devised strategies to influence public opinion and force change. The bus boycott in Montgomery, Alabama, is generally regarded as the turning-point in the political struggle for racial justice. Rosa Parks, a seamstress and part-time union worker was asked by the driver of her home-bound bus to give up her seat to a white patron. On refusing, she was arrested and taken to jail. In support of her protest, NAACP activists and church leaders met and agreed to call on all of Montgomery's black population to boycott the city's bus service until the segregated seating policy was overturned. In planning alternative transport and other organisational matters, they chose as their leader a then-unknown Baptist preacher, Dr Martin Luther King Jr. The boycott was successful after sixteen months. The Supreme Court ordered in *Browder* v. *Gayle* the desegregation of Montgomery's buses, striking down Alabama's laws under the Fourteenth Amendment.[10]

Other successes followed using this strategy of local resistance and Federal constitutional appeals. Segregation of facilities in public parks, pools and buildings was outlawed in a string of cases from 1958, including *New Orleans City Park Improvement Association* v. *Dittiege* (golf course, 1958), *Watson* v. *City of Memphis* (publicly owned recreational spaces, 1963), *Johnson* v. *Virginia* (courtrooms, 1963) and *Palmer* v. *Thompson* (swimming pools, 1971).[11]

In the early 1960s, Martin Luther King, the leader of the bus campaign, and his colleagues in the Southern Christian Leadership Conference, adopted a new strategy of civil disobedience inspired by the example of Gandhi. Sit-ins in the streets and at segregated lunch-counters affronted the police, who responded with force, thereby attracting television and newspaper coverage. During one such protest in Birmingham in 1963, King himself was arrested. Whilst he was in prison, white clergymen took out an advertisement deploring this strategy as un-Christian. King's *Letter from Birmingham Jail*, written in reply on scraps of paper, was a cogent and eloquent justification of his action and immediately became a classic of prison and civil-rights literature. It answers all the charges brought by his critics with reason and restraint. Specifically King draws on the natural law tradition within Christian theology to distinguish between just and unjust laws, between laws that must be obeyed, and those that 'degrade human personality' and must be resisted. To strengthen his case, King invokes notable exemplars of civil disobedience from the Bible, ancient Greece and revolutionary America. Positioning his non-violent direct action between the passive acceptance of injustice and the emerging alternative of black violence, King presents himself as a moderate, a sincere Christian and loyal American. He identifies with these revered traditions, proposing a powerful vision of shared values:

One day the South will know that when these disinherited children of God sat down at lunch counters, they were in reality standing up for what is best in the American dream and for the most sacred values in our Judaeo-Christian heritage, thereby bringing our nation back to those great wells of democracy which were dug deep by the founding fathers in their formulation of the Constitution and the Declaration of Independence.

With the long rhythmic sentences and extended metaphors characteristic of pulpit oratory, King's prose cuts across boundaries of black and white, sacred and secular, to exhort his readers to turn their idealism into action.[12] The gathering momentum of the Civil Rights Movement was evidenced four months later, when 250,000 people marched to Washington in support of reform and integration. Standing in front of the Lincoln Memorial, King elaborated his vision of racial harmony and political unity in his electrifying 'I Have a Dream' speech. Rhetoric and action achieved their aim when federal legislators passed the Civil Rights Act in 1964.

Other writers, from other races, were inspired by the struggle for equal rights. Jewish writers, having experienced the persecutions of the 1930s and 1940s, were among the first to engage in this struggle. In 1939, Abel Meeropol, under the pseudonym Lewis Allen, wrote the haunting anti-lynching lyric 'Strange Fruit'.

Harper Lee's *To Kill a Mockingbird*, which won the Pulitzer Prize in 1960 and has since sold 30 million copies, is set in Alabama in the 1930s. Presented with great immediacy through the eyes of a child, it utilises its historical distance and innocent perspective to create a vivid sense of horror and injustice at the fate of the black accused, Tom Robinson. All texts about the past are infused with the social agendas of their time of production, and the debates explored in *Brown* are rehearsed in the lawyer-hero Atticus Finch's address to the jury. Here various possible meanings of

Jefferson's words, 'All men are created equal', are pondered, including educational equality and equality before the law, in a ringing albeit ultimately unavailing endorsement of the rule of law.[13] The narrative crisis in *To Kill a Mockingbird* is set in motion by cross-racial sexual attraction, traditionally a taboo subject, but one soon to be legitimated by the Supreme Court in *Loving* v. *Virginia*.[14] Finally, this immensely popular text seeks to console its readers by invoking a form of poetic justice in its conclusion to redress the racist verdict of Tom Robinson's jury. When we recall the critiques of poetic justice mounted earlier in the century, this reversion to an older cultural formation seems a troubling fusion of literary imagining and legal idealism.[15]

The battle of African-Americans to establish a break between past and future is dramatised in Lorraine Hansberry's play, *A Raisin in the Sun*. Taking its title from a poem by Langston Hughes,

> What happens to a dream deferred?
> Does it dry up like a raisin in the sun?
> Does it fester like an old sore and run,
> Or, does it explode?[16]

the play is a realist family drama about the conflict between the dream of integration and its practical obstacles. As represented in *A Raisin in the Sun*, the latter include violent white resistance, poverty, and the fears and low self-esteem of blacks. This became the first play by an African-American woman to be produced on Broadway, in 1959. Hansberry's progressive social vision is seen not merely in her chosen 'dream', of home ownership in a neighbourhood not restricted by race, but also in her combining this with other new directions for her people's identity, namely a young woman's desire to train as a doctor, and a young man's engagement with African culture. Hansberry's parents had defied a racially exclusive housing covenant in Chicago during her childhood, by taking their case to the Supreme Court.[17] This activist impulse and transformative faith is registered in the play, which Amiri Baraka called 'the quintessential civil rights drama'.[18]

Perhaps the most acute and reflective writer to engage with the Civil Rights Movement was James Baldwin. Baldwin discovered his literary vocation early in life and stuck to it despite the opposition of his stepfather, a lay preacher. Despite his tense relationship with Christianity, Baldwin's writings are infused with the language and symbolism of the Bible. As a young African-American homosexual during the 1940s, his experience of vilification and discrimination was intense, and he followed the path of many American writers by emigrating to Paris. Expatriatism gave him new perspectives on America and new understandings of the ideology of racial difference in Western culture. Although he wrote fiction of great distinction, Baldwin found his *métier* in the genre of the personal essay. Here he was able to weave fragments of autobiography into searching reflections on the general significance of particular actions, creating an incisive and humane commentary on injustice, identity and perhaps above all on the role of race in American culture. In 'Stranger in the Village' (1953), for example, he uses his experience as the first 'negro' ever to live in a remote Swiss village as a paradigm for the social status of the African-American anywhere in the modern West, that of a spectacle of strangeness, an alien, an outsider. Yet from this existential insight, Baldwin proceeds to consider its historical origins, and to posit a difference between America and Europe in the matter of interracial contact and cultural identity:

The time has come to realise that the interracial drama acted out on the American continent has not only created a new black man, it has created a new white man, too. No road whatever will lead Americans back to the simplicity of this European village where white men still have the luxury of looking on me as a stranger. I am not, really, a stranger any longer for any American alive.[19]

In a complex and humane argument, Baldwin acknowledges black peoples' experience of racial prejudice but insists on their identity as Americans, and on their role in the formation of a distinctly American culture. With such a vision, it is little wonder that in 1957 Baldwin was inspired by newspaper photographs of black children being spat on as they tried to enter formerly white schools, to return and join the civil rights struggle in his native land.

Baldwin was a frank and courageous personal essayist. In *The Fire Next Time* (1963), he moves easily between confessional and prophetic modes of expression. Starting with his own experience, he explores the psychological and social effects of hatred on blacks and whites and probes the causes of the continuing oppression of African-Americans. In particular he reflects on their resort to violence in this situation. He notes the length, expense and difficulty of litigation and is especially clear-sighted about the link between white power and the law: 'white people ... had the judges, the juries, the shotguns, the law – in a word, the power'.[20] He is therefore sceptical of liberal confidence that *Brown* represented 'a change of heart', arguing rather that it was born of political pragmatism: 'Most of the Negroes I know do not believe that this immense concession would have been made if it were not for the competition of the Cold War.'[21] As a result,

Baldwin is less sanguine about the possibility of non-racial identity than in 'Stranger in the Village':

if we who can scarcely be considered a white nation persist in thinking of ourselves as one, we condemn ourselves with the truly white nations, to sterility and decay, whereas if we could accept ourselves *as we are*, we might bring new life to the Western achievements, and transform them. The price of this transformation is the essential freedom of the Negro . . . He is *the* key figure in his country, and the American future is precisely as bright or as dark as his. And the Negro recognises this, in a negative way. Hence the question: do I really *want* to be integrated into a burning house?

Given the violence invoked by whites in response to the non-violent protests and constitutional claims made by the Civil Rights Movement, as well as the resort to violence by blacks, Baldwin's 'burning house' is an apposite symbol of America at this time. His work concludes with an apocalyptic prophecy that forms the counter-current to the inclusive dream that Martin Luther King was to utter in the same year: 'God gave Noah the rainbow sign. No more water, the fire next time!'

REVOLUTION AND LIBERATION

James Baldwin bears witness to the African-American disenchantment with the symbolic promise of *Brown*. As he was writing, a more radical alternative to gradual integration and legality was being articulated, whose chief advocate was Malcolm X. A former prisoner, who converted to Islam while in gaol, Malcolm X saw white America as the enemy and scorned claims of progress through Civil Rights law as propaganda. He sought to demystify the political position of blacks in America, pointing to the continuation of white violence, in plain and direct language: 'We no longer endorse patience and turning the other cheek. We assert the right of self-defence by whatever means necessary, and reserve the right of maximum retaliation against our racist oppressors.'[22] In the same year, he posed the choice facing African-Americans in a speech titled, 'The Ballot or the Bullet'. He identified their 'political oppression, economic exploitation and social degradation', and concluded: 'Today it's time to stop singing and start swinging.'[23]

In the latter half of the 1960s, then, a more militant notion of 'Black Power' became the new rallying cry for racial justice. Inspired by this, young black writers such as Leroi Jones developed a more activist notion of literature, the Black Arts Movement, the cultural equivalent of Black Power. Rejecting the aesthetic dominance of white America along with

its political dominance, these writers sought individual and racial liberation through experiments in form, frankness in expression and an attentive
study of their African and African-American cultural heritages. This new
literature demanded alternative or collectivist forums of publication, like
Broadside Press, and new, less 'respectable' identities for writers. Leroi
Jones changed his name to Amiri Baraka. One of the first works published
by Dudley Randall's Broadside Press was *Poems from Prison* by Etheridge
Knight. Knight's 'Hard Rock Returns to Prison from the Hospital for the
Criminally Insane' registers in its opening an insider's perspective on the
violent economy of prisoner and warder:

> Hard Rock was 'known not to take no shit
> from nobody,' and he had the scars to prove it.[24]

Hard Rock's resistance has made him a hero to his fellow-inmates; but on
his return, 'we discovered that it took Hard Rock / Exactly 3 minutes to tell
you his first name.' The crushing of his spirit through electro-convulsive
therapy is recognised by the poet as a defeat for all of them:

> He had been our Destroyer, the doer of things
> We dreamed of doing but could not bring ourselves to do,
> The fear of years, like a biting whip
> Had cut grooves too deeply across our backs.

The physical precision of this concluding image leaves a powerful impression
of the terror of prison discipline, and with its echoes of slavery casts doubt on
the myth of progress and rehabilitation. The stripping away of identity and
freedom along with defiance is registered as an assault on human rights. The
recasting of resistance as insanity, and the consequent medicalisation of
punishment underscore the violence of the law, deepening Knight's critique.

Black Arts writers located their struggles for liberation in an international framework. Like Malcolm X, they drew inspiration from the
decolonising of African states, and they joined their voices to the choruses
of protest against the war in Vietnam and South African apartheid.
Women writers in the movement also drew on feminist critiques of sexual
oppression in modern Western society. June Jordan's 'Poem about My
Rights' juxtaposes this revolutionary fusion of gender and racial liberation
with the American discourse of individual rights. However, rather than
speaking this discourse, the poet proceeds by narrating her life history as a
litany of denial and oppression, of being identified as a problem, or as
'wrong'. From being unable to walk alone at night to the invasion of
Namibia by South Africa,

the problems
turn out to be
me
I am the history of rape
I am the history of the rejection of who I am
I am the history of the terrorised incarceration of
my self.[25]

With its incantatory repetition acting as a counterbalance to its graphic images of sexual violence, 'Poem about My Rights' finally articulates the frustrated rage of this generation of African-Americans:

I am not wrong: Wrong is not my name
My name is my own my own my own
and I can't tell you who the hell set things up like this
but I can tell you that from now on my resistance
my simple and daily and nightly self-determination
may very well cost you your life

Ending thus, without a full stop, June Jordan's free verse enables a strong protest against all oppressive systems. She does not petition the civil authorities for her rights but assumes the fundamental and innate right of 'self-determination', appropriating the spirit of the Bill of Rights to a new revolution.

One feature of the Black Arts–Black Power vision of self-determination was its recovery of an African-American historical tradition. Alice Walker has been a notable proponent of this quest, in her prose work *In Search of our Mothers' Gardens*, as well as in her fiction.[26] Like June Jordan, Walker combines a feminist with a black consciousness. She explores the conflicts between black liberation and women's liberation in her short story, 'Advancing Luna – and Ida B. Wells'. As a historical fiction, this story reconstructs the Civil Rights era, and its Black Power aftermath, by focusing on the interracial friendship between the narrator and a young white woman who meet during the voter registration campaign of 1965. Initially political idealism and sexual liberation harmonise around the phenomenon of interracial sex, however the friendship is tested when Luna, the white woman, is raped by a black man. In seeking to explain this event and its political meaning, Walker invokes the words of the turn-of-the-century anti-lynching campaigner, Ida B. Wells. Her counsel is to remain silent, and to question the evidence, a position which the contemporary feminist and writer rejects. The ensuing narrative presents alternative endings in its attempt to do justice to both Luna and her assailant. Using the resources of fiction, Walker 'advances' the freedom of both her sex and her race. Yet her fidelity to historical complexity ensures that this story also captures the continuing disempowerment and exploitation of blacks, the containment of the revolution.[27]

EQUAL RIGHTS FOR A MULTICULTURAL SOCIETY

Walker's award of the Pulitzer Prize for her novel *The Colour Purple* in 1982 was indicative of a broader pattern: the diversification of American literature as other ethnic and racial minorities adapted the principles of the Black Arts movement in using creative writing and performance to assert their cultural identity within the nation, and to protest their experience of oppression. The Native American writer N. Scott Momaday had won the Pulitzer Prize in 1969 for his novel *House Made of Dawn*, and in 1976 Maxine Hong Kingston had won the National Book Critics' Circle Award for *The Woman Warrior*. Literary prizes are a form of mainstream validation and are limited in number, but the 'black efflorescence' we have been tracing in this chapter was accompanied by what A. Robert Lee has called an 'ethnic renaissance', on the part of Native, Spanish and Asian American peoples, 'a bid for long-overdue empowerment . . . [and] also a major and continuing surge of imaginative self-expression'.[28] Several of the most significant literary texts produced by this renaissance embrace questions of race, culture and law. One of the most inventive of these is Maxine Hong Kingston's autobiographical fiction, *China Men*.

In a critical essay on this book, Alfred Wang observed: 'No other racial group have been subjected to worse *legalized* personal, collective and sexual deprivation than the Chinese male immigrants between 1868 . . . and 1952.'[29] *China Men* has as its central section a chapter entitled 'The Laws' which summarises, baldly and shockingly, the ways in which the machinery of the law was turned against the Chinese. For this disquisition, Kingston departs from the fantastic narrative mode of the rest of her book and employs a timeline:

1882: Encouraged by fanatical lobbying from California, the US Congress passed the first Chinese Exclusion Act. It banned the entrance of Chinese labourers, both skilled and unskilled, for ten years.

Anyone unqualified for citizenship could not come in – and by the terms of the Nationality Act of 1870, Chinese were not qualified for citizenship. Some merchants and scholars were granted temporary visas.

1884: Congress refined the Exclusion Act with An Act to Amend an Act. This raised fines and sentences and further defined 'merchants' to exclude 'hucksters, peddlers, or those engaged in taking, draying, or otherwise perserving shell or other fish for home consumption or exportation'.[30]

Kingston's analysis reveals how racist phobias and economic anxieties gave birth to these laws, and how the laws then consolidated and authorised a distorted image of the Chinese as threatening aliens. For those Chinese men who had already entered the country, and were working there, severely discriminatory laws were passed. 'Though the Chinese were filling and leveeing the San Joaquin Delta for thirteen cents a square yard, building the richest agricultural land in the world, they were prohibited from owning land or real estate. They could not apply for business licences.'[31] They were targeted explicitly or by implication, as when their economic and cultural practices were attacked in the 'pole law prohibiting the use of carrying baskets on poles'.

This epitome of specific enactments accumulates into a spare narrative of the legal subordination of the Chinese from the earliest xenophobic campaigns to the repeal of the Exclusion Act in 1943, and the eventual passage of a non-discriminatory immigration policy in 1978. Yet this is only one small section of the book, and as Donald Goellnicht has pointed out, its impersonal, documentary-style recital of facts seems 'anomalous' in the context of the detailed representation of the individual lives of Kingston's Chinese male ancestors. The effect, in Goellnicht's terms, is that the 'centric authority of American law is subverted and contested by the "eccentric" or marginal, but richly imaginative stories of China Men that surround it'.[32] The humanity, the vulnerability and courage of her great-grandfather, grandfather and father is thereby reclaimed through narratives of their arduous and ill-paid labour in such foundational American projects as Hawaiian sugar-cane plantations and transcontinental railways. Their attempts to find solace and meaning through adaptations of Chinese mythology to their new land, their attempts to become American through adoption of dress and language, their resistance to expulsion, their exploitation of immigration processes all work to retrieve their masculinity and their cultural dignity from the law's disempowering provisions.

The citation of legal statutes and judgments as one element in a polyphonic narrative that combines fiction and history illustrates Kingston's post-modern approach to cultural identity and justice. *China Men* is a pastiche of stories from Chinese and European literature, notably *The Romance of the Flowers in the Mirror*, an early nineteenth-century Chinese novel, *Robinson Crusoe* and even the Midas episode from Ovid's *Metamorphoses*, intertwined with oral traditions of her own family history and community in Stockton, California.[33]

China Men offers this reading of the American past not only to Kingston's own community, but to the nation of which that community is a part. National belonging is a deep desire for the characters, and the novel traces its long evolution. A new vision of American-ness emerges out of their work constructing the railroads: 'China Men banded the nation North and South, East and West, with crisscrossing steel. They were the binding and building ancestors of this place' (145). Brook Thomas argues cogently that the importance of *China Men* lies in its inclusive definition of 'We, the People', its ever-renewing concept of American identity, and its belief in the importance of citizenship as well as ethnic identity.[34] This commitment to inclusivity, founded on a portrait of the migrant as nation-builder, has redoubled the significance of Kingston's text in recent years. Since its publication, hostility towards migrants as a result of economic hardship has led to a less receptive social climate for Asians and other immigrant groups. This reaction is best illustrated by the revival of a discourse of 'illegal aliens' and the passage of the Immigration Reform and Control Act of 1986 and the Immigration Act of 1990 as retrenchments of the open policy celebrated by Kingston.[35]

Another migrant community that turned to literary expression and legal history for a defence of cultural identity in the early 1980s was the Chicano people. The evolution of pride in a distinctive Mexican-American ethnicity in the face of discrimination from a white-dominated legal system is shown in Luis Valdez's play, *Zoot Suit*. Valdez pioneered a community theatre among the agricultural workers of California while working with the union movement in a struggle to improve conditions for migrant workers in the 1960s. From this beginning, he founded El Teatro Campesino as a company located in San Juan Bautisto, California, with the express aim of representing on-stage the stories of the Chicano people. *Zoot Suit* was born in this environment, but it was produced as a play in a mainstream Los Angeles theatre, where it ran for eleven months to sell-out audiences.

Zoot Suit is based around the Sleepy Lagoon murder trials and attendant riots between white servicemen and the Mexican-American 'zootsuiters' in Los Angeles in 1942–3. The success of this historical re-creation, both on stage and subsequently in a 1981 film directed by Valdez, is evidence of an emergent multiculturalism in this period. *Zoot Suit* is experimental in form, part-musical and part-dramatised documentary, a 'construct of fact and fantasy'.[36] In its brilliant opening, 'a switchblade plunges through a newspaper' and the play's master of ceremonies, El Pachuco, steps on-stage. Wearing the zoot suit which served the 1940s generation of Mexican-American young men as the emblem of ethnic pride and masculinity, he orchestrates the play's representation of the Sleepy Lagoon case. With a bilingual commentary he initiates the audience into 'Pachuco realities', including segregated dances, traditional gender distinctions and the generational conflict often found in migrant stories, between the customs brought from the home country, and the freer behaviours of American modernity. Compounding this conflict are two contrasting strategies of the minority culture, to live quietly on the margins in accordance with the segregationist ethos, or to assert one's ethnic identity in the avenues of mainstream society. Music and dance function as markers of a more integrated popular culture, as the young protagonists, whom the press stigmatise as Mexican gang members, enjoy jazz and swing as well as more Latin-inflected music such as the mambo.[37] As well as prefiguring potential harmony and fusion in society, the dances are emblems of sexual and racial competition. Through commentary and scene-shifting, El Pachuco creates for the viewer the context of wartime Los Angeles, in which the zoot suit came to signify an internal enemy.

Within this world, the murder of José Díaz during a fight at a party was used by police as an excuse for indiscriminate arrests based on ethnic identity, and subsequently for a mass trial of twenty-two defendants. The accused were defended by seven lawyers, whose work was thwarted by the prejudice of the judge. Among other rulings, the defendants were refused fresh clothes and hair cuts, and made to stand whenever their names were mentioned so that the jury might distinguish them more easily. Unsurprisingly, seventeen of the defendants were convicted and imprisoned. The evident unfairness of the trial provoked protest and an immediate appeal campaign. In 1944, in *People* v. *Zammora*, the California Court of Appeals overturned the convictions and effectively declared mass trials to be illegal.[38]

Valdez draws on several of the more outrageous procedural rulings of the trial in his theatrical version. Overall, the legal action is reduced to its structural principles, with four defendants represented by one lawyer, and a minimalist set gesturing at legal process through highly selective props and personnel. The idea of a show trial is reinforced through musical conventions, such as when the ruling that defendants stand whenever their names are mentioned is illustrated to the accompaniment of a fast ragtime piano, mocking the perfunctoriness of the proceedings. Valdez also uses the Brechtian technique of alienation, inviting his audience to sit in judgment on the groundless 'expert testimony' that the Aztec roots of the Mexican culture proved a proclivity to violence among the defendants.

At one moment in the play, when El Pachuco is beaten and stripped of his zoot suit, Valdez constructs this character in terms of the sacrificial victim of Aztec ceremony.[39] However, it is the institutions of mainstream America, particularly 'the Press', that practise ritual violence and scapegoating. El Pachuco is a complex figure of myth, commanding respect in and for his ethnic difference and yet forced into an abject victimhood. As the *alter ego* of the chief protagonist, Henry Reyna, he narrates a story of ordeal and triumph, which suggests that the legal system 'still works' but, more importantly, shows the emergence of 'Chicano' as a new identity in the south-western states, one composed of elements of Mexican, Spanish and American origin. Like *China Men*, *Zoot Suit* is a story of cultural survival, of the conversion of what was originally a racist contraction of 'Mexicano' from a label of otherness into a proud diminutive of belonging, and thus an allegory for Los Angeles today.[40]

BAKKE-LASH

The law and literature of Civil Rights and the ethnic renaissance showed that real cultural progress towards equal justice was possible, but these new visions and vocabularies were not accompanied by structural change in society. To combat resistance and inertia, a programme of 'affirmative action' to increase the representation of minority or subordinate groups in higher education and the professions was instituted. No sooner had this legislative scheme been put in place by universities than disappointed white applicants sought to overthrow it as a violation of *their* rights under the Fourteenth Amendment. In the case of *Regents of University of California* v. *Bakke*, which began in 1973 and reached the Supreme Court in 1978, the special admissions programme at the new UC Davis medical school, which reserved sixteen positions for blacks, Asians, Chicanos and Native Americans, was challenged. In a finely balanced judgment, a bare majority of the nine justices upheld the challenge to the Davis scheme; however, one member of the majority accepted that affirmative action did not of itself contravene the Fourteenth Amendment and that another system of entry would be constitutional and so joined the dissenters to make a new majority for this proposition. The pivotal opinion in the case was that of Justice Lewis F. Powell.[41]

In stark contrast to its unanimity in the *Brown* judgment, the Court in *Bakke* was deeply divided over an issue of the competing entitlements of majority and minority applicants. A scheme to redress the effects of generations of exclusion and prejudice precluded some members of the dominant race from gaining access to medical school. Did this conform with the Fourteenth Amendment's guarantee of 'equal protection of the laws'? Again in contrast to the *Brown* decision, this complex question was answered not in plain prose but in abstruse legalese. Justice Powell's judgment is a measured and complex example of formal legal reasoning, employing the 'rhetoric of neutrality and universality' that Pierre Bourdieu has shown aims to situate the Court above the social conflict.[42] While such apparent separateness is a fundamental aspect of the law's claim to authority, Bourdieu perceives that the conflict cannot be wholly transformed into 'rule-bound exchanges of rational arguments'.[43] As a result, a judgment is 'a political compromise between irreconcilable demands, presented as the logical synthesis of antagonistic theses'. If this observation is not always borne out in judicial practice, it certainly explains the ideological manoeuvring visible in Powell's judgment.

Apart from the complexity of the result and the analysis, the discourses employed show Powell negotiating his way through the thicket of competing values. First he examines the effect of the Davis admissions scheme upon Bakke and, on the basis of a commonsense interpretation of the Fourteenth Amendment, concludes he was excluded on the basis of his race. Secondly, in dealing with arguments about the purpose of affirmative action, he interrogates the notions of 'majority' and 'minority' and claims that they are 'temporary arrangements' and that the majority is actually composed of various minorities. Accordingly, he believes, there is 'no principled basis for deciding which groups would merit "heightened judicial solicitude"'. Thirdly, in a less legalistic section of the argument, he examines the possible social effects of the scheme. He identifies problems with the idea of 'preference' itself, that it may reinforce stereotypes that certain groups can only get ahead with special treatment. Then, in a display of unconscious ideology, he argues that there is 'a measure of inequity in forcing innocent persons to bear the burden of redressing grievances not of their own making'.[44] His assumption that white persons are 'innocent' is revealing about both his attitude to his own race and his individualist notion of social responsibility. He proceeds to require 'specific instances of racial discrimination', rather than a general intention to remedy the effects of racism. However, he acknowledges that the university has a proper interest in obtaining a diverse student body, and on this basis alone, he finds it legitimate that some form of discretion in the racial composition of the student body be afforded to university administrators.

The only African-American on the bench, Justice Thurgood Marshall, penned a vigorous defence of affirmative action by locating the scheme in the history of racial discrimination and in the context of shifting interpretations of the Constitution. The main current of his opinion is a narrative of legal history, followed by evidence of systemic under-representation of blacks in the professions. In this context, racial disadvantage is a matter of record, not something requiring individual proof: 'While I applaud the judgment of the Court that a University may consider race in its admission process, it is more than a little ironic that, after several hundred years of class-based discrimination against negroes, the court is unwilling to hold that a class-based remedy for that discrimination may be permissible.'[45]

In an appreciative reading of Powell's judgment in *Bakke* written after the University of California had repudiated the principle of affirmative action in student enrolment, Robert Post argued that Powell's 'ideological construct' was worth supporting: 'He was determined both to achieve a pragmatic accommodation to the social necessity of affirmative action and to extract a patent symbolic commitment to the values of individualism.'[46] In the twenty-five years since *Bakke*, affirmative action has remained a contentious area of public opinion, and a site of ideological engagement in the press and the courts. While the theoretical and ideological limitations of Powell's approach are manifest, his 'pragmatic accommodation' has proven attractive to legal decision-makers. Reviewing the cases that have come before the Supreme Court, Cass Sunstein noted the lack of predictability and general principles, and concluded that 'the legitimacy of affirmative action programmes is best understood as a matter of particulars'.[47] With its focus on the details of each case, the Court has continued the Powell compromise. In the most recent Supreme Court cases concerning the admission schemes at the University of Michigan, the Law School procedure was upheld, while the affirmative action plan of the College of Literature, Arts and Sciences was struck down. Justice Sandra Day O'Connor in the majority opinion in *Grutter* v. *Bollinger*, the Law School case, conceded the continuing necessity of affirmative action programmes as a means of obtaining the goals validated in *Bakke* but expressed the view that they were a temporary expedient.[48]

Thus, the 'rhetoric of neutrality' adopted by Powell has proved highly serviceable to judges in questions of race and rights. Fewer and fewer have felt compelled to make use of the historical approach of Marshall, with the undoubted result that the law has become more interested in individual than in group rights. As Aviam Soifer has written, 'Judges today evince a profoundly ahistorical approach to groups that most obviously warrant special judicial concern on the basis of past wrongs.'[49] This trend is best exemplified in the dissent of Justice Clarence Thomas, the sole African-American member of the Court, in *Grutter* v. *Bollinger*. Thomas trenchantly rejected affirmative action as 'a faddish slogan of the cognoscenti' and buttressed his individualist approach with a literary quotation from Frederick Douglass arguing that a laissez-faire approach offers the best hope of advancement for blacks.[50]

TOWARDS A BELOVED COMMUNITY

In 1992 four police officers in Los Angeles were acquitted of the bashing of a motorist, Rodney King. Their assault had been filmed on a home video, but after minute frame-by-frame analysis, the white jury accepted the defendants' version of events that the force was necessary to subdue the apparent victim. Rioting followed this unjustifiable verdict, and a later Federal trial saw some of the officers convicted. Three years later, positions seemed reversed, as O. J. Simpson was acquitted of the murder of his wife. In a sensational trial that was telecast live and captivated the nation, the football star turned media celebrity triumphed despite strong evidence, the collection of which was compromised by overt police racism, and was cheered as a hero by African Americans, to the consternation of whites. The outcome seemed a racially determined verdict, and this reversal of the historical norm was viewed by the dominant race as a crisis for the legal system, rather than as evidence of the massive disaffection with the legal system among African-Americans, created by on-going daily racial injustice.

In this context of inadequate representation and failed justice, members of ethnic and racial minorities working in law schools began to apply the insights of a radical movement in legal education, Critical Legal Studies, to the systemic, but invisible, racism of the law. Drawing on the well-developed identity politics of the liberation movements and the methods of contemporary critical theory, they forged a new coalition between the discourses of law and literature, Critical Race Theory. Practitioners of Critical Race Theory, such as Derrick Bell, Richard Delgado and Patricia Williams, eschew the ideal of objectivity and the exclusive doctrinal focus of traditional legal scholarship and instead bring their personal histories and rhetorical and ideological analysis to bear on the operations of law.[51] Through the use of narrative, history and an attention to the construction of racial difference in legal language, they seek not merely to analyse, but to change the law. A specific subject of critique has been the prevailing ideal of colour-blindness in jurisprudence, which these scholars see as preserving the interests of the white race.

In addition to their critiques of existing law, Critical Race Theorists have promoted new causes of action, such as tortious claims for psychological damage sustained through racial abuse.[52] Some members of this movement have also sought to address a broader audience as cultural critics of racism and its persistence. In defiance of the defeats and the temptations to pessimism, Martin Luther King's ideal of a 'beloved community' has been revived as a goal for all Americans. The cultural critic, bell hooks, takes up this ideal in a 1995 essay, 'Beloved Community: A World without Racism'. She begins with her own experience of networks of friendship among people of various races and ethnicities, friendships developed through the struggle against racism. These small-scale communities give the lie to claims that racism is inevitable and separation the best practical policy. Whilst disappointed at the continuing hold of racist ideas in America, hooks invokes King's vision of 'beloved community' as a way forward. However, she draws on the insights of Critical Race Theory to qualify King's conception in one important particular: 'beloved community is formed not by the eradication of race-consciousness, but by its affirmation, by each of us claiming the identities and cultural legacies that shape who we are'.[53] In a more extended analysis, Anthony E. Cook draws out the theological vision of social justice underlying this concept, and its application to politics, in the spirit of Martin Luther King. Cook sees 'beloved community' as a value derived from progressive liberalism, and as a viable goal for this tradition in its fight against American conservatism. He defines its constituent elements as interdependency, love, equality and hope, and he suggests that the achievement of this goal will require attention to social, spiritual and strategic needs.[54] The literary critic Elizabeth Kella has used King's ideal as the title of a study of the fiction of Michael Ondaatje, Toni Morrison and Joy Kogawa. Her emphasis is on the 'nonviolent and racially inclusive' aspects of this goal.[55] Kella argues that 'the limited but nonetheless unprecedented gains made in the civil rights era continue to exert a strong influence on the ways in which communities can be imagined in American and Canadian fiction'.[56]

These commitments have indeed been demonstrated in recent American fiction. One example is the distinguished and very popular body of work written by the African-American novelist Ernest J. Gaines. Although he moved away from the South as a teenager, Gaines centres his fictional world on his birthplace, a single parish of Louisiana. His local stories, often written in the first person, fulfil a communicative and humanistic aim in holding up models of ethical challenge and growth for readers of all social groups. He retells the history of the African-American experience from the slave era to the dawn of the Civil Rights period in *The Autobiography of Miss Jane Pittman*. Several of his works involve the criminal law as one among a number of forums in which society judges and punishes offensive behaviour. *A Lesson Before Dying* is set in the late 1940s and features the encounter between a priggish schoolteacher and a teenager awaiting execution in the town jail. The novel is a brilliant portrait of conditions and attitudes in the segregated South, from the primitive school to the defective trial with its all-white jury and defence counsel describing his client as a 'hog' incapable of murder. The prisoner acts out this identity, while the teacher, a reluctant visitor at first, labours to reach him, but in doing so, allows new ethical sensibilities to emerge in the town, as attention is focused on the young man and the elderly woman who has raised him. As his pupil's humanity is affirmed, so the teacher acquires self-respect, and some whites in the town begin to question the justice of the harsh law which condemned so many young African-American men to death.[57] With its attention drawn fearfully towards the jail, the town becomes an image of a new community in process.[58]

Toni Morrison, who was awarded the Nobel Prize for Literature in 1993, addresses the issue of how to imagine a 'beloved community' in the face of a history of traumatic violence. Her novel *Beloved* is a searing exploration of the brutality of slavery, and the psychic burdens it placed on survivors. Her initial inspiration for the plot was a legal case concerning a runaway slave, Margaret Garner, who killed her child rather than see her return to slavery, but who was tried not for murder, but for stealing the property of her master. However, the novel is less focused on the act than on the horrific consequences of slavery, so it eschews the realism of legal narrative for a mythic and gothic mode of storytelling. The dead baby, known only by the sole word on her grave, 'Beloved', returns as a ghost, disrupting the lives of her mother Sethe, her grandmother Baby Suggs and her siblings. The novel voices the perceptions and memories of all characters using modernist narrative devices such as stream-of-consciousness, refusing any objective exterior viewpoints. From the opening sentence, '124 was spiteful', the result, in Morrison's words, is that the reader is 'snatched, yanked, thrown into an environment completely foreign, . . . just as the slaves were from one place to another, from anyplace to another, without preparation and without defence'.[59] Another animating principle of the novel is a commitment to the curative value of frankness, so Morrison seeks to reveal the unspeakable degradation that earlier writers repressed. She notes that many writers of slave narratives set limits to their accounts through formulae like 'but let us drop a veil over these proceedings too terrible to relate', and believes that the writer's job is to find 'how to rip that veil . . ., to fill in the blanks' in the interests of historical truth.[60] Thus the crime of child murder is recontextualised in a frame of other abuses normalised in the totalitarian order of slavery. The indirect acceptance of such degradation under American law, through the Fugitive Slave Act, under which escaped slaves could be recaptured in free states and returned to their owners, impelled Sethe to choose between two evils at the crucial moment of the text. The normative worlds of master and slave are re-created with great economy in this 'extended meditation on the law'.[61]

This preoccupation with the past in *Beloved* and contemporary literature more generally makes a decided contrast with the refusal of courts to adopt the historical perspective since *Bakke*. The novel stresses the interconnection between past and present, and its treatment of this is well articulated by Mae G. Henderson when she links narrative, suffering and the desire for justice. Quoting the philosopher Paul Ricoeur, 'The whole history of suffering cries out for vengeance and calls out for narrative', Henderson argues that the novel transforms a story of oppression into one of liberation.[62] The family at '124' are eventually liberated from the psychic bondage of their legalised dehumanisation, but only after a long struggle with the spirits of their infant victims. The novel forces readers to consider the justice of Sethe's act, and in doing so forces us to reconsider our own categories of judgment. The individual story of Beloved is also tied to the community's attitude to the members of that household. In addition to a narrative of maternal love, the novel represents the struggle for a beloved community.

James Alan McPherson was eleven years old and living in Savannah, Georgia, when the *Brown* case was decided. McPherson studied law at Harvard University but decided to become a writer upon graduation in 1968. His early story, 'An Act of Prostitution', reveals his interest in deep characterisation, with the irrepressible prostitute whose jive-talking is a way of resisting the racist officers of justice, and the condescending advocate whose attitudes are undermined in the tale.[63] After his second collection of stories, *Elbow Room* (1977), which won the Pulitzer Prize for Literature, McPherson turned to essays and memoirs. In the essays collected in *A Region Not Home* McPherson writes of his many long-standing friendships with people of other races, and of the 'rising tensions' between various groups in many American cities.[64] In 'Ukiyo', a reflective autobiographical essay, he invokes Martin Luther King's ideal as an answer to the question of how to 'create meaningful communities, even across racial lines'.[65] McPherson's ethical quest is matched by his social observation: 'It is a very hard fact of life that there exists no such community in any part of the country. But at the same time it *does* exist in every part of the country, among selected individuals from every possible background.' Even more than bell hooks, McPherson applies King's ideal in the private sphere, in a virtual community composed of far-flung individuals connected by shared commitments and experiences that have blossomed into friendship, and that is carried on as much in writing as in person. Drawing on a Japanese concept he defines this community as 'a floating world, a *ukiyo*'.[66] This shadowy world, his 'substitute for a hometown', is not nostalgic, but future-oriented. In representing it McPherson draws upon the range of his experience as a law student, a teacher of writing, a writer and a citizen in various American towns and cities.

McPherson's model reflects his lifetime of travel and uprootedness. For this reason, perhaps, he is drawn to connecting his own *ukiyo* with another 'imagined community', the nation. In the opening essay in the collection, 'On Becoming an American Writer', he structures his quest for identity in terms of citizenship, rather than race. Growing up black he could not ignore racial difference, but at a crucial moment, during a class on American constitutional law, his imagination was seized by the possibility that legal interpretation might open up new modes of being for the individual and the society:

I began to play with the idea that the Fourteenth Amendment was not just a legislative instrument designed to give former slaves legal equality with other Americans. Looking at the slow but steady way in which the basic guarantees of the Bill of Rights had, through judicial interpretation, been incorporated into the clauses of that amendment, I began to see the outlines of a new identity.[67]

This insight was confirmed some years later when, in the Library of Congress, McPherson read the brief prepared by the lawyer-novelist, Albion W. Tourgee, for the 1896 case of *Plessy* v. *Ferguson*: 'This provision *creates* a new citizenship of the United States embracing *new* rights, privileges and immunities.'[68] Tourgee's argument was rejected by the Supreme Court, but McPherson recommends it as literature, as a prophetic multicultural imagining: 'that each United States citizen would attempt to approximate the ideals of the nation, be on at least conversant terms with all its diversity, carry the mainstream of the culture inside himself'.[69]

The fiftieth anniversary of *Brown* v. *Board of Education* has come and gone. The dream of a racially integrated and equal America that the case inspired has not been fully realised. Yet the legal world-making set in motion by *Brown* continues, illustrating Robert Cover's thesis that law is a bridge between an existent reality and a transformed future. Despite the manifold inequities of contemporary American life, the labour of transformation goes on. In legal writs and other cultural texts the movement of the disempowered is assisted, as the poet Cyrus Cassells puts it in a poem dedicated to Elizabeth Eckford, the student who ran the gauntlet at Little Rock,

> Up, up from the shadows of gallows trees
> To the other shore.[70]

Conclusion

The intersection of law and literature remains a vital subject of study in contemporary culture. In December 2000 a high school student in eastern Ontario, who had been bullied by his classmates, read out a creative writing assignment in which the protagonist made preparations for bombing his school. The student was placed in juvenile detention for thirty-four days, and was finally charged with making threats. Leading Canadian writers, including Margaret Atwood and Michael Ondaatje, protested on his behalf, arguing that his imprisonment violated freedom of expression. The case was controversial, with the school and police denying that the boy's story was the cause of his detention. Rather, they argued, he had made verbal threats against fellow students. However, a police search found no weapons or explosives at his home, and the charges against him were dropped. Other students were charged with assaulting him.

Apart from its freedom of speech issue, the story illustrates how writing may occupy a contested territory, how it may be subject to the jurisdiction of both literature and law. Using the terminology of Wittgenstein discussed in our Introduction, we could say that the authorities in the case failed to identify the kinds of sentences or the 'language-game' performed in the student's text, mistaking an imaginative scenario for a criminal intention. The episode suggests the need for greater recognition of the role of literary activity in our cultural conversation. As Michael Oakeshott argued fifty years ago, the dominant discourses in modern society are practical and scientific, at the expense of the 'poetic voice'.[1] Poetry, writing that is imaginative rather than instrumental, is a way of envisaging alternative worlds, of coming to terms with traumatic experience by embodying it in verbal imagery and narrative. And yet, as this book has shown through many examples, creative writing does not involve a retreat into some lonely tower of the poetic imagination. Rather, the publication of such images and stories is a way of intervening in the world, of reshaping understandings and challenging relationships of power. The student's story supports the philosopher Paul Ricoeur's thesis that 'the whole history of suffering cries out for vengeance and calls for narrative'.[2] An understanding of the nature of literature in this case led Atwood and her colleagues not just to defend free speech, but to seek justice for the teenager.

This case illustrates the importance of fostering the ancient dialogue between literature and law. The eighteenth-century legal writer, Edward Wynne, noting the emergence of disciplinary isolation, put the case for 'mutual intercourse' in his dialogue on English law, *Eunomus*:

> I am persuaded that all arts and sciences have some form or connection with one another; and that 'Law', as one of these, is not . . . like one left on a desart island [sic], and shut off from all society. But that there is mutual intercourse and assistance constantly kept up between the law and other sciences; the first by protecting the latter, and the latter by the various lights and illustrations they afford in the study of the law.[3]

Something of Blackstone's complacency animates Wynne's assurance that law always protects the other arts and sciences with which it necessarily comes in contact. Nonetheless, as we noted in chapter 2, in the last fifty years law has offered limited recognition of, and protection to, literature as a valuable category of expression. As a consequence, many provocative works, challenging values and hierarchies, have been published.

Wynne's belief in the illumination conferred by bringing the insights of other disciplines to the law distils one of the major conclusions to be drawn from this study. The influence of economics and modern philosophy on Oliver Wendell Holmes, or that of psychology on the Warren court in *Brown* provides examples of law's openness to new discourses. However, Caroline Norton's experience of the rigid application of legal rules, and the exclusion of discourses of justice and maternal feeling, is more typical of the workings of the juridical field in modern society. The Law-and-Literature dialogue cannot be carried on solely by erudite individuals. It flourishes when supported by institutions of law and civil society. Historically, male conclaves like the Inns of Court during the Renaissance and Dr Johnson's Literary Club provided influential forums for the dialogue, but since the nineteenth century, disempowered communities seeking to reform the laws and ideologies that oppress them have formed their own institutions, such as the Langham Place Group in Norton's time and Howard University in post-Civil War America. These bodies have used the linguistic tools of law and literature in their quests for social justice. Today, the various law and literature associations, and law and culture conferences, are demonstrating the 'mutual assistance' to scholars, students and the profession that a revival of the legal-literary dialogue can provide.[4] However, despite increased recognition of the value of external perspectives in legal education, 'law and literature' has not yet returned to the core of the law school curriculum.[5]

Whatever the fluctuations in the institutional status of the two disciplines, the 'mutual intercourse' between the two fields continues unabated. One of the findings of Part II of this study is the extent to which writing produced within the literary sphere has drawn on legal events, and been directed to issues of law and justice. This aspect of literature's social responsibility was memorably declared during the English Civil War by Andrew Marvell in 'Tom May's Death':

> When the sword glitters o'er the judge's head
> And fear has coward churchmen silencèd,
> Then is the poet's time, 'tis then he draws
> And single fights forsaken virtue's cause.
> He, when the wheel of empire whirleth back,
> And though the world's disjointed axle crack,
> Still sings of ancient rights and better times,
> Seeks wretched good, arraigns successful crimes.[6]

Tom May was a writer who changed sides to become a propagandist for Cromwell. Marvell's humanistic vision of poetry's alliance with 'virtue's cause' is therefore informed by an awareness that this ideal is not automatically upheld by all writers. Yet, as we have seen, from Cavendish and Dickens down to Morrison and Soyinka, many have borne witness to evils performed by powerful groups, have infused their representations with legal discourse and imagined 'better times' through narratives of redress.

Another vital form of the 'mutual intercourse' between law and literature is the poetics of the law. The literary and cultural studies perspectives brought to bear on law in these pages illuminate the rhetorical strategies and the influence of cultural narratives and symbols in legal utterances. As the pioneering work of Peter Goodrich has shown, the law makes use of the aesthetic resources of the surrounding culture – eloquent words, visual spectacles, architecture, ritualised forms of procedure – to solicit the voluntary obedience of its subjects. Caroline Norton described such a spectacle when Queen Victoria opened a new hall in Lincoln's Inn in 1845:

It was the very poetry of allegiance, when the Lord Chancellor and the other great law officers did obeisance in that Hall to their Queen; and the Treasurer knelt at a woman's feet, to read of the amendments in that great stern science by which governments themselves are governed . . . on that vantage ground of Justice where students are taught, by sublime theories, how Right can be defended against Might, the poor against the rich, the weak against the strong, in their legal practice.[7]

We have seen how jurists from Coke to Mortimer have employed the tropes of this 'poetry of allegiance' to praise the justice of the common law. Even a critic of law's deficiencies like Norton can be swayed by its poetry to accept its ideology. Outside the law, satirists from Swift to Stead have mocked this resort to aesthetics. The study of law and literature enables an understanding of this strategy, and an evaluation of its effects.

Edward Wynne recognises this discursive traffic across law's border, quoting a startling image from the seventeenth-century jurist Henry Finch: 'the sparks of all sciences are raked up in the ashes of the law'.[8] The fire of the law is kept alive by outside fuel, but in the process law appears a voracious consumer of other discourses! Law's discursive dominance affects its neighbours, including literature. In the names that writers give to actions and roles, the categories of the law are strongly felt. Pierre Bourdieu describes Wynne's 'mutual assistance' in more realistic terms: discussing law's possession of the 'symbolic power of naming', he argues that 'it would not be excessive to say that it *creates* the social world, but only if we remember that it is this world which first creates the law'.[9] The process of naming or representation, which is so fundamental to human cognition and to the recognition of others, is shared by law and literature, as can be seen in the emergence of contract out of the culture of the Renaissance, or that of the tort of negligence in industrial modernity. Apart from being a cognitive process, however, naming is also a political one. As is particularly evident in the final chapter on race, law and literature in contemporary America, some social groups possess the power to name and thereby dominate others, so that symbolic power is fought for, fought over. Such discursive battles are particularly intense in postcolonial, multilingual societies. Often they pit the symbolic power of literature against that of law. The intense engagement of writers on the Indian subcontinent with the British decision in 1947 to 'partition' India is a case in point.

The raking of the sparks of other disciplines into the ashes of the law suggests, in Mieke Bal's words, that 'law [is] a follower not maker of culture'.[10] However, the process also operates in reverse, as culture draws from the law. Owen Barfield has shown how many words in common use, even ones so widespread as 'person' and 'cause', have a legal origin.[11] To adapt section 92 of the Australian Constitution, the linguistic 'trade, commerce and intercourse' between the domains of law and literature is extensive if not 'absolutely free'. It is part of the modern polyglot world of 'active, mutual cause-and-effect and inter-illumination'.[12] Bakhtin, whose theory I am using here, argues that languages 'throw light on each other: one language can, after all, see itself only in the light of another language'. Not only do the languages of law and literature engage with each other, borrowing phrases and images through the operation of intertextuality; the study of 'law and literature' also enables students in each field to gain a better understanding of their own discipline and its discourse.

'Law and literature', according to Mieke Bal, 'serves the project of *interdisciplinary cultural analysis*.'[13] This book has presented a history of the unfolding relationship between these two disciplines in Anglophone culture. It has shown how the composition of the two fields has changed over the last 500 years, and with it the boundary between them.[14] As such, it contributes to the on-going 'understanding of interdisciplinarity' in general, by presenting a history of one particular field.[15] An integrated legal-literary approach to the Ontario case would acknowledge the interests of both creative freedom and social safety; would affirm the need to find the truth and the difficulty of doing so; and would analyse all the narratives circulating in and around the case, the fictional, the factual and the unspoken scripts about human behaviour, as a means of seeking a just interpretation of the event. To do this would entail drawing on concepts and methods from both law and literary studies.

Under the auspices of this interdisciplinary project, ethics and aesthetics become active partners with politics in creating the normative basis for a just society. The Irish poet Eavan Boland captures this imperative in 'The Laws of Love', a poem dedicated to Mary Robinson, the former United Nations Human Rights Commissioner and Irish President. As 'new found sisters', early in their friendship they 'began to trade / Salmond for Shakespeare'.[16] This exchange between law and literature (Salmond was the author of textbooks on torts and jurisprudence) could not remain a private or an intellectual dialogue; rather it developed into a cultural and political quest to use their professional resources to understand and change the position of women in a violent society. Inter-illuminated, their 'separate speech' worked to a common end as law and literature pleaded for:

> Another world for whose horizons,
> For whose anguish no reprieve
> Exists unless new citizens,
> And, as we found, the laws of love –

The sentence is suspended, just as the wish for the otherworld of justice is 'Ungranted, / . . . Yet still there.' Both poet and lawyer are 'haunted' by that gulf between desire and reality. Their words, and the dialogue between law and literature which they enact, aim to bring into being 'laws of love'.[17] That this was a joint discovery, a shared quest ('as *we* found'), suggests that in this dialogue it is not the role of literature to introduce love into an aridly rationalist law. Rather, that suggestively open phrase, 'the laws of love', encompasses some important discourses of law, such as the tradition of equity, the construction of a general duty of care, and the development of human rights law, as well as ethical insights that emerge from literature, philosophy and other disciplines. In her turn, Mary Robinson drew on literary discourses in formulating her vision of 'a new, pluralist Ireland'. In the penultimate paragraph of her Inaugural Speech as President of Ireland she invoked the poetry of her friend to place on the agenda of her presidency their shared project of writing women 'back into history, in the words of Eavan Boland, "finding a voice where they have found a vision" '.[18] Recognising the link between justice and narrative, she proceeded:

I want this Presidency to promote the telling of stories – stories of celebration through the arts and stories of conscience and of social justice.

The friendship between Robinson and Boland is a compelling contemporary instance of both the vitality and the potential of the interdisciplinary dialogue between law and literature.

Notes

INTRODUCTION

1. 514 U.S. 211, 131 L. Ed. 2d 328. Subsequent page references to this report are placed parenthetically in the text.
2. For an introduction to legal narrative studies see Brooks and Gewirtz (eds.), *Law's Stories*.
3. Cover, 'Foreword: *Nomos* and Narrative', p. 4.
4. See 'Supreme Court Poetry Seminar', p. 4. I am indebted to this article for first drawing my attention to this case.
5. Frost, 'Mending Wall', in *Poetry of Robert Frost*, p. 33.
6. See Cramer, *Robert Frost among His Poems*, p. 30.
7. *Ibid.*
8. *Ibid.*
9. Culler, *Literary Theory*, p. 40.
10. Bakhtin, 'Discourse in the Novel', in *Dialogic Imagination*, p. 342.
11. *Ibid.*, p. 343.
12. Sarat, Constable, Engel *et al.* (eds.), *Crossing Boundaries*, pp. 3–4. Certain references have been omitted from the text quoted. See also Nedelsky, 'Law, Boundaries and the Bounded Self'.
13. Plato, *The Laws*, p. 343.
14. Arendt, *The Human Condition*, pp. 63, 190.
15. Magris, 'Who Is on the Other Side?', p. 22.
16. For a lawyer's argument that English literature is deeply 'antinomian' or hostile to law, see Julius, 'Dickens the Lawbreaker', p. 63.
17. Gunn and Greenblatt, *Redrawing the Boundaries*, p. 5.
18. On subversion in Frost's text see Poirier, *Robert Frost*, p. 106.
19. Magris, 'Who Is on the Other Side?', p. 9.
20. Other scholars of law and literature have used variations on the metaphor of the boundary in describing this interdisciplinary field of study. See especially Weisberg, 'Literature's Twenty-Year Crossing'; Kayman, 'Law-and-Literature' and Petch, 'Borderline Judgments'.
21. Thomas, 'Reflections on the Law and Literature Revival', p. 533.
22. Wittgenstein, *Philosophical Investigations I*, pp. 11e–12e.
23. Thomas, 'Reflections on the Law and Literature Revival', p. 533 n. 43.
24. Auden, 'In Memory of W. B. Yeats', *The English Auden*, pp. 241–3.

25. Beer, *Open Fields*, p. 1.
26. *Ibid.*, p. 115.
27. Hanafin, Geary and Brooker (eds.), *Law and Literature*, p. 1.
28. See Weisberg, 'Literature's Twenty-Year Crossing'. For the dynamic and multifaceted notion of a Law *and* Literature project, I am indebted to Maria Aristodemou, *Law and Literature*, pp. 28, 262–3. The beginnings of this project as a current subject of study are usually traced to the 1973 publication by James Boyd White, *The Legal Imagination*.
29. Weisberg and Barricelli, 'Literature and the Law', p. 150.
30. Cover, 'Violence and the Word', p. 1609.
31. Posner, *Law and Literature*, p. 363.
32. *Ibid.*, p. 353.
33. Beer, *Open Fields*, p. x.
34. Bourdieu, 'The Force of Law', p. 838.
35. Terdiman, 'Translator's Introduction', *Hastings Law Review* 38 (1987), 805.
36. Bourdieu, *Field of Cultural Production*.
37. Bourdieu, 'The Intellectual Field', p. 146.
38. *Ibid.*, p. 149.
39. Bourdieu, 'The Force of Law', p. 839.
40. *Ibid.*
41. For an account of this context see Cornish and Clark, *Law and Society in England*, pp. 450–4.
42. Leckie, 'The Force of Law and Literature', p. 131.
43. For an example of such a study, see Moddelmog, *Reconstituting Authority*.
44. Bourdieu, 'The Intellectual Field', p. 146.
45. Pritchard, *Frost*, p. 241.
46. Richardson, *The Ordeal of Robert Frost*, p. 33.
47. Frost, 'For John F. Kennedy His Inauguration', in *In the Clearing*, p. 30.
48. Pritchard, *Frost*, p. 255.
49. *Ibid.*, p. 250.
50. Ellmann, *Eminent Domain*, p. 4.

1 LAW'S LANGUAGE

1. For a full account of the case, see Culhane, *Pleasure of the Crown*, chapter 2.
2. *Ibid.*, p. 31.
3. *Ibid.*, p. 21.
4. Sarat and Kearns, 'Editorial Introduction', in *Rhetoric of Law*, pp. 1–2.
5. Vickers, *In Defence of Rhetoric*, p. 1.
6. Aristotle, *Art of Rhetoric*, pp. 69–70.
7. *Ibid.*, p. 75.
8. See Harris, 'Law and Oratory'.
9. Frost's *Introduction to Classical Legal Rhetoric* is a practical guide to this tradition.
10. For more details, see chapter 3 below.

11. See Schoeck, 'Lawyers and Rhetoric,' p. 278.
12. Hollander, 'Legal Rhetoric,' p. 177.
13. See Meehan, 'Authorship and Imagination,' and Robert A. Ferguson, *Law and Letters* respectively.
14. See Burke, *Rhetoric of Motives*. On the Chicago school, see Booth, *Rhetoric of Fiction* and Crane (ed.), *Critics and Criticism*. Perelman and Obrechts-Tyteca's *New Rhetoric* was a major attempt to revivify the tradition.
15. White gives a clear retrospective of the development of his ideas in the introduction to his *Justice as Translation*.
16. See White, *Heracles' Bow*, p. 35.
17. See White, *Acts of Hope*, pp. 124–5.
18. White, *Heracles' Bow*, p. 41.
19. For analyses of White's work, see Gaakeer, *Hope Springs Eternal*, and Minda, 'Cool Jazz But Not So Hot Literary Text'. On 'huge stabilities', see Threadgold, 'Performativity, Regulative Fictions, Huge Stabilities'.
20. See Goodrich, *Reading the Law*, chapter 6.
21. Goodrich, 'Antirrhesis'.
22. Goodrich, *Languages of Law*, chapter 2. The psychoanalytic discourse of repression is deliberately invoked here: psychoanalysis becomes a major theoretical resource in Goodrich's later work, beginning with *Languages of Law* and going on to *Oedipus Lex* and *Law and the Postmodern Mind*.
23. Goodrich, *Languages of Law*, p. 7.
24. See Meehan, 'An Anatomy of Australian Law'; Duncan, *Romantic Criminals, Beloved Prisons*, especially Part III: 'In Slime and Darkness'; and Hibbitts, 'Making Sense of Metaphors'.
25. Blom-Cooper (ed.), *Law as Literature*, p. ix.
26. *Ibid.*, p. x.
27. See Elwyn-Jones, 'Law as Literature'.
28. See chapter 2 below for examples.
29. See Weisberg, *Poethics*, pp. 24–8, where Cardozo's opinion is reprinted. See also Weisberg and Barricelli, 'Literature and the Law'.
30. *Buck* v. *Bell* 274 US 200, 207 (1927).
31. Posner, *Law and Literature*, 2nd edn, p. 273.
32. For the tendency of ideological factors to influence traditional evaluative literary criticism, see Eagleton, *Literary Theory*, chapter 1.
33. Ferguson, 'On the Judicial Opinion as a Literary Genre', p. 201. See also his ' "We do Ordain and Establish" '.
34. Ferguson, ' "We do Ordain and Establish" ', p. 25.
35. For an excellent demonstration of this, see Klinck's analysis of Lord Denning's writings in 'This Other Eden'.
36. Resnik and Heilbrun, 'Convergences', p. 1912.
37. See, for example, Douzinas and Warrington, *Justice Miscarried*.
38. Diamond, *Primitive Law*, p. 45.
39. Bourdieu, 'The Force of Law', p. 814.
40. *Ibid.*, p. 820.

41. Balkin, 'A Night in the Topics', p. 216.
42. Jackson, *Law, Fact and Narrative Coherence*.
43. Goodrich, *Languages of Law*, pp. 4, 209–10.
44. See Barthes, *Mythologies*, pp. 43–6.
45. Alison Young, 'The Body of Criminality'.
46. See Brooks, *Troubling Confessions*.
47. E.g. Cardozo's judgment in *Hynes* v. *New York Central Railroad Co.*, discussed above.
48. Brooks, 'Narrative and Rhetoric in the Law', p. 16.
49. Cover, '*Nomos* and Narrative', pp. 3–4. For a full account of Cover's theory, see the collection of his essays, *Narrative, Violence and the Law*; see also Dolin, *Fiction and the Law*, chapter 1.
50. Cover, '*Nomos* and Narrative', p. 17.
51. Simpson, *Cannibalism and the Common Law*.
52. See White, *Content of the Form*.
53. See Scheppele, 'Foreword: Telling Stories', and Delgado, 'Storytelling for Oppositionists and Others'.
54. West, *Caring for Justice*, p. 210.
55. Heinzelman, ' "Going Somewhere" '.
56. Ferguson, 'Untold Stories in the Law', p. 85.
57. West, *Caring for Justice*, p. 211.
58. *Ibid.*, p. 212.
59. See Ferguson's 'Untold Stories in the Law', and his 'Story and Transcription in the Trial of John Brown'. Another famous trial narrative which utilises the concept of the trial as social drama is Michael Grossberg, *A Judgment for Solomon*. For an incisive review of the issues involved in such narrative studies, see Thomas, 'Michael Grossberg's Telling Tale'.
60. Felman, *Juridical Unconscious*, p. 12.
61. *Ibid.*, p. 16.
62. *R.* v. *Duffy* [1949] All ER 932.
63. *Ibid.*, p. 933.
64. Fish, 'The Law Wishes to Have a Formal Existence'.
65. On this point, see Meehan, 'Anatomy of Australian Law'.
66. Melville, *Billy Budd, Sailor*, p. 387.
67. For two very different discussions of this issue, see Noonan, *Persons and Masks of the Law* and Conklin, *Phenomenology of Modern Legal Discourse*.
68. Devlin, *Enforcement of Morals*. In addition to lectures on various aspects of the law, Devlin also wrote an autobiographical essay, *Taken at the Flood* and a study of a trial over which he presided, *Easing the Passing*. On the latter, see my 'The Case of Doctor John Bodkin Adams'.
69. Bakhtin, 'Discourse in the Novel', in *Dialogic Imagination*, p. 342.
70. See Bruns, 'Law and Language', pp. 30–1.
71. Kennedy, *Eve Was Framed*, chapter 8.
72. Raitt and Zeedyk, *Implicit Relation of Psychology and Law*, p. 75.

73. *Lavallée* v. *The Queen* [1990] S. C. R. 852, 872. Subsequent page references to this report are placed parenthetically in the text.
74. Bourdieu, 'The Force of Law', p. 819.

2 LITERATURE UNDER THE LAW

1. Quoted in Sutherland, *Offensive Literature*, p. 3.
2. See Kayman, 'Lawful Writing', p. 779.
3. See Julius, 'Dickens the Lawbreaker', p. 44.
4. *James* v. *Commonwealth* (1936) 55 CLR 1 (Privy Council decision).
5. *Halsbury's Laws of Australia*, paragraph 80–1945.
6. See Highet, *Juvenal the Satirist*, chapter 3, for a full account of the case.
7. Quoted by Patterson, *Criticism and Interpretation*, p. 12.
8. Levy, *Treason against God*, p. 307.
9. See Ian Hunter, Saunders and Williamson, *On Pornography*, p. 89.
10. Quoted by Kendrick, *Secret Museum*, p. 117. For a full account of the circumstances of the cases, and the campaign against pornography in London, see Nead, *Victorian Babylon*, III. 3.
11. Kendrick, *Secret Museum*, p. 118.
12. Hunter, Saunders and Williamson, *On Pornography*, p. 71.
13. See Waugh, *Revolutions of the Word*; and MacCabe, *James Joyce and the Revolution of the Word*.
14. Pease, *Modernism, Mass Culture and the Aesthetics of Obscenity*.
15. Quoted in Vanderham, 'Lifting the Ban on *Ulysses*', p. 192.
16. It has been anthologized in Robbins (ed.), *Law*, pp. 299–301.
17. *Roth* v. *US* 354 US 476 (1957), quoted in Craig, *Banned Books*, p. 152.
18. Quoted in Craig, *Banned Books*, p. 157.
19. *Ibid.*, p. 160.
20. Rembar, *The End of Obscenity. The Trials of Lady Chatterley, Tropic of Cancer and Fanny Hill* The on-going struggle against prosecutions for obscenity is made clear in an excellent book by another of the counsel defending *Tropic of Cancer*: see Edward de Grazia, *Girls Lean Back Everywhere*.
21. Quoted in Craig, p. 124.
22. Rolph (ed.), *Trial of Lady Chatterley*. See p. 17.
23. Sutherland, *Offensive Literature*, p. 2.
24. Hunter, Saunders and Williamson, *On Pornography*, p. 153.
25. Millett, *Sexual Politics*.
26. See Downs, *New Politics of Pornography*.
27. *R.* v. *Butler* 89 Dominion Law Reports 449 (1992), *per* Sopinka J. at 483.
28. The debate among feminist thinkers is well represented in Chester and Dickey (eds.), *Feminism and Censorship*. Easton, *Problem of Pornography*, reviews the issues well and concludes that incitement to sexual hatred, along the lines of proscriptions against race hate-speech, may offer a more effective legal attack on the harms created by pornography.

29. *New York* v. *Ferber* 458 US 747 (1982).
30. Levy, *Treason against God*, p. 4.
31. *Ibid.* See also Marsh, *Word Crimes*.
32. Webster, *Brief History of Blasphemy*, pp. 22–3, referring to the case of John Taylor.
33. Carter-Ruck, Walker and Starte, *Libel and Slander*, p. 187.
34. Alan King-Hamilton QC cited in *R* v. *Chief Metropolitan Stipendiary Magistrate ex p Choudhury* [1991] 1 QB 429 at 444 [*Satanic Verses case*]. Carter-Ruck, Walker and Starte, *Libel and Slander*, pp. 187–8.
35. For a lively account of the case see Robertson, *Justice Game*, chapter 6.
36. Webster, *Brief History of Blasphemy*, p. 24. This judgment reflected Coleridge's own intellectual journey away from Christianity: see Geary, ' "Born Pious, Literary and Legal" ', pp. 463–80.
37. Marsh, *Word Crimes*, p. 9.
38. For a discussion of this case, see *ibid.*, pp. 60–77.
39. *Ibid.*, p. 98.
40. [1917] A.C. 459, and 464 respectively.
41. The latter suggestion is noted in Webster, *Brief History of Blasphemy*, p. 67.
42. Carter-Ruck, Walker and Starte, *Libel and Slander*, pp. 188–9.
43. Hamburger, 'The Development of the Law of Seditious Libel'.
44. These cases are discussed in chapter 4, below.
45. Lieberman, *A Practical Companion to the Constitution*, p. 450.
46. *A Brief Narrative of the Case and Tryal of John Peter Zenger*, quoted in Robbins (ed.), *Law*, p. 152.
47. *Abrams* v. *US* 250 US 616 (1919).
48. Carter-Ruck, Walker and Starte, *Libel and Slander*, p. 189. At the time of writing, the Australian Government is strengthening sedition laws as part of its counter-terrorism legislation.
49. This speech is reprinted in Blom-Cooper (ed.), *Law as Literature*, pp. 100–1: for other cases see Barak, *Bankshall Court*.
50. Carter-Ruck, Walker and Starte, *Libel and Slander*, p. 2.
51. Edw I c 34 (1275). See Carter-Ruck, Walker and Starte, *Libel and Slander*, p. 20.
52. Stone, *Crisis of the Aristocracy*, p. 25.
53. Kaplan, *Culture of Slander*, pp. 19–20.
54. See Perry, ' "If Proclamation will not Serve" '.
55. Carter-Ruck, Walker and Starte, *Libel and Slander*, p. 21.
56. Kegl, *Rhetoric of Concealment*, p. 119.
57. Carter-Ruck, Walker and Starte, *Libel and slander*, p. 23.
58. Shakespeare, *Othello*, III.iii.155–61.
59. George Puttenham, *The Art of English Poesy* (1589), quoted in Kaplan, *Culture of Slander*, p. 30.
60. Quoted from the case *de Libellis famosis* (1606) by Kaplan, *Culture of Slander*, p. 30.
61. Seidel, 'Satire, Lampoon, Libel, Slander', p. 33.

62. *Ibid.*, p. 42.
63. Pope, *Poems of Alexander Pope*, p. 613.
64. Carter-Ruck, Walker and Starte, *Libel and Slander*, p. 107.
65. *Ibid.*, p. 28.
66. See Hooper, *Reputations under Fire*, p. 416.
67. See Barendt, 'Defamation and Fiction', p. 482. This article is a comprehensive treatment of the topic. Posner, *Law and Literature*, chapter 11, also explores the issues surrounding defamation by fiction.
68. See Weatherby, *Salman Rushdie*, p. 50.
69. *Costello* v. *Random House Australia* [1999] ACTSC 13.
70. *New York Times* v. *Sullivan* 376 US 254 (1964).
71. For a study of this context see chapter 8 below.
72. See Hooper, *Reputations under Fire*, chapter 5. For an American criticism of the law, see Leval, 'The No-Money, No-Fault Libel Suit'.
73. *Garrison* v. *Louisiana* 379 US 64, 130 (1964).
74. *Ibid.*, p. 135.
75. See Armstrong, *Frank Hardy and the Making of* Power Without Glory, for a full account of the case.
76. Snyder, *Hypertext*.
77. See Nelson, *Literary Machines* 93.1, front cover.
78. *Ibid.*, p. 3/19.
79. *Laurence Godfrey* v. *Demon Internet Limited* [1999] 4 All ER 342.
80. See Communications Decency Act 1996, section 230.
81. *Dow Jones* v. *Gutnick* [2002] HCA 56.
82. Defoe, *Essay on the Regulation of the Press*. An electronic edition is available at http://darkwing.uoregon.edu/~rbear/defoe2.html.
83. For a good discussion of Defoe's ideas and their place in the unfolding history of copyright, see Rose, *Authors and Owners*, pp. 34ff.
84. *Oxford English Dictionary* (2nd edn).
85. Muir, *Sources of Shakespeare's Plays*.
86. Orgel, 'The Renaissance Artist as Plagiarist', pp. 493–4. Accusations of plagiarism did still surface, especially in relation to women playwrights, as Rosenthal shows: *Playwrights and Plagiarists*.
87. de Grazia, 'Sanctioning Voice', pp. 288–9.
88. See Loewenstein, *Ben Jonson*; and his *The Author's Due*.
89. See Hart, *Samuel Johnson*.
90. See Patterson, *Copyright*, p. 4.
91. *Ibid.*, p. 143.
92. *Donaldson* v. *Becket* 4 Burr 2408, 98 ER 257.
93. For a full account see Rose, *Authors and Owners*. See also Patterson, *Copyright*, chapter 8, and Saunders, *Authorship and Copyright*, chapter 3.
94. Young, *Conjectures on Original Composition*, p. 9. Italics and capitals in original.
95. See Wordsworth, *Prose Works*, vol. I, p. 126.
96. Wordsworth, 'Essay, Supplementary to the Preface', in *Prose Works*, vol. III, p. 80.

97. Jaszi and Woodmansee, 'The Ethical Reaches of Authorship', p. 947. On Dorothy's role, see Woodmansee, 'The Cultural Work of Copyright', pp. 65–96.
98. For full historical studies, see Woodmansee, 'The Cultural Work of Copyright'; Vanden Bossche, 'The Value of Literature'; and Eilenberg, 'Mortal Pages: Wordsworth and the Reform of Copyright'. On the personal criticism of Wordsworth by opponents, see Chandler, 'Dickens on Wordsworth'.
99. Woodmansee, 'The Cultural Work of Copyright', p. 67.
100. Rose, *Authors and Owners*, pp. 1–2.
101. Saunders, *Authorship and Copyright*, p. 151.
102. Patterson, *Copyright*, chapter 10, discusses the close relations between reporter and court.
103. McGill, 'The Matter of the Text', p. 24.
104. *Stowe v. Thomas* 23 F.Cas. 201 (1853).
105. *Burrow-Giles Lithographic Co. v. Sarony* 111 US 53 (1884).
106. *Bleistein v. Donaldson Lithographing Co.* 158 US 239 (1903).
107. *Alfred Bell & Co. v. Catalda Fine Arts* 191 F. 2d 99 (1951).
108. Jaszi, 'Toward a Theory of Copyright', p. 87.
109. I allude to Wordsworth's poem, 'The Solitary Reaper', available in many anthologies.
110. Spoo, 'Injuries, Remedies, Moral Rights'. This article is part of a special issue on Joyce and the law.
111. *Ibid.*, p. 342.
112. See the Canadian Internet Policy and Public Interest Clinic website, http://cippic.ca/en/projects-cases/icommons-canada/moral-rights.html (accessed 14 Sept. 2004). The internal quotation is from *Morang and Co. v. LeSueur* (1911), 45 S.C.R. 95.
113. Benjamin, 'The Work of Art in an Age of Mechanical Reproduction'.
114. Woodmansee and Jaszi, 'The Ethical Reaches of Authorship', p. 948.
115. *Ibid.*, p. 972.
116. See Robertson, *Justice Game*, p. 240.
117. See Harlow, *Barred*.
118. See Racial Hatred Act 1995 (Australia); Racial Vilification Amendment Act 1989 (NSW) especially ss. 20C, 20D; Race Relations Act 1965 s.6 (UK); Public Order Act 1986, especially s. 18.

3 RENAISSANCE HUMANISM AND CONTRACT

1. Bacon, *Advancement of Learning*, in *Works*, p. 288.
2. Shakespeare, *Hamlet*, II.ii.286–8.
3. Grafton and Jardine, *From Humanism to the Humanities*, p. xiii.
4. Parker, *Shakespeare from the Margins*, p. 18. For an informed account of Bacon's same-sex relations, see Alan Stewart, 'Bribery, Buggery and the Fall of Lord Chancellor Bacon', Kahn and Hutson (eds.), *Rhetoric and Law*, pp. 125–42.

5. Parker, *Shakespeare from the Margins*, p. 18.
6. Bacon, 'Letter to Lord Burghley', in *Works*, vol. XII, pp. 5–6.
7. Bacon, 'Of Heresies', in *Works*, vol. I, p. 219.
8. See Jardine, *Worldly Goods*.
9. Thorne, 'Tudor Social Transformation and Legal Change', in *Essays in Legal History*, p. 206.
10. Sheen and Hutson (eds.), *Literature, Politics and Law*, p. 3.
11. White, *Natural Law*, p. 74.
12. *Ibid.*, p. 73.
13. Finkelpearl, *John Marston*, p. 5.
14. *Ibid.*, p. 19.
15. This summary is drawn from *ibid.*, chapters 3 and 4.
16. See Axton (ed.), *Three Rastell Plays*.
17. Cunningham, *Imaginary Betrayals*, p. 25.
18. Hutson, *Usurer's Daughter*, p. 74.
19. Kahn and Hutson (eds.), *Rhetoric and Law*, is an excellent collection of recent studies in the field.
20. Wilson, *Arte*, p. 25.
21. Horace, 'On the Art of Poetry', p. 90.
22. Quoted by Derrick, 'Introduction', in Wilson, *Arte*, p. lxxxviii.
23. Wilson, *Arte*, pp. 203–4.
24. *Ibid*, pp. 315–16.
25. Parker, *Literary Fat Ladies*, p. 97.
26. Lewis, *English Literature in the Sixteenth Century*, p. 60.
27. Yeats, 'Anima Hominis', *Essays*, p. 492.
28. Heninger, *Sidney and Spenser*, p. 224.
29. Sidney, *Apology for Poetry*, p. 101.
30. Quoted by White, *Natural Law*, p. 72.
31. Goodrich, *Languages of Law*, p. 142.
32. The quoted phrase is from Cormack, 'Practicing Law and Literature', p. 81. For a full discussion of the legal poetics of order in the Inns, see Raffield, *Images and Cultures*.
33. See Bradbrook, *John Webster*, pp. 33–6; Finkelpearl, *John Marston*, chapter 4.
34. Cunningham, *Imaginary Betrayals*, p. 35.
35. Prest, *Inns of Court*, p. 159.
36. On Coke's writing, see Helgerson, *Forms of Nationhood*.
37. Donne, 'Satire 2', in Carey (ed.), *John Donne*, p. 23.
38. See generally Jeremy Maule, 'Donne and the Words of the Law', in Colclough, *Donne's Professional Lives*, pp. 19–36.
39. Prest, *Inns of Court*, p. 156.
40. Whitney, 'Last Wyll and Testament', in Stevenson and Davidson (eds.), *Early Modern Women Poets*, p. 59.
41. Baker, *Legal Profession*, p. 476.
42. See Ziolkowski, *Mirror of Justice*, pp. 167–8.
43. Quoted by Eden, *Poetic and Legal Fiction*, p. 42n.

44. *Ibid.*, pp. 41–2.
45. Quoted in *ibid.*, p. 42n.
46. I have drawn on the work of John Guy, *Thomas More*, pp. 130–7.
47. See Guy, 'Law, Equity and Conscience', p. 185 and throughout.
48. See Thorne, *Essays in English Legal History*, chapter 11.
49. Hutson, *Usurer's Daughter*, p. 146.
50. Cicero is quoted by Altman, *Tudor Play of Mind*, p. 390.
51. Habermann, 'Femininity as Challenge', in Sheen and Hutson (eds.), *Literature, Politics and Law*, p. 100.
52. *Ibid.*, p. 103.
53. Kahn and Hutson, 'Introduction', in Kahn and Hutson (eds.), *Rhetoric and Law*, pp. 4–5.
54. Hutson, *Usurer's Daughter*, chapter 5.
55. Shakespeare, *Comedy of Errors*, I.i.97.
56. Ward, *Shakespeare and the Legal Imagination*, p. 115.
57. Agnew, *Worlds Apart*, p. 41.
58. Goodrich, *Languages of Law*, pp. 153–4, notes that this etymology carries with it negative implications of contraction or narrowing.
59. Maine, *Ancient Law*, p. 170.
60. See MacFarlane, 'Some Contributions', p. 130.
61. Weber, *Max Weber on Law in Economy and Society*, p. 101.
62. Agnew, *Worlds Apart*, p. 9.
63. *Ibid.*, p. 53.
64. Quoted by Wilson, *Theatres of Intention*, p. 77.
65. Thorne, *Essays in English Legal History*, p. 208.
66. Sacks, 'Slade's Case in Perspective', in Kahn and Hutson (eds.), *Rhetoric and Law*, p. 44.
67. Wilson, *Theatres of Intention*, pp. 76–82.
68. Hutson, *Usurer's Daughter*, pp. 146–7.
69. Baker, 'English Law and the Renaissance', in Baker, *Legal Profession*, p. 468.
70. Sacks, 'Slade's Case in Perspective', in Kahn and Hutson (eds.), *Rhetoric and Law*, p. 45.
71. Selden, *Table-Talk*, p. 69.
72. Wilson, *Theatres of Intention*, p. 71.
73. Agnew, *Worlds Apart*, p. 54.
74. See 'Introduction', in Marlowe, *Doctor Faustus*, p. xliii.
75. Agnew, *Worlds Apart*, pp. 112–13.
76. *Ibid.*, pp. 11–12.
77. Wilson, *Theatres of Intention*, p. 112.
78. W. H. Auden, paraphrased by Phillips, *Shakespeare and the Lawyers*, p. 39.
79. Cavendish, *New Blazing World*, p. 42.
80. Lilley, 'Introduction', in Cavendish, *New Blazing World*, p. xx.
81. Kahn, 'Margaret Cavendish, and the Romance of Contract', in Hutson (ed.), *Feminism and Renaissance Studies*, pp. 286–316.
82. Cohen, 'Quality of Mercy', p. 43.

83. Shakespeare, *MV*, 1.3.141–4. Subsequent references appear parenthetically in the text.
84. Mesquita, 'Travesties of Justice', p. 122.
85. Ward, *Shakespeare and the Legal Imagination*, p. 121.
86. Quoted in *ibid*, p. 124.
87. Bacon, 'Of Usury', in *Works*, pp. 422, 424.
88. See White, *Natural Law*, pp. 159–61, and Ziolkowski, *Mirror of Justice*, chapter 9.
89. For Sokol and Sokol, *Shakespeare, Law and Marriage*, p. 8, the 'fantastical moot' is one of Shakespeare's characteristic modes of deploying legal ideas.
90. White, *Natural Law*, p. 167.
91. Bal, 'Legal Lust'.
92. For a similar conclusion, see Weisberg, *Poethics*, p. 100.
93. Ward, *Shakespeare and the Legal Imagination*, p. 128.

4 CRIME AND PUNISHMENT IN THE EIGHTEENTH CENTURY

1. Percy Bysshe Shelley, *A Defence of Poetry*, in *Shelley's Poetry and Prose*, p. 535.
2. Pope, *An Essay on Criticism*, lines 88–91, in *Poems of Alexander Pope*, p. 146.
3. Johnson, *Samuel Johnson*, p. 353.
4. Goldsmith, *An Enquiry into the Present State of Polite Learning in Europe*, ch. 10, *Selected Writings*, pp. 90–1.
5. Legal language is ubiquitous in critical writing of the period: see Meehan, 'Neo-Classical Criticism'.
6. Wertenbaker, *Our Country's Good*, p. 59.
7. See Hay, 'Property, Authority and the Criminal Law'.
8. Bentham, *Panopticon Writings*.
9. The quoted phrase is from Sharpe, *Crime in Early Modern England*, p. 145. On anti-lawyer satire, see Tucker, *Intruder into Eden*, chapter 5.
10. Pope, *The Rape of the Lock*, canto III, lines 21–2, in *Poems of Alexander Pope*, p. 227.
11. Montagu, *Essays and Poems and Simplicity, a Comedy*, p. 232. For general studies of the position of women in eighteenth-century law and society, see Jones (ed.), *Women and Literature in Britain 1700–1800*.
12. See McLynn, *Crime and Punishment*.
13. Thompson, *Whigs and Hunters*.
14. Swift, *Complete Poems*, p. 316.
15. See Borowitz, *Blood and Ink*, p. 419.
16. Gladfelder, *Criminality and Narrative*, p. 5.
17. For a full analysis of the genre, see Faller, *Turned to Account*.
18. These collections are both now available in electronic form: http://www.oldbaileyonline.org/.
19. See Faller, *Defoe and Crime*, chapter 1; see also Doody, 'The Law, the Page and the Body of the Woman', p. 133.

20. Doody, 'The Law, the Page and the Body of the Woman', p. 136.
21. For accessible editions of the biographies, see Holmes (ed.), *Defoe on Sheppard and Wild*.
22. This paragraph draws on the work of Davis, *Factual Fictions*, chapter 7. See also Gladfelder, *Criminality and Narative*; and Faller, *Defoe and Crime*.
23. See McLynn, *Crime and Punishment*, p. 127.
24. Gladfelder, *Criminality and Narrative*, pp. 98–100.
25. Defoe, *Moll Flanders*, p. 266. All subsequent references are to this edition and are incorporated parenthetically in the text.
26. Backscheider, *Moll Flanders*, pp. 48–53, argues that the novel propagandises for transportation.
27. 'Essay on the Life and Genius of Henry Fielding', quoted in Battestin, *Henry Fielding*, p. 273.
28. Welsh, *Strong Representations*, p. 58.
29. Empson, 'Tom Jones', p. 249.
30. Welsh, *Strong Representations*, chapter 2.
31. Shapiro, 'The Concept "Fact"'.
32. Fielding, *A Charge Delivered to the Grand Jury*, repr. in *Enquiry*, pp. 4, 24.
33. For a good account of the controversy, and tensions within Fielding's texts, see Gladfelder, 'Obscenity, Censorship and the Eighteenth-Century Novel'.
34. On the Blandy case, see Welsh, *Strong Representations*, pp. 18–31; Doody, 'The Law, the Page and the Body of the Woman'; and Heinzelman, 'Guilty in Law, Implausible in Fiction'.
35. Fielding, *Enquiry*, p. 75
36. King, *Crime, Justice and Discretion*, p. 353.
37. Fielding, *Tom Jones*, Book VIII, chapter 11.
38. Fielding, *Enquiry*, p. 166.
39. See *ibid.*, p. 164, and King, *Crime, Justice and Discretion*, p. 327f.
40. Gladfelder, *Criminality and Narrative*, p. 161.
41. Fielding's nostalgia for the feudal manor is discussed by Schmidgen, *Eighteenth-Century Fiction*.
42. *The Law-Suit* (1738), quoted in Lemmings, *Professors of the Law*, p. 1.
43. *Letters on the Study and Use of History* (Dublin, n.d. [1752]), quoted in Lemmings, *Professors of the Law*, p. 21.
44. Blackstone, 'The Lawyer's Farewell to his Muse'.
45. Jones, *Henry Fielding*, p. 80.
46. Sir William Jones, *An Essay on the Law of Bailments*, quoted by Meehan, 'Authorship and Imagination', p. 115.
47. Blackstone, *Commentaries*, vol. I, p. 35.
48. See Lobban, *Common Law and English Jurisprudence*, chapter 2.
49. For an appreciative study, see Forbes, 'Johnson, Blackstone and the Tradition of Natural Law'. For an ideological analysis, see Bell, *Literature and Crime*, pp. 6–12.
50. Meehan, 'Authorship and Imagination', p. 121.
51. Bell, *Literature and Crime*, pp. 6–12, traces these contradictions well.

52. Blackstone, *Commentaries*, vol. IV, p. 4.

53. Beccaria, *On Crimes and Punishments*; Blackstone, *Commentaries*, vol. IV, p. 3.

54. Wynne, *Eunomus*, p. 102. On the disappearance of this genre from legal writing, see Hibbitts, 'Making Sense of Metaphors', p. 262.

55. Wynne, *Eunomus*, p. 103.

56. Quoted by Curley, *Sir Robert Chambers*, p. 126.

57. Johnson, 'Preface', *Dictionary of the English Language*, in *Samuel Johnson*, p. 307.

58. See Crystal, *Cambridge Encyclopedia of the English Language*, pp. 77–8.

59. Johnson, 'Preface', *Dictionary of the English Language*; in *Samuel Johnson*, p. 310.

60. Rogers, *Samuel Johnson*, p. 67.

61. Boswell, *Life of Samuel Johnson*, vol. III. pp. 302–7.

62. Piozzi, *Anecdotes*, p. 58.

63. See e.g. McNair, *Dr Johnson and the Law*.

64. Johnson, *The Rambler* No. 114 (Saturday April 20, 1751) repr. *Samuel Johnson*, p. 214.

65. The new approach is highlighted in the title of Foucault's history, *Discipline and Punish*.

66. This and other quotations are drawn from the trial transcript reproduced in *A Constellation of Genius*, p. 14.

67. *Ibid.*, p. 16.

68. Boswell, *Life of Samuel Johnson*, vol. II, p. 97.

69. Gatrell, *Hanging Tree*, p. 294. My details of the case are drawn from Gatrell's study.

70. Chambers, *Course of Lectures on the English Law*, vol. I, p. 84.

71. *Ibid.*, p. 313.

72. Curley, 'Editor's Introduction', in *ibid.*, pp. 56, 58.

73. Richardson, *Clarissa*, p. 1019.

74. See Rubin, *Identity, Crime and Legal Responsibility*, pp. 71–6, and Zomchick, *Family and the Law*, pp. 92–101.

75. See entry in *Newgate Calendar*, available online: http://www.exclassics.com/newgate/ng441.htm (accessed 26 April 2005).

76. On Radcliffe's representation of prison, see Swan, *Fictions of Law*, pp. 193–204.

77. Foucault, *Discipline and Punish*, p. 14.

78. Fielding, *A Proposal for Making an Effectual Provision for the Poor* (1753), repr. in *Enquiry*, pp. 219–78.

79. Goldsmith, *Vicar of Wakefield*, p. 150.

80. See Bender, 'Prison Reform'.

81. Johnson, *The Idler*, No. 38 [Debtor's Prisons (2)], repr. *Samuel Johnson*, p. 289, quoted by Howard, *The State of the Prisons* (1777; repr. London: J. M. Dent, 1929), p. 10.

82. Böker, 'The Prison and the Penitentiary', p. 231.

83. See Bentham, *Panopticon Writings*, with Bozovic's careful introduction.

84. Foucault's *Discipline and Punish* brilliantly demonstrates the diffusion of the panopticon principle throughout modern society. For a study of Foucault's thesis in relation to reform of crime and punishment in England, see Hutchings, *Criminal Spectre.*
85. Byron, 'Sonnet on Chillon', in *Byron's Poems*, vol. I, p. 351.
86. See Fludernik, 'Carceral Topography'.
87. See Barrell, *Imagining the King's Death.*
88. Quoted in Böker, 'The Prison and the Penitentiary', p. 226.
89. Quoted in *ibid.*, p. 228.
90. See Hays, *Victim of Prejudice*, p. 117.
91. Gladfelder, *Criminality and Narrative*, p. 214.
92. Hazlitt, 'Illustrations of "The Times" Newspaper', p. 142.

5 THE WOMAN QUESTION IN VICTORIAN ENGLAND

1. For a concise account of positivist theory and its operation in legal and literary practice, see Petch, 'Walks of Life: Legal'.
2. See Brantlinger, *Spirit of Reform*, Kestner, *Protest and Reform*, and most recently, Krueger, 'Victorian Narrative Jurisprudence'.
3. Blackstone, *Commentaries*, vol. I, p. 430.
4. Cobbe, 'Criminals, Idiots, Women and Minors', p. 111.
5. Patmore, 'The Angel in the House', Canto IX, p. 52.
6. Korobkin, *Criminal Conversations*, p. 39.
7. Blackstone, *Commentaries*, vol. I, p. 433.
8. Warner, *Monuments and Maidens*, p. 126.
9. Maine, *Ancient Law*, p. 164.
10. Chase and Levenson, *Spectacle of Intimacy*, p. 13.
11. My account of Norton's marriage draws on Chedzoy, *Scandalous Woman.*
12. Chase and Levenson, *Spectacle of Intimacy*, pp. 43–5.
13. Norton, *Letter to the Queen*, p. 77.
14. Teresa De Lauretis, quoted by Michie, *Outside the Pale*, p. 4.
15. Norton, *Letter to the Queen*, p. 62.
16. Poovey, *Uneven Developments*, p. 65.
17. Norton, *English Laws for Women*, p. 141.
18. See my 'Transfigurations of Caroline Norton', for a fuller discussion of this image.
19. Smith, *Brief Summary*, p. 25.
20. Oliphant, 'The Laws Concerning Women', p. 306.
21. For excellent studies of gender and Victorian journalism see Onslow, *Women of the Press*, and Fraser, Green and Johnston, *Gender and the Victorian Periodical.*
22. Cornwallis, 'Capabilities and Disabilities of Women', p. 313.
23. 'A Petition for Women's Rights' (1856).
24. Cobbe, 'Criminals, Idiots, Women and Minors', pp. 112f.
25. Cobbe, 'Wife-Torture in England'. See Mitchell, *Frances Power Cobbe.*

26. Dickens, *Pickwick Papers*, p. 563. Chedzoy, *Scandalous Woman*, p. 13, establishes Dickens's source. Craig, *Promising Language*, pp. 111–13, compares the novel and the trial transcript.
27. Clarke, *Thackeray and Women*, p. 34.
28. Thackeray, *The Newcomes*, p. 734.
29. Pollock, *For My Grandson*, p. 79.
30. Meredith, *Diana of the Crossways*, p. 160.
31. See Schramm, *Testimony and Advocacy*, for a historical study of this convention.
32. My understanding of this novel owes much to Dolin, *Mistress of the House*, chapter 6.
33. Dickens, 'Doctors' Commons', in *Sketches by Boz*, p. 90.
34. Dickens, '"A Truly British Judge"', in *Dickens' Journalism: The Amusements of the People*, p. 127. For another example see 'Judicial Special Pleading', in *ibid.*, pp. 137–42.
35. Dickens, 'The Murdered Person', in *Gone Astray*, p. 400.
36. See Cornish and Clark, *Law and Society in England*, p. 384.
37. 'Divorce: sentence of Mr Justice W. H. Maule in R. v. Thomas Hall (1845)', *English Historical Documents*, vol. 12 (1), pp. 528–9.
38. See Stone, *Road to Divorce*, pp. 368–9 for a more highly evolved version.
39. Baird, 'Divorce and Matrimonial Causes', p. 410; Asche, 'Dickens and the Law', p. 85.
40. Dickens, *Hard Times*, p. 58.
41. Baird, 'Divorce and Matrimonial Causes', pioneered this reading.
42. See Julius, 'Dickens the Lawbreaker', p. 50.
43. Dickens, *Bleak House*, p. 22.
44. For a fuller discussion, see my *Fiction and the Law*, chapter 4.
45. James, 'Mary Elizabeth Braddon', p. 742.
46. *Ibid.*, p. 743.
47. For a fine discussion of the case and the novel, see Leckie, *Culture and Adultery*.
48. On Braddon's engagement with the law, see Tromp, *Private Rod*.
49. Brantlinger, 'What is "Sensational" about the "Sensation Novel"?' p. 34.
50. See O'Neill, *Wilkie Collins*, p. 158.
51. This plot was inspired in part by the Madeleine Smith trial: see Jacobson, 'Plain Faces'.

6 THE COMMON LAW AND THE ACHE OF MODERNISM

1. Arnold, 'Heinrich Heine' (1863), *Matthew Arnold's Essays*, p. 104.
2. Arnold, 'The Scholar-Gypsy', lines 143–6, in *Matthew Arnold: Selected Poems and Prose*, p. 112.
3. Berman, *All That Is Solid Melts into Air*, p. 15.
4. Hardy, *Tess of the D'Urbervilles*, p. 124.

5. Douzinas and Nead (eds.), *Law and the Image*, p. 1.
6. See Garber, 'Cinema Scopes', p. 124 (a full account of the case and its cultural impact).
7. See Holland, *Irish Peacock and Scarlet Marquis*, p. 106 (a complete transcript).
8. For cultural analyses of this trial, on which I have drawn, see Chamberlin, 'Oscar Wilde'; and two essays by Ed Cohen, 'Writing Gone Wilde', and 'Typing Wilde'.
9. See my *Fiction and the Law*, chapter 7.
10. Weisberg, *Failure of the Word* and *Poethics*, chapter 2. For a full study of Faulkner's lawyers, see Watson, *Forensic Fictions*.
11. See Grey, *Wallace Stevens Case*, and Crotty, *Law's Interior*, chapter 3.
12. Hine, *Confessions of an Un-Common Attorney*.
13. Jones, 'Pollock, Sir Frederick', p. 421.
14. *Ibid.*, p. 423.
15. *Ibid.*, p. 421.
16. See Sugarman, 'Legal Theory, the Common Law Mind and the Making of the Text-Book Tradition', p. 54.
17. Quoted in Cosgrove, *Our Lady the Common Law*, p. 139.
18. Pollock, *Genius of the Common Law*, p. 2.
19. For a study of how a modernist legal challenge to this gender order failed, see Williams's analysis of the *Viscountess Rhondda* case, *Empty Justice*, chapter 3.
20. Tennyson, 'Guinevere', lines 465–80, in *Poems of Tennyson*, vol. III, p. 542.
21. See Dworkin, *Law's Empire*, p. 239. For an excellent study of how this identity was constructed, see Ferguson, 'Holmes and the Judicial Figure'.
22. Holmes, Jr, *Common Law*, p. 5.
23. Novick, *Honorable Justice* is a comprehensive biography. See also Gibian, 'Opening and Closing the Conversation', p. 205.
24. Holmes, 'The Law', in Marke (ed.), *Holmes Reader*, p. 62.
25. Moddelmog, *Reconstituting Authority*, p. 8.
26. Holmes, 'The Law', in Marke (ed.), *Holmes Reader*, p. 63.
27. Eliot, '*Ulysses*, Order and Myth' (1923), p. 103.
28. Kaplan, 'Encounters with O. W. Holmes, Jr', p. 1840, quoted in Cosgrove, *Our Lady the Common Law*, pp. 125–6.
29. Holmes, 'The Path of the Law', in Marke (ed.), *Holmes Reader*, p. 43.
30. Grey, 'Holmes and Legal Pragmatism', p. 826. On Holmes's pragmatism and Social Darwinism, see also Duxbury, *Patterns of American Jurisprudence*, pp. 33–47.
31. See Gordon, "Introduction," *Legacy of Oliver Wendell Holmes*, p. 7.
32. Holmes, 'The Soldier's Faith', in Marke (ed.), *Holmes Reader*, p. 101.
33. Grey, 'Holmes and Legal Pragmatism', p. 858.
34. For a case study of a Holmes decision in which the litigants 'disappeared from sight', see Noonan, *Persons and Masks of the Law*, chapter 3.
35. Dimock, *Residues of Justice*, pp. 151–2.
36. *Ibid.*, p. 158.

37. Woolf, 'Hours in a Library' (1916), quoted in Reichman, '"New Forms for our New Sensations"'.
38. Sinclair, *The Jungle*, p. 159.
39. *Ibid.*, p. 160.
40. See Tavernier-Courbin, '*The Call of the Wild* and *The Jungle*', for a full discussion.
41. See Forché, *Against Forgetting*, and Gifford, *Poetry in a Divided World*.
42. Reznikoff, quoted by Davidson, 'On *Testimony*'.
43. Reznikoff, from *Testimony*, p. 435. The first stanzas of the sequence were published in 1934, but the complete work did not appear till 1968.
44. Green, *Living*.
45. Stead, 'Day of Wrath', in *Salzburg Tales*, pp. 329–31. For further discussion of this volume of short stories see the section on 'Modernist critiques of law', below.
46. Dark, *Waterway*. For the most recent historical study of the disaster, see Brew, *Greycliffe: Stolen Lives*.
47. Rosenberg, *Hidden Holmes*, p. 3.
48. For a good general summary of these developments see Goodman, *Shifting the Blame*, chapter 1. On the fellow-servant rule, see Thomas, *Cross-Examinations*, pp. 167–9. On the 'radius of pertinence' and causation, see Dimock, *Residues of Justice*, pp. 158–76.
49. See Rosenberg, *Hidden Holmes*, p. 4.
50. Cardozo, 'Law and Literature', p. 342.
51. *Hynes* v. *New York Central Railroad* 231 NY 229 (1921). The opinion is reprinted and discussed approvingly in Weisberg, *Poethics*, pp. 16–28.
52. *Palsgraf* v. *Long Island Railroad* 248 NY 339 (1928).
53. *MacPherson* v. *Buick* 217 NY 382 (1916), p. 391.
54. See *Donoghue* v. *Stevenson* [1932] AC 532, 580.
55. Lewis, *Lord Atkin*, p. 61.
56. *Ibid.*, p 63.
57. Quoted by Lewis, *ibid.*, p. 67.
58. The full story of the case, and its consequences for the law are explored in a memorial volume, Burns (ed.), *Donoghue* v. *Stevenson and the Modern Law of Negligence*.
59. Reichman, '"New Forms for our New Sensations"', p. 4, citing *Dulieu* v. *White* [1901] 2 KB 669.
60. See Fleming, *Law of Torts*, p. 159.
61. *Chester* v. *Waverley Corporation* (1939) 63 CLR. 12, 13 respectively.
62. See Pierce, *The Country of Lost Children* for a full study of this cultural myth. For analysis of Evatt's judgment, see Petch, 'Borderline Judgements', pp. 7–9; Meehan, 'The Good, the Bad and the Ugly', pp. 437–9.
63. Barfield, 'Poetic Diction and Legal Fiction', pp. 114–15.
64. See Bryan, 'Stories in Fiction and in Fact'.
65. Jesse, *A Pin to See the Peepshow*. The original case was included in the Notable British Trials series: Young, *Trial of Bywaters and Thompson*. See also Weis, *Criminal Justice: The Story of Edith Thompson*.

66. Joyce, *Ulysses*, p. 587.
67. See Valente, *James Joyce and the Problem of Justice*, p. 245.
68. Kelley, *Human Measure*, p. 281.
69. For important readings of this parable see Derrida, 'Before the Law', and Potter, 'Waiting at the Entrance to the Law'.
70. Kafka, 'The Problem of Our Laws', p. 437.
71. See Robinson, 'Law of the State in Kafka's *The Trial*'.
72. Steiner, 'Introduction', in Kafka, *The Trial*, p. v.
73. Kafka, *The Trial*, pp. 160–1.
74. 'A Twentieth-Century Decameron', unsigned review, *The Times* (30 January 1934), p. 9. Quoted by Harris, 'Christina Stead and her Critics', p. 263 n. 5. For a fine study of Hofmannsthal's significance as a symbol of liberal legality, and the revolt of younger writers against this tradition, see Schorske, *Fin-de-Siècle Vienna*.
75. Stead, *Salzburg Tales*, p. 312.
76. 'Justice', *OED* V, 640 (1961).
77. Douzinas and Nead (eds.), *Law and the Image*, p. 1.

7 LAW AND LITERATURE IN POST-COLONIAL
SOCIETY

1. Pue, 'Editorial', *Law, Social Justice and Global Development* (2003).
2. For a general introduction, see Ashcroft, Griffiths and Tiffin, *Empire Writes Back*.
3. Fitzpatrick and Darian-Smith, 'Laws of the Postcolonial', p. 4.
4. Soyinka, *Ibadan*, p. 362.
5. Mortimer, *Clinging to the Wreckage*, pp. 152–3. Mortimer acknowledges that his conception of the 'long road' to Ibadan is indebted to Soyinka's play, *The Road*. The compliment of influence is repaid by Soyinka in *Isara: A Voyage Round Essay*, which takes its subtitle from Mortimer's play, *A Voyage Round My Father*.
6. Arnold, 'The Function of Criticism at the Present Time', p. 198.
7. Chanock, *Law, Custom and Social Change*, p. 5.
8. See Moore's encyclopedia entry, 'Law in Africa: Colonial and Contemporary', for a succinct overview.
9. Widner, *Building the Rule of Law*, p. 31.
10. Benton, *Law and Colonial Cultures*, p. 11. For one example of such a jurisdictional conflict see Manji, 'Law, Literature and the Politics of Culture in Kenya'.
11. Macaulay, Speech to the House of Commons, 'Government of India', 10 July 1833, in *Life and Works*, vol. VIII, p. 142.
12. Mortimer, *Second Rumpole Omnibus*, p. 243. The story originally appeared in *Rumpole and the Golden Thread*.
13. Booth, *Writers and Politics in Nigeria*, p. 23, quoting Basil Davidson, *Can Africa Survive?*, p. 60.

14. [1935] A. C. 481 *per* Viscount Sankey L. C.
15. Williams, *Proof of Guilt*, pp. 130–1.
16. Still and Worton, 'Introduction', in *Intertextuality*, pp. 1–2.
17. *Ibid.*, p. 9.
18. See Said, *Orientalism*.
19. Flecker, *Collected Poems*, pp. 147–8.
20. This process is described as a 'manichean allegory' by JanMohamed, *Manichean Aesthetics*, p. 4.
21. Wallace, *Sanders of the River*, p. 273.
22. Christopher L. Miller, *Blank Darkness*, p. 20.
23. Wallace, *Sanders of the River*, p. 224.
24. Boire, '*Ratione Officii*', p. 199.
25. Naipaul, *Mimic Men*, p. 175.
26. Fanon, *Wretched of the Earth*, p. 311.
27. Bhabha, *Location of Cultures*, chapter 4.
28. Oputa, *Conduct at the Bar*, p. 1.
29. Achebe, *Things Fall Apart*.
30. For another post-colonial study of Achebe's fictional representation of law, see Manji, '"Like a Mask Dancing"', pp. 626–42. See also her 'Law, Literature and the Politics of Culture in Kenya'.
31. Oputa, *Conduct at the Bar*, p. 17. (Bold type in original text.)
32. Achebe, *Man of the People*, p. 82.
33. Soyinka, *The Interpreters*, p. 142.
34. See Jones, *Writings of Wole Soyinka*, pp. xiii–xiv.
35. Soyinka, *The Man Died*, p. 21.
36. See Gibbs, '"Eshu Confuser of Men"', pp. 119–30.
37. Soyinka, *Ibadan*, p. 379.
38. Soyinka, *Open Sore of a Continent*, p. 134.
39. Soyinka, *The Man Died*, p. 95.
40. Gandhi, *Postcolonial Theory*, p. 121.

8 RACE AND REPRESENTATION IN CONTEMPORARY AMERICA

1. Thomas, *Cross-Examinations*, p. 5.
2. See Weisberg, *Vichy Law*; and Crenshaw et al. (eds.), *Critical Race Theory*.
3. 163 US 537 (1896).
4. See Ackerman, *We the People*, vol. I: *Foundations*, p. 131.
5. The full story of the case is told in Kluger, *Simple Justice*.
6. Greenhouse, 'A Federal Life'.
7. 349 US 294 (1955).
8. Brooks, *Selected Poems*, p. 87.
9. *Ibid.*, p. 75.
10. 352 US 903 (1956).

11. See, respectively, 358 US 54 (1958); 373 US 526 (1963); 373 US 61 (1963); and 403 US 217 (1971).
12. For an interesting law-and-literature reading of King's text, see Tiefenbrun, 'Semiotics'.
13. Lee, *To Kill a Mockingbird*, p. 226.
14. *Loving* v. *Virginia* 388 US 1 (1967).
15. There is an extensive secondary literature on this novel in American law reviews. For a full and illuminating exploration, see Atkinson, 'Liberating Lawyers'.
16. Hughes, *Montage of a Dream Deferred*.
17. *Hansberry* v. *Lee* 311 US 32 (1940).
18. Quoted in Gates and Mackay (eds.), *Norton Anthology of African American Literature*, p. 1726.
19. Baldwin, 'A Stranger in the Village', in Gates and Mackay (eds.), *Norton Anthology of African American Literature*, p. 1679.
20. Baldwin, *The Fire Next Time*, p. 28.
21. *Ibid.*, p. 75. Subsequent research has confirmed this insight. See Delgado and Stefancic, *Critical Race Theory*, pp. 18–20, citing the work of Derrick Bell and Mary Dudziak.
22. Malcolm X, 'Speech to African Summit Conference, Cairo, Egypt', in Hill (ed.), *Call and Response*, p. 1419.
23. Malcolm X, 'The Ballot or the Bullet', in Lauter (ed.), *Heath Anthology of American Literature*, pp. 2542–55.
24. Knight, 'Hard Rock Returns to Prison from the Hospital for the Criminally Insane', in Gates and Mackay (eds.), *Norton Anthology of African American Literature*, p. 1868.
25. Jordan, 'Poem about My Rights', in Gates and Mackay (ed.), *Norton Anthology of African American Literature*, p. 2233.
26. Walker, *In Search of our Mothers' Gardens*.
27. Walker, 'Advancing Luna – and Ida B. Wells', pp. 85–104.
28. Lee, 'Ethnic Renaissance', pp. 140–1.
29. Quoted by Goellnicht, 'Tang Ao in America', p. 197.
30. Hong Kingston, *China Men*, p. 153.
31. *Ibid.*, p. 152.
32. Goellnicht, 'Tang Ao in America', p. 197.
33. On Kingston's use of the Chinese classics, see Ning Yu, 'A Strategy against Marginalization'; on *Robinson Crusoe* see Chiu, 'Being Human in the Wor(l)d'.
34. Thomas, '*China Men*, *United States* v. *Wong Kim Ark* and the Question of Citizenship'.
35. For a discussion of the context see Walker, 'California's Collision of Race and Class', p. 294. See also Chang, 'Toward an Asian American Scholarship', for a good study of the Chinese American legal experience.
36. Valdez, *Zoot Suit and other Plays*, p. 25.
37. See Huerta, 'Introduction', in Valdez, *Zoot Suit*, p. 14.

38. The Public Broadcasting Service website has a highly informative section on the case: http://www.pbs.org/wgbh/amex/zoot/.
39. Huerta, 'Introduction', in Valdez, *Zoot Suit*, pp. 14–15.
40. For a multicultural study of recent trends in law and immigration in California, see Hing, *To Be an American*.
41. *Regents* v. *Bakke* 438 US 265 (1978).
42. Bourdieu, 'The Force of Law', p. 819.
43. *Ibid.*, p. 830.
44. *Regents* v. *Bakke* 438 US 265, 298.
45. *Ibid.*, p. 400.
46. Post, 'Introduction', in Post and Rogin (eds.), *Race and Representation*, p. 17.
47. Sunstein, 'Casuistry', p. 316.
48. Delivered 23 June 2003. 539 US 244 (2003).
49. Soifer, *Law and the Company We Keep*, p. 127.
50. See note 48 above.
51. For an excellent anthology see Delgado (ed.), *Critical Race Theory*.
52. See Matsuda, *Words That Wound*.
53. bell hooks, *Killing Rage*, p. 267.
54. See Cook, *The Least of These*.
55. Kella, *Beloved Communities*, p. 22.
56. *Ibid.*, p. 11.
57. Gaines, *A Lesson before Dying*.
58. The importance of community in the novel is argued by Doyle, *Voices from the Quarters*, p. 206.
59. See Morrison, *Beloved*, p. 3; and 'The Opening Sentences of *Beloved*', pp. 91–2.
60. Quoted by Henderson, 'Toni Morrison's *Beloved*', p. 63.
61. Suggs, *Whispered Consolations*, p. 290.
62. Henderson, 'Toni Morrison's *Beloved*', pp. 62, 79.
63. McPherson, 'An Act of Prostitution', from his *Hue and Cry* (1969), repr. in *Trial and Error*, pp. 388–401. For a study of law in this short story, see Beavers, *Wrestling Angels into Song*, chapter 6.
64. McPherson, *Region Not Home*, p. 186.
65. *Ibid.*, pp. 289–90.
66. *Ibid.*, p. 290.
67. *Ibid.*, p. 23.
68. Tourgee, quoted by McPherson, *ibid.*, p. 24.
69. McPherson, *Region Not Home*, p. 25.
70. Cassells, *Soul Make a Path Through Shouting*.

CONCLUSION

1. Oakeshott, *Voice of Poetry in the Conversation of Mankind*.
2. Ricoeur, *Time and Narrative*, vol. I, p. 75.
3. Wynne, *Eunomus*, p. 103.
4. Thomas, 'Reflections on the Law and Literature Revival'.

5. See Resnik, 'On the Margins'.
6. Marvell, *Complete English Poems*, pp. 59–60.
7. Norton, *Letter to the Queen*, p. 7.
8. Wynne, *Eunomus*, p. 120.
9. Bourdieu, 'The Force of Law', p. 839.
10. Bal, 'Legal Lust', p. 13.
11. Barfield, *History in Language*, pp. 55–8.
12. Bakhtin, *Dialogic Imagination*, p. 12.
13. Bal, 'Legal Lust', p. 5. Italics in original.
14. Jane Baron stresses the importance in interdisciplinary scholarship of examining 'how we categorize knowledge and why' in 'Law, Literature and the Problems of Interdisciplinarity'. For a critical discussion of how law and literature have attributed various qualities to each other in the unfolding interdisciplinary encounter, see Peters, 'Law, Literature and the Vanishing Real'.
15. Thompson, *Interdisciplinarity*, pp. 195–6.
16. Boland, 'The Laws of Love', in *Collected Poems*, pp. 34–5.
17. Cf. Kahn, *Law and Love*.
18. Robinson, 'The Inaugural Speech', p. 255, quoting Boland, 'The Singers'.

Bibliography

Abrams v. *US* 250 US 616 (1919).

Achebe, Chinua. *Things Fall Apart*. London: Heinemann, 1958.

A Man of the People. London: Heinemann, 1966.

Ackerman, Bruce. *We the People*. Vol. I: *Foundations*. Cambridge: Belknap Press of Harvard University Press, 1991.

Agnew, Jean-Christophe. *Worlds Apart: The Market and the Theatre in Anglo-American Thought, 1550–1750*. Cambridge: Cambridge University Press, 1986.

Alfred Bell & Co. v. *Catalda Fine Arts* 191 F. 2d 99 (1951).

Altman, Joel. *The Tudor Play of Mind*. Berkeley: University of California Press, 1978.

Arendt, Hannah. *The Human Condition*. Chicago: University of Chicago Press, 1958.

Aristodemou, Maria. *Law and Literature: Journeys from Her to Eternity*. Oxford: Oxford University Press, 2000.

Aristotle. *The Art of Rhetoric*. Trans. Hugh Lawson-Tancred. London: Penguin, 1991.

Armstrong, Pauline. *Frank Hardy and the Making of* Power Without Glory. Carlton South: Melbourne University Press, 2000.

Arnold, Matthew. *Matthew Arnold's Essays*. Ed. G. K. Chesterton. London: Dent, 1906.

'The Function of Criticism at the Present Time'. In *Matthew Arnold: Selected Poems and Prose*, pp. 189–201.

Matthew Arnold: Selected Poems and Prose. Ed. Miriam Allott. London: Dent, 1978.

Asche, K. J. A. 'Dickens and the Law'. In Turner and Williams (eds.), *The Happy Couple*, pp. 81–93.

Ashcroft, Bill, Gareth Griffiths and Helen Tiffin. *The Empire Writes Back: Theory and Practice in Post-Colonial Literatures*. 2nd edn. London: Routledge, 2002.

Atkinson, Rob. 'Liberating Lawyers: Divergent Parallels in *Intruder in the Dust* and *To Kill a Mockingbird*'. *Duke Law Journal* 49 (1999), 601–748.

Auden, W. H. *The English Auden*. Ed. Edward Mendelson. New York: Random House, 1977.

Axton, Richard (ed.). *Three Rastell Plays*. Cambridge: D. S. Brewer, 1979.

Backscheider, Paula R. Moll Flanders: *The Making of a Criminal Mind*. Boston: Twayne Publishers, 1990.

Bacon, Francis. *The Works of Francis Bacon*. Ed. James Spedding, Robert Leslie Ellis and Douglas Denon Heath. 14 vols. London: Longman, 1858–74.

The Major Works. Ed. Brian Vickers. Oxford: Oxford University Press, 1996.

Baird, John D. 'Divorce and Matrimonial Causes: An Aspect of *Hard Times*'. *Victorian Studies* 20 (1977), 401–12.

Baker, J. H. *The Legal Profession and the Common Law: Historical Essays*. London: Hambledon Press, 1986.

Bakhtin, M. M. *The Dialogic Imagination: Four Essays*. Trans. Caryl Emerson and Michael Holquist. Austin: University of Texas Press, 1981.

Bal, Mieke. 'Legal Lust: Literary Litigations'. *Australian Feminist Law Journal* 15 (2001), 1–22.

Baldwin, James. *The Fire Next Time*. Harmondsworth: Penguin, 1963.

Balkin, J. M. 'A Night in the Topics: The Reason of Legal Rhetoric and the Rhetoric of Legal Reason'. In Brooks and Gewirtz (eds.), *Law's Stories*, pp. 211–24.

Barak, B. *Bankshall Court: Some Memorable Trials*. Calcutta: B. Mitra, 1977.

Barendt, Eric. 'Defamation and Fiction'. In Freeman and Lewis (eds.), *Law and Literature*, pp. 481–98.

Barfield, Owen. 'Poetic Diction and Legal Fiction'. In *Essays Presented to Charles Williams*. London: Oxford University Press, 1947, pp. 106–27.

History in Language. London: Faber and Faber, 1954.

Baron, Jane B. 'Law, Literature and the Problems of Interdisciplinarity'. *Yale Law Journal* 108 (1998), 1059–85.

Barrell, John. *Imagining the King's Death: Figurative Treason, Fantasies of Regicide, 1793–1796*. Oxford: Oxford University Press, 2000.

Barthes, Roland. *Mythologies*. Trans. Annette Lavers. 1957; repr. St Albans: Paladin, 1973.

Battestin, Martin C. *Henry Fielding: A Life*. London: Routledge, 1989.

Beavers, Herman. *Wrestling Angels into Song: The Fictions of Ernest J. Gaines and James Alan McPherson*. Philadelphia: University of Pennsylvania Press, 1995.

Beccaria, Cesare. *On Crimes and Punishments*. Ed. Richard Bellamy. Cambridge: Cambridge University Press, 1995.

Beer, Gillian. *Open Fields: Science in Cultural Encounter*. Oxford: Oxford University Press, 1996.

Bell, Ian A. *Literature and Crime in Augustan England*. London: Routledge, 1991.

Bell, Susan Groag and Karen M. Offen (eds.). *Women, the Family and Freedom*. 2 vols. Stanford: Stanford University Press, 1983.

Bender, John. 'Prison Reform and the Sentence of Narration in *The Vicar of Wakefield*'. In *The New Eighteenth Century*. Ed. Felicity Nussbaum and Laura Brown. New York: Methuen, 1987, pp. 168–88.

Benjamin, Walter. 'The Work of Art in an Age of Mechanical Reproduction'. In *Illuminations*. Trans. Harry Zohn. London: Collins Fontana, 1973, pp. 211–44.

Bentham, Jeremy. *The Panopticon Writings*. Ed. Miran Bozovic. London: Verso, 1995.

Benton, Lauren. *Law and Colonial Cultures: Legal Regimes in World History 1400–1900*. Cambridge: Cambridge University Press, 2002.

Berman, Marshall. *All That Is Solid Melts into Air: The Experience of Modernity*. London: Verso, 1983.

Bhabha, Homi. *The Location of Cultures*. London: Routledge, 1994.

Blackstone, Sir William. 'The Lawyer's Farewell to his Muse'. In *Specimens with Memoirs of the Lesser-Known British Poets*. Ed. George Gilfillan, 1860. Project Gutenberg ebook. http://www2.cddc.vt.edu./gutenberg/etext06/71bp310.txt.

Commentaries on the Laws of England. 4 vols. Chicago: University of Chicago Press, 1979.

Bleistein v. *Donaldson Lithographing Co.* 158 US 239 (1903).

Blom-Cooper, Louis (ed.). *The Law as Literature: An Anthology of Great Writing in and about the Law*. London: Bodley Head, 1961.

Boire, Gary. '*Ratione Officii*: Representing Law in Postcolonial Literatures'. *Mosaic* 27/4 (1994), 199–214.

Böker, Uwe. 'The Prison and the Penitentiary as Sites of Public Counter-Discourse'. In *Sites of Discourse: Public and Private Spheres – Legal Culture*. Ed. Uwe Böker and Julie A. Hibbard. Amsterdam: Rodopi, 2002, pp. 211–47.

Boland, Eavan. *Collected Poems*. Manchester: Carcanet Press, 1995.

Booth, James. *Writers and Politics in Nigeria*. New York: Africana Publishing, 1981.

Booth, Wayne. *The Rhetoric of Fiction*. Chicago: University of Chicago Press, 1961.

Borowitz, Albert. *Blood and Ink: An International Guide to Fact-Based Crime Literature*. Kent: Kent State University Press, 2002.

Boswell, James. *The Life of Samuel Johnson*, 6 vols. 1791; London: Oxford University Press, 1887.

Bourdieu, Pierre. 'The Force of Law: Towards a Sociology of the Juridical Field'. *Hastings Law Review* 38 (1987), 814–53.

'The Intellectual Field: A World Apart'. *In Other Words: Essays on a Reflexive Sociology*. Trans. Matthew Adamson. Cambridge: Polity Press, 1990, pp. 140–9.

The Field of Cultural Production: Essays on Art and Literature. Ed. Randal Johnson. Cambridge: Polity Press, 1993.

Bowman v. *Secular Society* [1917] A.C. 406.

Bradbrook, M. C. *John Webster*. London: Weidenfeld and Nicolson, 1980.

Brantlinger, Patrick. *The Spirit of Reform*. Cambridge: Harvard University Press, 1977.

'What is "Sensational" about the "Sensation Novel"?' In *Wilkie Collins*. Ed. Lyn Pykett. Basingstoke: Macmillan, 1998, pp. 30–57.

Brew, Steve. *Greycliffe: Stolen Lives*. Sydney: Navarine Publishers, 2003.

Brooks, Gwendolyn. *Selected Poems*. New York: Harper and Row, 1963.

Brooks, Peter. 'Narrative and Rhetoric in the Law'. In Brooks and Gewirtz (eds.). *Law's Stories*, pp. 14–21.

Troubling Confessions. Chicago: University of Chicago Press, 2000.

Brooks, Peter and Paul Gewirtz (eds.). *Law's Stories*. New Haven: Yale University Press, 1996.

Browder v. *Gayle* 352 US 903 (1956).

Brown v. *Board of Education* (No. 2) 349 US 294 (1955).

Brown v. *Board of Education* 347 US 483 (1954).

Bruns, Gerald L. 'Law and Language: A Hermeneutics of the Legal Text'. In *Legal Hermeneutics*. Ed. Gregory Leyh. Berkeley: University of California Press, 1992, pp. 23–40.

Bryan, Patricia L. 'Stories in Fiction and in Fact: Susan Glaspell's "A Jury of Her Peers" and the 1902 Murder Trial of Margaret Hossack'. *Stanford Law Review* 49 (1997), 1293–363.

Buck v. *Bell* 274 US 200 (1927).

Burke, Kenneth. *A Rhetoric of Motives*. 1950; Berkeley: University of California Press, 1969.

Burns, Peter T. (ed.). *Donoghue* v. *Stevenson and the Modern Law of Negligence*. Vancouver: Continuing Legal Education Society of British Columbia, 1990.

Burrow-Giles Lithographic Co. v. *Sarony* 111 US 53 (1884).

Byron, George Gordon, Lord. *Byron's Poems*. Ed. V. de Sola Pinto. London: Everyman's Library, 1968.

Canadian Internet Policy and Public Interest Clinic website: http://cippic.ca/en/projects-cases/icommons-canada/moral-rights.html.

Cardozo, Benjamin N. 'Law and Literature'. In *Selected Writings*. Ed. Margaret Hall. New York: Fallon Publications, 1947, pp. 339–56.

Carter-Ruck, Peter, Richard Walker and Harvey N. A. Starte. *Carter-Ruck on Libel and Slander*, 4th edn. London: Butterworths, 1992.

Cassells, Cyrus. *Soul Make a Path through Shouting*. Port Townsend: Copper Canyon Press, 1994.

Cavendish, Margaret. *New Blazing World and Other Writings*. Ed. Kate Lilley. New York: New York University Press, 1992.

Chamberlin, J. E. 'Oscar Wilde'. In *Rough Justice: Essays on Crime in Literature*. Ed. Martin L. Friedland. Toronto: University of Toronto Press, 1991, pp. 141–56.

Chambers, Sir Robert. *A Course of Lectures on the English Law, 1767–1773*. Ed. Thomas M. Curley. Madison: University of Wisconsin Press, 1986.

Chandler, David. 'Dickens on Wordsworth: *Nicholas Nickleby* and the Copyright Question'. *English Language Notes* 41 (2004), 62–9.

Chang, Robert. 'Toward an Asian American Scholarship: Critical Race Theory, Post-Structuralism and Narrative Space'. *California Law Review* 81 (1993), 1241–323.

Chanock, Martin. *Law, Custom and Social Change*. London: Oxford University Press, 1985.

Chase, Karen and Michael Levenson. *The Spectacle of Intimacy: A Public Life for the Victorian Family*. Princeton: Princeton University Press, 2000.

Chedzoy, Alan. *A Scandalous Woman: The Story of Caroline Norton*. London: Allison and Busby, 1992.

Chester v. *Waverley Corporation* (1939) 63 CLR. 1.

Chester, Gail and Julienne Dickey (eds.). *Feminism and Censorship: The Current Debate*. Bridport: Prism Press, 1988.

Chiu, Monica. 'Being Human in the Wor(l)d: Chinese Men and Maxine Hong Kingston's Reworking of *Robinson Crusoe*'. *Journal of American Studies* 34 (2000), 187–206.

Clarke, Micael M. *Thackeray and Women*. DeKalb: Northern Illinois University Press, 1995.

Cobbe, Frances Power. 'Criminals, Idiots, Women and Minors: Is the Classification Sound?' *Fraser's Magazine* (1868). In Hamilton (ed.), *Criminals, Idiots, Women and Minors*, pp. 108–32.

'Wife-Torture in England', *Contemporary Review* (1878). In Hamilton (ed.), *Criminals, Idiots, Women and Minors*, pp. 133–70.

Cohen, Ed. 'Writing Gone Wilde: Homoerotic Desire in the Closet of Representation'. *Publications of the Modern Language Association of America* 102 (1987), 801–13.

Cohen, Ed. 'Typing Wilde: Construing "the Desire to Appear to be a Person Inclined to the Commission of the Gravest of All Offences"'. *Yale Journal of Law and the Humanities* 5 (1993), 1–49.

Cohen, Stephen A. ' "The Quality of Mercy": Law, Equity and Ideology in *The Merchant of Venice*'. *Mosaic* 27/4 (1994), 35–54.

Colclough, David (ed.). *John Donne's Professional Lives*. Cambridge: D. S. Brewer, 2003.

Coleman, Peter. *Obscenity, Blasphemy and Sedition: 100 Years of Censorship in Australia*. Sydney: Angus and Robertson, 1974.

Conklin, William E. *The Phenomenology of Modern Legal Discourse*. Portsmouth: Ashgate, 1998.

A Constellation of Genius. Intro. H. W. L. New Haven: Yale University Press / Grolier Club, 1958.

Cook, Anthony E. *The Least of These: Race, Law and Religion in American Culture*. New York: Routledge, 1997.

Cormack, Bradin. 'Practicing Law and Literature in Early Modern England'. *Modern Philology* 101 (2003), 79–91.

Cornish, W. R. and G. de N. Clark. *Law and Society in England 1750–1950*. London: Sweet and Maxwell, 1989.

Cornwallis, Caroline Frances. 'Capabilities and Disabilities of Women'. *Westminster Review* 67 (1857). In Bell and Offen (eds.), *Women, the Family and Freedom*. Vol. I, pp. 310–13.

Cosgrove, Richard A. *Our Lady the Common Law: An Anglo-American Legal Community 1870–1930*. New York: New York University Press, 1987.

Costello v. *Random House Australia* [1999] ACTSC 13.

Cover, Robert M. 'Foreword: *Nomos* and Narrative'. *Harvard Law Review* 97 (1983–4), 4–68.

'Violence and the Word'. *Yale Law Journal* 95 (1986), 1601–29.

Narrative, Violence and the Law. Ed. Martha Minow, Michael Ryan and Austin Sarat. Ann Arbor: University of Michigan Press, 1993.

Craig, Alec. *The Banned Books of England and Other Countries*. London: Allen and Unwin, 1962.

Craig, Randall. *Promising Language: Betrothal in Victorian Law and Fiction*. Albany: State University of New York Press, 2000.

Cramer, Jeffrey S. *Robert Frost among His Poems: A Literary Companion to the Poet's Own Biographical Contexts and Associations*. Jefferson: McFarland and Co, 1996.

Crane, R. S. (ed.). *Critics and Criticism*. Chicago: University of Chicago Press, 1952.

Crenshaw, Kimberlé et al. (eds.). *Critical Race Theory: The Key Writings that Formed the Movement*. New York: New Press, 1995.

Crotty, Kevin. *Law's Interior: Legal and Literary Constructions of the Self*. Ithaca: Cornell University Press, 2001.

Crystal, David. *The Cambridge Encyclopedia of the English Language*. Cambridge: Cambridge University Press, 1995.

Culhane, Dara. *The Pleasure of the Crown: Anthropology, Law and First Nations*. Burnaby: Talon Books, 1998.

Culler, Jonathan. *Literary Theory: A Very Short Introduction*. Oxford: Oxford University Press, 1997.

Cunningham, Karen. *Imaginary Betrayals: Subjectivity and the Discourses of Treason in Early Modern England*. Philadelphia: University of Pennsylvania Press, 2002.

Curley, Thomas M. *Sir Robert Chambers: Law, Literature and Empire in the Age of Johnson*. Madison: University of Wisconsin Press, 1998.

Dark, Eleanor. *Waterway*. 1938; repr. Sydney: Collins/Angus and Robertson, 1990.

Davidson, Basil. *Can Africa Survive?* Boston: Little, Brown and Co., 1974.

Davidson, Michael. 'On *Testimony*'. http://www.english.uiuc.edu/maps/poets/ m_r/reznikoff/davidson.htm.

Davis, Lennard J. *Factual Fictions: The Origins of the English Novel*. New York: Columbia University Press, 1983.

de Grazia, Edward. *Girls Lean Back Everywhere: The Law of Obscenity and the Assault on Genius*. New York: Random House, 1992.

de Grazia, Margreta. 'Sanctioning Voice: Marks, the Abolition of Torture and the Fifth Amendment'. In Jaszi and Woodmansee (eds.), *Construction of Authorship*, pp. 281–302.

Defoe, Daniel. *An Essay on the Regulation of the Press*. London, 1704. http:// darkwing.uoregon.edu/~rbear/defoe2.html.

Moll Flanders. Ed. David Blewett. London: Penguin, 1989.

Delgado, Richard. 'Storytelling for Oppositionists and Others: A Plea for Narrative'. *Michigan Law Review* 87 (1989), 2411–41.

(ed.). *Critical Race Theory: The Cutting Edge*. Philadelphia: Temple University Press, 1995.

Delgado, Richard and Jean Stefancic. *Critical Race Theory: An Introduction*. New York: New York University Press, 2001.

Derrida, Jacques. 'Before the Law'. In *Acts of Literature*. Ed. Derek Attridge. London: Routledge, 1992, pp. 181–220.

Devlin, Patrick. *The Enforcement of Morals*. London: Oxford University Press, 1965.

Easing the Passing. London: Bodley Head, 1985.

Taken at the Flood. East Harling: Taverner, 1996.

Diamond, A. S. *Primitive Law: Past and Present*. London: Methuen, 1971.

Dickens, Charles. *Hard Times*. Ed. George H. Ford and Sylvère Monod. New York: Norton, 1967.

The Pickwick Papers. Ed. Robert L. Patten. 1836–7; London: Penguin, 1972.

Bleak House. Ed. George H. Ford and Sylvère Monod. New York: Norton, 1977.

Dickens' Journalism: Sketches by Boz and other Early Papers. Ed. Michael Slater. London: Dent, 1994.

Dickens' Journalism: The Amusements of the People and other Papers. Ed. Michael Slater. London: Dent, 1996.

'Gone Astray' and Other Papers from Household Words. Ed. Michael Slater. London: Dent, 1998.

Dimock, Wai Chee. *Residues of Justice: Literature, Law, Philosophy*. Berkeley: University of California Press, 1996.

'Divorce: Sentence of Mr Justice W. H. Maule in R. v. Thomas Hall (1845)'. Repr. *English Historical Documents*. Vol. 12 (1). Ed. G. M. Young and W. D. Hancock. London: Eyre and Spottiswoode, 1953, pp. 528–9.

Dolin, Kieran. *Fiction and the Law: Legal Discourse in Victorian and Modernist Literature*. Cambridge: Cambridge University Press, 1999.

'The Case of Doctor John Bodkin Adams: A "Notable" Trial and its Narratives'. *REAL: Yearbook of Research in English and American Literature* 18 (2002), 145–66.

'The Transfigurations of Caroline Norton'. *Victorian Literature and Culture* 30 (2002), 503–27.

Dolin, Tim. *Mistress of the House: Women of Property in the Victorian Novel*. Aldershot: Ashgate, 1997.

Donaldson v. *Becket* (1774) 4 Burr 2408, 98 ER 257.

Donne, John. *John Donne: The Oxford Authors*. Ed. John Carey. Oxford: Oxford University Press, 1996.

Donoghue v. *Stevenson* [1932] A.C. 532.

Doody, Margaret Anne. 'The Law, the Page and the Body of the Woman: Murder and Murderesses in the Age of Johnson'. *The Age of Johnson* 1 (1987), 127–60.

Douzinas, Costas and Lynda Nead (eds.). *Law and the Image: The Authority of Art and the Aesthetics of Law*. Chicago: University of Chicago Press, 1999.

Douzinas, Costas and Ronnie Warrington. *Postmodern Jurisprudence: The Law of Text in the Texts of Law*. London: Routledge, 1991.

Justice Miscarried: Ethics and Aesthetics in Law. New York: Columbia University Press, 1997.

Dow Jones v. *Gutnick* [2002] HCA 56.

Downs, Donald Alexander. *The New Politics of Pornography*. Chicago: University of Chicago Press, 1989.

Doyle, Mary Ellen. *Voices from the Quarters: The Fiction of Ernest J. Gaines*. Baton Rouge: Louisiana State University Press, 2002.

Duncan, Martha Grace. *Romantic Criminals, Beloved Prisons*. New York: New York University Press, 1996.

Duxbury, Neil. *Patterns of American Jurisprudence*. Oxford: Clarendon Press, 1995.

Dworkin, Ronald. *Law's Empire*. London: Fontana, 1986.

Eagleton, Terry. *Literary Theory: An Introduction*. Oxford: Blackwell, 1983.

Easton, Susan M. *The Problem of Pornography: Regulation and the Right to Free Speech*. London: Routledge, 1994.

Eden, Kathy. *Poetic and Legal Fiction in the Aristotelian Tradition*. Princeton: Princeton University Press, 1986.

Eilenberg, Susan. 'Mortal Pages: Wordsworth and the Reform of Copyright'. *Journal of English Literary History* 56 (1985), 351–74.

Eliot, T. S. '*Ulysses*, Order and Myth' (1923). In *A Modernist Reader*. Ed. Peter Faulkner. London: Batsford, 1986, pp. 100–4.

Ellmann, Richard. *Eminent Domain: Yeats Among Wilde, Joyce, Pound, Eliot and Auden*. New York: Oxford University Press, 1967.

Elwyn-Jones, Lord. 'Law as Literature'. *Saskatchewan Law Review* 47 (1983), 341–51.

Empson, William. 'Tom Jones'. *Kenyon Review* 20 (1958), 217–49.

Faller, Lincoln B. *Defoe and Crime: A New Kind of Writing*. Cambridge: Cambridge University Press, 1993.

　Turned to Account: The Forms and Functions of Criminal Biography in the Late Seventeenth and Early Eighteenth Centuries. Cambridge: Cambridge University Press, 1987.

Fanon, Frantz. *The Wretched of the Earth*. Trans. Constance Farrington. New York: Grove Weidenfeld, 1968.

Farquhar, George. *The Recruiting Officer*. Ed. John Ross. London: Ernest Benn, 1977.

Felman, Shoshana. *The Juridical Unconscious: Trials and Traumas in the Twentieth Century*. Cambridge: Harvard University Press, 2002.

Ferguson, Robert A. *Law and Letters in American Culture*. Cambridge: Harvard University Press, 1984.

　' "We Do Ordain and Establish": The Constitution as Literary Text'. *William and Mary Law Review* 29 (1987), 3–25.

　'On the Judicial Opinion as a Literary Genre'. *Yale Journal of Law and the Humanities* 2 (1990), 201–19.

　'Holmes and the Judicial Figure'. In Gordon (ed.), *Legacy of Oliver Wendell Holmes*, pp. 155–85.

　'Story and Transcription in the Trial of John Brown'. *Yale Journal of Law and Humanities* 6 (1994), 37–73.

　'Untold Stories in the Law'. In Brooks and Gewirtz (eds.), *Law's Stories*, pp. 84–98.

Fielding, Henry. *Tom Jones*. Ed. Sheridan Baker. New York: Norton, 1973.

　Joseph Andrews. Ed. R. F. Brissenden. Harmondsworth: Penguin, 1977.

An Enquiry into the Causes of the Late Increase of Robbers and Related Writings. Ed. Malvin R. Zirker. Oxford: Clarendon, 1988.

Finkelpearl, Philip J. *John Marston of the Middle Temple.* Cambridge: Harvard University Press, 1969.

Fish, Stanley. 'The Law Wishes to Have a Formal Existence'. In *The Fate of Law.* Ed. Austin Sarat and Thomas R. Kearns. Ann Arbor: University of Michigan Press, 1991, pp. 159–208.

Fitzpatrick, Peter and Eve Darian-Smith. 'Laws of the Postcolonial: An Insistent Introduction'. In *Laws of the Postcolonial.* Ed. E. Darien-Smith and P. Fitzpatrick. Ann Arbor: University of Michigan Press, 1999, pp. 1–15.

Flecker, James Elroy. *The Collected Poems of James Elroy Flecker.* Ed. J. C. Squire. London: Martin Secker, 1916.

Fleming, John G. *The Law of Torts.* 8th edn., Sydney: Law Book Co., 1992.

Fludernik, Monika. 'Carceral Topography: Spatiality, Temporality and Liminality in the Literary Prison'. *Textual Practice* 13 (1999), 43–77.

Forbes, Alexander M. 'Johnson, Blackstone and the Tradition of Natural Law'. *Mosaic* 27/4 (1994), 81–98.

Forché, Caroline. *Against Forgetting: Twentieth-Century Poetry of Witness.* New York: Norton, 1993.

Foucault, Michel. *Discipline and Punish: The Birth of the Prison.* Trans. Alan Sheridan. London: Penguin, 1977.

Fraser, Hilary, Stephanie Green and Judith Johnston. *Gender and the Victorian Periodical.* Cambridge: Cambridge University Press, 2003.

Freeman, Michael and Andrew D. E. Lewis (eds.). *Law and Literature.* Oxford: Oxford University Press, 1999.

Frost, Michael H. *Introduction to Classical Legal Rhetoric: A Lost Heritage.* Aldershot: Ashgate, 2005.

Frost, Robert. *In the Clearing.* London: Holt, Rinehart and Winston, 1962.
  The Poetry of Robert Frost. Ed. Edward Connery Lathem. New York: Holt, Rinehart and Winston, 1969.

Gaakeer, Jeanne. *Hope Springs Eternal: An Introduction to the Work of James Boyd White.* Amsterdam: Amsterdam University Press, 1998.

Gaines, Ernest J. *A Lesson before Dying.* New York: Knopf, 1993.

Gandhi, Leela. *Postcolonial Theory: An Introduction.* Sydney: Allen and Unwin, 1998.

Garber, Marjorie. 'Cinema Scopes'. In *Law in the Domains of Culture.* Ed. Austin Sarat and Thomas R. Kearns. Ann Arbor: University of Michigan Press, 1998, pp. 121–59.

Garrison v. *Louisiana* 379 US 64 (1964).

Gates, Henry Louis and Nellie Y. Mackay (eds.). *The Norton Anthology of African American Literature.* New York: Norton, 1997.

Gatrell, V. A. C. *The Hanging Tree: Execution and the English People 1770–1868.* Oxford: Oxford University Press, 1994.

Geary, Ray. ' "Born Pious, Literary and Legal": Lord Coleridge's Criticisms in Law and Literature'. In Freeman and Lewis (eds.), *Law and Literature*, pp. 463–80.

Gibbs, James. ' "Eshu Confuser of Men!": Questions Prompted by *Ibadan: The Penkelemes Years, a Memoir 1946–65*'. In *The Contact and the Culmination: Essays in Honour of Hena Maes-Jelinek*. Ed. Marc Delrez and Bénédicte Ledent. Liège: Liège Language and Literature, 1997, pp. 119–30.

Gibian, Peter. 'Opening and Closing the Conversation: Style and Stance from Holmes Senior to Holmes Junior'. In Gordon (ed.), *Legacy of Oliver Wendell Holmes*, pp. 186–215.

Gifford, Henry. *Poetry in a Divided World*. Cambridge: Cambridge University Press, 1985.

Gladfelder, Hal. *Criminality and Narrative in Eighteenth-Century England: Beyond the Law*. Baltimore: Johns Hopkins University Press, 2001.

'Obscenity, Censorship and the Eighteenth-Century Novel: The Case of John Cleland'. *Wordsworth Circle* 35 (2004), 123–7.

Goellnicht, Donald C. 'Tang Ao in America: Male Subject Positions in *China Men*'. In *Reading the Literatures of Asian America*. Ed. Shirley Geok-lin Lim and Amy Ling. Philadelphia: Temple University Press, 1992, pp. 191–212.

Goldsmith, Oliver. *The Vicar of Wakefield*. 1766; London: Oxford University Press, 1974.

Oliver Goldsmith: Selected Writings. Ed. John Lucas. Manchester: Carcanet, 1988.

Goodman, Nan. *Shifting the Blame: Literature, Law and the Theory of Accidents in Nineteenth-Century America*. Princeton: Princeton University Press, 1998.

Goodrich, Peter. *Reading the Law: A Critical Introduction to Legal Method and Techniques*. Oxford: Blackwell, 1986.

Languages of Law: From Logics of Memory to Nomadic Masks. London: Weidenfeld and Nicolson, 1990.

'Antirrhesis'. In Sarat and Kearns (eds.), *Rhetoric of Law*, pp. 57–102.

Oedipus Lex: Psychoanalysis, History, Law. Berkeley: University of California Press, 1995.

Goodrich, Peter and David Gray Carlson (eds.). *Law and the Postmodern Mind: Essays on Psychoanalysis and Jurisprudence*. Ann Arbor: University of Michigan Press, 1998.

Gordon, Robert W. (ed.). *The Legacy of Oliver Wendell Holmes, Jr*. Edinburgh: Edinburgh University Press, 1992.

Grafton, Anthony and Lisa Jardine. *From Humanism to the Humanities*. London: Duckworth, 1986.

Green, Henry. *Living*. London: J. M. Dent, 1929.

Greenhouse, Carol J. 'A Federal Life: *Brown* and the Nationalization of the Life Story'. In Sarat (ed.), *Race, Law and Culture*, pp. 170–89.

Grey, Thomas C. 'Holmes and Legal Pragmatism'. *Stanford Law Review* 41 (1989), 787–870.

The Wallace Stevens Case. Cambridge: Harvard University Press, 1991.

Grossberg, Michael. *A Judgment for Solomon: The D'Hauteville Case and Legal Experience in Antebellum America*. Cambridge: Cambridge University Press, 1996.

Grutter v. *Bollinger* 539 US 244 (2003).

Gunn, Giles and Stephen Greenblatt. *Redrawing the Boundaries: The Transformation of English and American Literary Studies*. New York: MLA, 1992.

Guy, John. 'Law, Equity and Conscience in Henrician Juristic Thought'. In *Reassessing the Henrician Age*. Ed. Alistair Fox and John Guy. Oxford: Basil Blackwell, 1986, pp. 179–98.

Thomas More. London: Edward Arnold, 2000.

Halsbury's Laws of Australia. Sydney: Butterworths, 1991.

Hamburger, Philip. 'The Development of the Law of Seditious Libel and the Control of the Press'. *Stanford Law Review* 37 (1985), 661–765.

Hamilton, Susan (ed.). *Criminals, Idiots, Women and Minors: Nineteenth-Century Writing by Women on Women*. Peterborough: Broadview Press, 1995.

Hanafin, Patrick, Adam Gearey and Joseph Brooker (eds.). *Law and Literature*. Oxford: Blackwell, 2004.

Hansberry v. *Lee* 311 US 32 (1940).

Hardy, Thomas. *Tess of the D'Urbervilles*. Ed. Tim Dolin. 1891; repr. London: Penguin, 1998.

Harlow, Barbara. *Barred: Women, Writing and Political Detention*. Hanover: Wesleyan University Press, 1992.

Harris, Edward M. 'Law and Oratory'. In *Persuasion: Greek Rhetoric in Action*. Ed. Ian Worthington. London: Routledge, 1994, pp. 130–50.

Harris, Margaret. 'Christina Stead and her Critics'. In *The Magic Phrase: Critical Essays on Christina Stead*. Ed. Margaret Harris. St Lucia: University of Queensland Press, 2000, pp. 1–22.

Hart, Kevin. *Samuel Johnson and the Culture of Property*. Cambridge: Cambridge University Press, 1999.

Hay, Douglas. 'Property, Authority and the Criminal Law'. In *Albion's Fatal Tree: Crime and Society in Eighteenth-Century England*. Ed. Hay et al. London: Allen Lane, 1975, pp. 17–63.

Hays, Mary. *The Victim of Prejudice*. Ed. Eleanor Ty. 1799; repr. Peterborough: Broadview, 1998.

Hazlitt, William. 'Illustrations of "The Times" Newspaper: On Modern Lawyers and Poets'. *Political Essays*, in *The Complete Works of William Hazlitt*. Ed. P. P. Howe. Vol. IX. London: J. M. Dent, 1932, pp. 137–45.

Heinzelman, Susan Sage. 'Guilty in Law, Implausible in Fiction: Jurisprudential and Literary Narratives in the Case of Mary Blandy, Parricide'. In *Representing Women: Law, Literature and Feminism*. Ed. Heinzelman and Zipporah Batshaw Wiseman. Baltimore: Duke University Press, 1994, pp. 309–36.

' "Going Somewhere": Maternal Infanticide and the Ethics of Judgment'. In *Literature and Legal Problem Solving: Law and Literature as Ethical Discourse*. Durham: Carolina Academic Press, 1998, pp. 73–98.

Helgerson, Richard. *Forms of Nationhood: The Elizabethan Writing of England*. Chicago: University of Chicago Press, 1992.

Henderson, Mae G. 'Toni Morrison's *Beloved*: Re-Membering the Body as Historical Text'. In *Comparative American Identities*. Ed. Hortense J. Spillers. New York: Routledge, 1991, pp. 62–86.

Heninger, S. K. *Sidney and Spenser: The Poet as Maker*. London: Pennsylvania State University Press, 1989.

Hibbitts, Bernard J. 'Making Sense of Metaphors. Visuality, Aurality and the Reconfiguration of American Legal Discourse'. *Cardozo Law Review* 16 (1994), 229–356.

Highet, Gilbert. *Juvenal the Satirist*. Oxford: Clarendon Press, 1954.

Hill, Patricia Liggins (ed.). *Call and Response: The Riverside Anthology of the African American Literary Tradition*. Boston: Houghton Mifflin, 1998.

Hine, Reginald L. *Confessions of an Un-Common Attorney*. London: Dent, 1945.

Hing, Bill Ong. *To Be an American: Cultural Pluralism and the Rhetoric of Assimilation*. New York: Oxford University Press, 1997.

Holland, Merlin. *Irish Peacock and Scarlet Marquis: The Real Trial of Oscar Wilde*. London: Fourth Estate, 2003.

Hollander, John. 'Legal Rhetoric'. In Brooks and Gewirtz (eds.), *Law's Stories*, pp. 176–86.

Holmes, O. W., Jr. *The Common Law*. Ed. Mark DeWolfe Howe. Boston: Little, Brown, 1963.

Holmes, Richard (ed.). *Defoe on Sheppard and Wild*. London: Harper Perennial, 2004.

Hong Kingston, Maxine. *China Men*. London: Picador, 1981.

hooks, bell. *Killing Rage*. New York: Henry Holt, 1995.

Hooper, David. *Reputations under Fire: Winners and Losers in the Libel Business*. London: Little, Brown and Co., 2000.

Horace. 'On the Art of Poetry'. In *Classical Literary Criticism*. Trans. T. S. Dorsch. Harmondsworth: Penguin, 1965.

Howard, John. *The State of the Prisons*. 1777; repr. London: J. M. Dent, 1929.

Huerta, Jorge. 'Introduction'. In Valdez, *Zoot Suit and Other Plays*, pp. 7–20.

Hughes, Langston. *Montage of a Dream Deferred*. New York: Henry Holt, 1951.

Hunter, Ian, David Saunders and Dugald Williamson. *On Pornography: Literature, Sexuality and Obscenity Law*. Basingstoke: Macmillan, 1993.

Hutchings, Peter J. *The Criminal Spectre in Law, Literature and Aesthetics: Incriminating Subjects*. London: Routledge, 2001.

Hutson, Lorna. *The Usurer's Daughter: Male Friendship and Fictions of Women in Sixteenth-Century England*. London: Routledge, 1994.

(ed.). *Feminism and Renaissance Studies*. Oxford: Oxford University Press, 1999.

Hynes v. *New York Central Railroad* 231 NY 229 (1921).

International Covenant on Civil and Political Rights (United Nations) 1977.

Jackson, Bernard S. *Law, Fact and Narrative Coherence*. Liverpool: Deborah Charles, 1988.

Jacobson, Karin. 'Plain Faces, Weird Cases: Domesticating the Law in Collins's *The Law and the Lady* and the Trial of Madeleine Smith'. In *Reality's Dark Light: The Sensational Wilkie Collins*. Ed. Maria K.

Bachman and Don Richard Cox. Knoxville: University of Tennessee Press, 2003, pp. 283–312.

James v. *Commonwealth* (1936) 55 CLR 1.

James, Henry. 'Mary Elizabeth Braddon'. In Henry James. *Literary Criticism*. Vol. I. New York: Library of America, 1984, pp. 741–6.

JanMohamed, Abdul R. *Manichean Aesthetics: The Politics of Literature in Colonial Africa*. Amherst: University of Massachusetts Press, 1983.

Jardine, Lisa. *Worldly Goods: A New History of the Renaissance*. London: Macmillan, 1996.

Jaszi, Peter. 'Toward a Theory of Copyright: The Metamorphoses of "Authorship"'. *Duke Law Journal* (1991), 455–502.

Jaszi, Peter and Martha Woodmansee. 'The Ethical Reaches of Authorship'. *South Atlantic Quarterly* 95 (1996), 947–77.

(eds.). *The Construction of Authorship: Textual Appropriation in Law and Literature*. Durham: Duke University Press, 1994.

Jesse, F. Tennyson. *A Pin to See the Peepshow*. 1934; repr. London: Virago, 1979.

Johnson v. *Virginia* 373 US 61 (1963).

Johnson, Samuel. *Samuel Johnson*. Ed. Donald Greene. Oxford: Oxford University Press, 1984.

Jones, B. M. *Henry Fielding: Novelist and Magistrate*. London: George Allen and Unwin, 1933.

Jones, Eldred Durosimi. *The Writings of Wole Soyinka*, 3rd edn. London: James Currey, 1989.

Jones, Gareth H. 'Pollock, Sir Frederick'. In *Biographical Dictionary of the Common Law*. Ed. A. W. B. Simpson. London: Butterworths, 1984, pp. 421–3.

Jones, Vivien (ed.). *Women and Literature in Britain 1700–1800*. Cambridge: Cambridge University Press, 2000.

Joyce, James. *Ulysses*. [Annotated Student's Edition] London: Penguin, 1992.

Julius, Antony. 'Dickens the Lawbreaker'. *Critical Quarterly* 40/3 (1998), 43–66.

Kafka, Franz. 'The Problem of Our Laws'. Trans. Willa and Edwin Muir. In *The Penguin Complete Short Stories of Franz Kafka*. London: Allen Lane, 1983, pp. 437–8.

The Trial. New York: Knopf/Everyman's Library, 1992.

Kahn, Paul W. *Law and Love: The Trials of King Lear*. New Haven: Yale University Press, 2000.

Kahn, Victoria and Lorna Hutson (eds.). *Rhetoric and Law in Early Modern England*. New Haven: Yale University Press, 2001.

Kaplan, Benjamin. 'Encounters with O. W. Holmes, Jr'. *Harvard Law Review* 96 (1983), 1828–52.

Kaplan, M. Lindsay. *The Culture of Slander in Early Modern England*. Cambridge: Cambridge University Press, 1997.

Kayman, Martin A. 'Lawful Writing: Common Law, Statute and the Properties of Literature'. *New Literary History* 27 (1996), 761–83.

Kayman, Martin A. 'Law-and-Literature: Questions of Jurisdiction'. *REAL: Yearbook of Research in English and American Literature* 18 (2002), 1–20.

Kegl, Rosemary. *The Rhetoric of Concealment: Figuring Gender and Class in Renaissance Literature*. Ithaca: Cornell University Press, 1994.

Kella, Elizabeth. *Beloved Communities: Solidarity and Difference in Fiction by Michael Ondaatje, Toni Morrison and Joy Kogawa*. Uppsala: Acta Universitatis Uppsaliensis, 2000.

Kelley, Donald R. *The Human Measure: Social Thought in the Western Legal Tradition*. Cambridge: Harvard University Press, 1990.

Kendrick, Walter. *The Secret Museum: Pornography in Modern Culture*. Berkeley: University of California Press, 1996.

Kennedy, Helena. *Eve Was Framed*. London: Vintage, 1993.

Kestner, Joseph A. *Protest and Reform: The British Social Narrative by Women, 1827–1867*. London: Methuen, 1985.

King, Peter. *Crime, Justice and Discretion 1740–1820*. Oxford: Oxford University Press, 2000.

Klinck, Dennis. 'This Other Eden: Lord Denning's Pastoral Vision'. *Oxford Journal of Legal Studies* 14 (1994), 25–56.

Kluger, Richard. *Simple Justice*. New York: Knopf, 1975.

Knapp, Andrew, and William Baldwin. *The Newgate Calendar*. London, 1824–28. http://www.exclassics.com/newgate/ngintro.htm.

Kornstein, Daniel J. *Kill All the Lawyers? Shakespeare's Legal Appeal*. Princeton: Princeton University Press, 1994.

Korobkin, Laura Hanft. *Criminal Conversations: Sentimentality and Nineteenth-Century Legal Stories of Adultery*. New York: Columbia University Press, 1998.

Krueger, Christine L. 'Victorian Narrative Jurisprudence'. In Freeman and Lewis (eds.), *Law and Literature*, pp. 437–61.

Laurence Godfrey v. *Demon Internet Limited* [1999] 4 All ER 342.

Lauter, Paul (ed.). *The Heath Anthology of American Literature*, 4th edn. Boston: Houghton Mifflin, 2001.

Lavallée v. *The Queen* [1990] S.C.R. 852.

Leckie, Barbara. 'The Force of Law and Literature: Critiques of Ideology in Derrida and Bourdieu'. *Mosaic* 28 (1995), 109–36.

Culture and Adultery. Philadelphia: University of Pennsylvania Press, 1999.

Lee, A. Robert. 'Ethnic Renaissance: Rudolfo Anaya, Louise Erdrich and Maxine Hong Kingston'. In *The New American Writing*. Ed. Graham Clarke. London: Vision Press, 1990, pp. 139–64.

Lee, Harper. *To Kill a Mockingbird*. 1960; London: Arrow Books, 1997.

Lemmings, David. *Professors of the Law: Barristers and English Legal Culture in the Eighteenth Century*. Oxford: Oxford University Press, 2000.

Leval, Pierre N. 'The No-Money, No-Fault Libel Suit: Keeping *Sullivan* in its Proper Place'. In *Reforming Libel Law*. Ed. John Soloski and Randall P. Bezanson. New York: Guildford Press, 1992, pp. 211–28.

Levy, Leonard W. *Treason against God: A History of the Offence of Blasphemy*. New York: Schocken Books, 1981.

Lewis, C. S. *English Literature in the Sixteenth Century, Excluding Drama*. Oxford History of English Literature Vol. III. Oxford: Clarendon Press, 1954.

Lewis, Geoffrey. *Lord Atkin*. London: Butterworths, 1983.

Lieberman, Jethro K. *A Practical Companion to the Constitution*. Berkeley: University of California Press, 1999.

Lobban, Michael. *The Common Law and English Jurisprudence, 1760–1850*. Oxford: Clarendon, 1991.

Loewenstein, Joseph. *Ben Jonson and Possessive Authorship*. Cambridge: Cambridge University Press, 2002.

  The Author's Due: Printing and the Prehistory of Copyright. Chicago: University of Chicago Press, 2002.

Loving v. *Virginia* 388 US 1 (1967).

Macaulay, Thomas Babington. 'Government of India'. In *Life and Works of Lord Macaulay*. Vol. VIII. London: Longmans, Green, 1904, pp. 111–42.

MacCabe, Colin. *James Joyce and the Revolution of the Word*. Basingstoke: Macmillan, 1978.

MacFarlane, Alan D. J. 'Some Contributions of Maine to History and Anthropology'. In *The Victorian Achievement of Sir Henry Maine*. Ed. Alan Diamond. Cambridge: Cambridge University Press, 1991, pp. 111–42.

McGill, Meredith L. 'The Matter of the Text: Commerce, Print Culture, and the Authority of the State in American Copyright Law'. *American Literary History* 9 (1997), 24–59.

McLynn, Frank. *Crime and Punishment in Eighteenth-Century England*. London: Routledge, 1989.

McNair, Arnold. *Dr Johnson and the Law*. Cambridge: Cambridge University Press, 1948.

McPherson, James Alan. 'An Act of Prostitution'. In *Trial and Error: An Oxford Anthology of Legal Stories*. Ed. Fred R. Shapiro and Jane Garry. New York: Oxford University Press, 1998, pp. 388–401.

  A Region Not Home. New York: Simon and Schuster, 2000.

MacPherson v. *Buick* 217 NY 382 (1916).

Magris, Claudio. 'Who Is on the Other Side? Considerations about Frontiers'. In *Frontiers*. Ed. Christopher MacLehose. London: HarperCollins, 1994, pp. 8–25.

Maine, Henry Sumner. *Ancient Law: Its Connection with the Early History of Society and its Relation to Modern Ideas*. 1861; London: John Murray, 1906.

Malamud, Bernard. *The Complete Stories*. Ed. Robert Giroux. New York: Farrer, Straus and Giroux, 1997.

Manji, Ambreena. ' "Like a Mask Dancing": Law and Colonialism in Chinua Achebe's *Arrow of God*'. *Journal of Law and Society* 27 (2000), 626–42.

  'Of the Laws of Kenya and Burials and All That'. *Law and Literature* 14 (2002), 436–88.

  'Law, Literature and the Politics of Culture in Kenya'. *Law, Social Justice and Global Development Journal* 2 (2003), http://elj.warwick.ac.uk/global/2003-2/manji.html.

Marke, Julius J. (ed.). *The Holmes Reader*. Dobbs Ferry: Oceana Publications, 1964.

Marlowe, Christopher. *Doctor Faustus: The A-Text*. Ed. David Ormerod and Christopher Wortham. Nedlands: University Of Western Australia Press, 1989.

Marsh, Joss. *Word Crimes: Blasphemy, Culture and Literature in Nineteenth-Century England*. Chicago: University of Chicago Press, 1998.

Marvell, Andrew. *The Complete English Poems*. Ed. Elizabeth Story Donno. London: Allen Lane, 1974.

Matsuda, Mari. *Words That Wound*. Boulder: Westview Press, 1993.

Meehan, Michael. 'The Good, the Bad and the Ugly: Judicial Literacy and the Australian Cultural Cringe'. *Adelaide Law Review* 12 (1990), 431–48.

'Neo-Classical Criticism'. In *Encyclopedia of Literature and Criticism*. Ed. John Peck and Martin Coyle. London: Routledge, 1991, pp. 666–81.

'Authorship and Imagination in Blackstone's *Commentaries on the Laws of England*'. *Eighteenth-Century Life* 16 (1992), 111–26.

'An Anatomy of Australian Law'. In Turner and Williams (eds.), *The Happy Couple*, pp. 376–89.

Melville, Herman. *Billy Budd, Sailor*. Ed. Harold Beaver. Harmondsworth: Penguin, 1967.

Meredith, George. *Diana of the Crossways*. London: Constable, 1922.

Mesquita, Filomena. 'Travesties of Justice: Portia in the Courtroom'. In *Shakespeare and the Law*. Ed. Daniela Carpi. Ravenna: Longo Editore, 2003, pp. 117–25.

Michie, Elsie B. *Outside the Pale: Cultural Exclusion, Gender Difference and the Victorian Woman Writer*. Ithaca: Cornell University Press, 1993.

Miller, Christopher L. *Blank Darkness: Africanist Writing in French*. Chicago: University of Chicago Press, 1985.

Millett, Kate. *Sexual Politics*. London: Hart-Davis, 1971.

Minda, Gary. 'Cool Jazz But Not So Hot Literary Text in *Lawyerland*: James Boyd White's Improvisations of Law as Literature'. *Cardozo Studies in Law and Literature* 13 (2001), 157–91.

Mitchell, Sally. *Frances Power Cobbe: Victorian Feminist, Journalist, Reformer*. Charlottesville: University of Virginia Press, 2004.

Moddelmog, William E. *Reconstituting Authority: American Fiction in the Province of the Law 1880–1920*. Iowa City: University of Iowa Press, 2000.

Montagu, Lady Mary Wortley. *Essays and Poems and Simplicity, a Comedy*. Ed. Robert Halsband and Isobel Grundy. Oxford: Clarendon Press, 1993.

Moore, Sally Falk. 'Law in Africa: Colonial and Contemporary'. In *Africana: The Encyclopedia of the African and African American Experience*. Ed. Kwame Anthony Appiah and Henry Louis Gates. New York: Basic Civitas Books, 1999, 1137–39.

Morang and Co. v. *LeSueur* (1911), 45 S.C.R. 95.

Morrison, Toni. *Beloved*. 1987; New York: Vintage, 1997.

'The Opening Sentences of *Beloved*'. In *Critical Essays on Beloved*. Ed. Barbara H. Solomon. New York: G. K. Hall, 1998, 91–2.

Mortimer, John. *A Voyage Round My Father*. London: Methuen, 1971.

Clinging to the Wreckage: A Part of Life. London: Weidenfeld and Nicolson, 1982.

Rumpole and the Golden Thread. Harmondsworth: Penguin, 1983.

The Second Rumpole Omnibus. London: Viking, 1987.

Muir, Kenneth. *The Sources of Shakespeare's Plays*. London: Methuen, 1977.

Naipaul, V. S. *The Mimic Men*. London: Andre Deutsch, 1967.

Nead, Lynda. *Victorian Babylon: People, Streets and Images in Nineteenth-Century London*. New Haven: Yale University Press, 2000.

Nedelsky, Jennifer. 'Law, Boundaries and the Bounded Self'. In *Law and the Order of Culture*. Ed. Robert Post. Berkeley: University of California Press, 1991, pp. 162–89.

Nelson, Theodor Holm. *Literary Machines 93.1*. Sausalito: Mindful Press, 1992.

New Orleans City Park Improvement Association v. *Dittiege* 358 US 54 (1958).

New York Times v. *Sullivan* 376 US 254 (1964).

New York v. *Ferber* 458 US 747 (1982).

Noonan, John T. *Persons and Masks of the Law*. New York: Farrar, Straus and Giroux, 1977.

Norton, Caroline. *English Laws for Women*. London, 1854.

A Letter to the Queen on Lord Chancellor Cranworth's Marriage and Divorce Bill. London: Longman, 1855.

Novick, Sheldon M. *Honorable Justice: The Life of Oliver Wendell Holmes*. Boston: Little, Brown, 1989.

Oakeshott, Michael. *The Voice of Poetry in the Conversation of Mankind*. Cambridge: Bowes and Bowes, 1953.

Old Bailey Session Papers http://www.oldbaileyonline.org/.

Oliphant, Margaret. 'The Laws Concerning Women'. *Blackwood's Edinburgh Magazine 79* (1856). In Bell and Offen (eds.), *Women, the Family and Freedom*. Vol. I, pp. 305–10.

O'Neill, Philip. *Wilkie Collins: Women, Property and Propriety*. Basingstoke: Macmillan, 1988.

Onslow, Barbara. *Women of the Press in Nineteenth-Century Britain*. Houndmills: Macmillan, 2000.

Oputa, Mr Justice C. A. *Conduct at the Bar and the Unwritten Laws of the Legal Profession*. 1976; Holmes Beach, Florida: Wm. W. Gaunt and Sons, 1982.

Ordinary of Newgate's Accounts http://www.oldbaileyonline.org/.

Orgel, Stephen. 'The Renaissance Artist as Plagiarist'. *Journal of English Literary History* 48 (1981), 476–95.

Oxford English Dictionary, 2nd edn. Oxford: Oxford University Press, 1989.

Palmer v. *Thompson* 403 US 217 (1971).

Palsgraf v. *Long Island Railroad* 248 NY 339 (1928).

Parker, Patricia A. *Literary Fat Ladies: Rhetoric, Gender, Property*. London: Methuen, 1987.

Shakespeare from the Margins: Language, Culture, Context. Chicago: University of Chicago Press, 1996.

Patmore, Coventry. 'The Angel in the House'. In *Poems*. London: G. Bell and Sons, 1915, pp. 3–145.

Patterson, Annabel. *Criticism and Interpretation: The Conditions of Writing and Reading in Early Modern England*. Madison: University of Wisconsin Press, 1984.

Patterson, Lyman Ray. *Copyright in Historical Perspective*. Nashville: Vanderbilt University Press, 1968.

Pease, Allison. *Modernism, Mass Culture and the Aesthetics of Obscenity*. Cambridge: Cambridge University Press, 2000.

Perelman, Chaim and L. Obrechts-Tyteca. *The New Rhetoric*. Notre Dame: University of Notre Dame Press, 1969.

Perry, Curtis. '"If Proclamation will not Serve": The Late Manuscript Poetry of James I and the Culture of Libel'. In *Royal Subjects: Essays on the Writing of James VI and I*. Ed. Daniel Fischlin and Mark Fortier. Detroit: Wayne State University Press, 2002, pp. 205–32.

Petch, Simon. 'Borderline Judgments: Law or Literature?' *Australian Journal of Law and Society* 7 (1991), 3–15.

 'Walks of Life: Legal'. In *A Companion to Victorian Literature and Culture*. Ed. Herbert F. Tucker. Oxford: Blackwell, 1999, pp. 155–69.

Peters, Julie Stone. 'Law, Literature and the Vanishing Real: On the Future of an Interdisciplinary Illusion'. *Publications of the Modern Language Association of America* 120 (2005), 442–53.

'A Petition for Women's Rights' (1856). In *Sources of English Legal History 1750–1950*. Ed. A. H. Manchester. London: Butterworths, 1984, p. 401.

Phillips, O. Hood. *Shakespeare and the Lawyers*. London: Methuen, 1972.

Pierce, Peter. *The Country of Lost Children*. Melbourne: Cambridge University Press, 1999.

Piozzi, Hester Lynch. *Anecdotes of the Late Samuel Johnson LL.D.* London, 1786.

Plato. *The Laws*. Trans. Trevor J. Saunders. Harmondsworth: Penguin, 1970.

Plaut v. *Spendthrift Farm* 514 US 211, 131 L. Ed. 2d 328 (1995).

Plessy v. *Ferguson* 163 US 537 (1896).

Poirier, Richard. *Robert Frost: The Work of Knowing*. New York: Oxford University Press, 1977.

Pollock, Sir Frederick. *The Genius of the Common Law*. New York: Columbia University Press, 1912.

 For My Grandson: Remembrances of an Ancient Victorian. London: John Murray, 1933.

Poovey, Mary. *Uneven Developments: The Ideological Work of Gender in Mid-Victorian England*. London: Virago, 1988.

Pope, Alexander. *The Poems of Alexander Pope*. Ed. John Butt. London: Methuen, 1965.

Posner, Richard A. *Law and Literature: A Misunderstood Relation*. Cambridge: Harvard University Press, 1988.

 Law and Literature, 2nd edn. Cambridge: Harvard University Press, 1998.

Post, Robert. 'Introduction: After *Bakke*'. In Post and Rogin (eds.), *Race and Representation*, pp. 13–28.

Post, Robert and Michael Rogin (eds.). *Race and Representation: Affirmative Action*. New York: Zone Books, 1998.

Potter, Rachel. 'Waiting at the Entrance to the Law: Modernism, Gender and Democracy'. *Textual Practice* 14 (2000), 253–63.

Prest, W. R. *The Inns of Court under Elizabeth I and the Early Stuarts 1590–1640*. London: Longman, 1972.

Pritchard, William H. *Frost: A Literary Life Reconsidered*, 2nd edn. Amherst: University of Massachusetts Press, 1993.

Public Broadcasting Service website: http://www.pbs.org/wgbh/amex/zoot/.

Pue, W. Wesley. 'Editorial', *Law. Social Justice and Global Development* 1 (2003), http://elj.warwick.ac.uk/global/issue/2003-1/editorial.html.

R. v. Chief Metropolitan Stipendiary Magistrate ex p Choudhury [1991] 1 QB 429.

R. v. Butler 89 Dominion Law Reports 449 (1992).

R. v. Duffy [1949] All ER 932.

Raffield, Paul. *Images and Cultures of Law in Early Modern England: Justice and Political Power, 1558–1660*. Cambridge: Cambridge University Press, 2004.

Raitt, Fiona and Suzanne Zeedyk. *The Implicit Relation of Psychology and Law*. London: Routledge, 2000.

Regents of the University of California v. *Bakke* 438 US 265 (1978).

Reichman, Ravit. '"New Forms for our New Sensations": Woolf and the Lesson of Torts'. *Novel: A Forum on Fiction* 36 (2003), 398–423.

Rembar, Charles. *The End of Obscenity: The Trials of Lady Chatterley, Tropic of Cancer and Fanny Hill*. London: Andre Deutsch, 1968.

Resnik, Judith. 'On the Margin: Humanities and Law'. *Yale Journal of Law and the Humanities* 10 (1998), 413–20.

Resnik, Judith and Carolyn Heilbrun. 'Convergences: Law, Literature and Feminism'. *Yale Law Journal* 99 (1990), 1913–53.

Reznikoff, Charles. 'From *Testimony*'. In *The Columbia Anthology of American Poetry*. Ed. Jay Parini. New York: Columbia University Press, 1995, pp. 434–5.

Richardson, Mark. *The Ordeal of Robert Frost*. Urbana: University of Illinois Press, 1997.

Richardson, Samuel. *Clarissa*. Ed. Angus Ross. Harmondsworth: Viking, 1985.

Ricoeur, Paul. *Time and Narrative*. Trans. Kathleen McLaughlin and David Pellauer. 3 vols. Chicago: University of Chicago Press, 1985.

Robbins, Sara (ed.). *Law: A Treasury of Art and Literature*. New York: Hugh Lauter Levin Associates, 1990.

Robertson, Geoffrey. *The Justice Game*. London: Vintage, 1999.

Robinson, Martha S. 'The Law of the State in Kafka's *The Trial*'. *American Legal Studies Association Forum* 6 (1982), 127–44.

Robinson, Mary. 'The Inaugural Speech'. In *Ireland's Women: Writings Past and Present*. Ed. Katie Donovan, A. Norman Jeffares and Brendan Kennelly. London: Kyle Cathie, 1994, pp. 253–56.

Rogers, Pat. *Samuel Johnson*. Oxford: Oxford University Press, 1993.

Rolph, C. H. (ed.). *The Trial of Lady Chatterley*. Harmondsworth: Penguin Books, 1961.

Rose, Mark. *Authors and Owners: The Invention of Copyright*. Cambridge: Harvard University Press, 1993.

Rosenberg, David. *The Hidden Holmes: His Theory of Torts in History*. Cambridge: Harvard University Press, 1995.

Rosenthal, Laura J. *Playwrights and Plagiarists in Early Modern England*. Cambridge: Cambridge University Press, 1996.

Roth v. *U.S.* 354 US 476 (1957).

Rubin, Dana Y. *Identity, Crime and Legal Responsibility in Eighteenth-Century England*. Houndmills: Palgrave, 2004.

Said, Edward W. *Orientalism*. London: Chatto and Windus, 1978.

Sarat, Austin. 'The Continuing Contest about Race in American Law and Culture: On Reading the Meaning of *Brown*'. In Sarat (ed.), *Race, Law and Culture*, pp. 3–19.

(ed.). *Race, Law and Culture: Reflections on Brown* v. *Board of Education*. New York: Oxford University Press, 1997.

Sarat, Austin and Thomas R. Kearns. 'Editorial Introduction'. *The Rhetoric of Law*. Ann Arbor: University of Michigan Press, 1994, pp. 1–27.

Sarat, Austin, Marianne Constable, Donald Engel et al. (eds.). *Crossing Boundaries: Traditions and Transformations in Law and Society Research*. Evanston: Northwestern University Press/American Bar Foundation, 1998.

Saunders, David. *Authorship and Copyright*. London: Routledge, 1992.

Scheppele, Kim Lane. 'Foreword: Telling Stories'. *Michigan Law Review* 87 (1989), 2073–98.

Schmidgen, Wolfram. *Eighteenth-Century Fiction and the Law of Property*. Cambridge: Cambridge University Press, 2002.

Schoeck, Richard J. 'Lawyers and Rhetoric in Sixteenth-Century England'. In *Renaissance Eloquence*. Ed. James J. Murphy. Berkeley: University of California Press, 1983, pp. 274–91.

Schorske, Carl E. *Fin-de-Siècle Vienna*. New York: Vintage, 1981.

Schramm, Jan-Melissa. *Testimony and Advocacy in Victorian Law, Literature and Theology*. Cambridge: Cambridge University Press, 2000.

Seidel, Michael. 'Satire, Lampoon, Libel, Slander'. In *The Cambridge Companion to English Literature, 1650–1740*. Ed. Steven N. Zwicker. Cambridge: Cambridge University Press, 1998, pp. 33–57.

Selden, John. *Table-Talk of John Selden*. Ed. Frederick Pollock. London: Quaritch, 1927.

Shakespeare, William. *Othello*. Ed. Norman Sanders. Cambridge: Cambridge University Press, 1984.

Hamlet. Ed. Philip Edwards. Cambridge: Cambridge University Press, 1985.

The Comedy of Errors. Ed. T. S. Dorsch. Cambridge: Cambridge University Press, 1988.

The Merchant of Venice. Ed. M. M. Mahood. Cambridge: Cambridge University Press, 1987.

The Sonnets. Ed. G. Blakemore Evans. Cambridge: Cambridge University Press, 1996.

Shapiro, Barbara. 'The Concept "Fact": Legal Origins and Cultural Diffusion'. *Albion* 26 (1994), 227–52.

Sharpe, J. A. *Crime in Early Modern England, 1550–1750*. London: Longman, 1984.

Sheen, Erica and Lorna Hutson (eds.). *Literature, Politics and Law in Renaissance England*. Basingstoke: Palgrave, 2005.

Shelley, Percy Bysshe. *Shelley's Poetry and Prose*. Ed. Donald H. Reiman and Neil Fraistat. New York: Norton, 2002.

Sidney, Philip. *An Apology for Poetry*. Ed. Geoffrey Shepherd. London: Nelson, 1965.

Simpson, A. W. Brian. *Cannibalism and the Common Law*. Harmondsworth: Penguin Books, 1986.

Sinclair, Upton. *The Jungle*. 1906; rpt. Cambridge: Robert Bentley, 1946.

Smith, Barbara Leigh. *A Brief Summary, in Plain Language, of the Most Important Laws Concerning Women: together with a Few Observations Thereon*. In *Barbara Leigh Smith Bodichon and the Langham Place Group*. Ed. Candida Ann Lacey. London: Routledge and Kegan Paul, 1986, pp. 23–35.

Snyder, Ilana. *Hypertext: The Electronic Labyrinth*. Carlton South: Melbourne University Press, 1990.

Soifer, Aviam. *Law and the Company We Keep*. Cambridge: Harvard University Press, 1995.

Sokol, B. J. and Mary Sokol. *Shakespeare, Law and Marriage*. Cambridge: Cambridge University Press, 2003.

Soyinka, Wole. *The Interpreters*. London: Heinemann, 1965.

The Road. London: Oxford University Press, 1965.

The Man Died: Prison Notes 1967–69. London: Rex Collings, 1972.

Isara: A Voyage Round Essay. Ibadan: Fountain Publications, 1989.

Ibadan: The Penkelemes Years. London: Minerva, 1995.

The Open Sore of a Continent: A Personal Narrative of the Nigerian Crisis. Oxford: Oxford University Press, 1996.

Spoo, Robert. 'Injuries, Remedies, Moral Rights and the Public Domain'. *James Joyce Quarterly* 37 (2000), 233–66.

Stead, Christina. *The Salzburg Tales*. 1934; repr. Melbourne: Sun Books, 1966.

Steiner, George. 'Introduction'. In Kafka, *The Trial*.

Stevenson, Jane and Peter Davidson (eds.). *Early Modern Women Poets: An Anthology*. Oxford: Oxford University Press, 2001.

Still, Judith and Michael Worton, 'Introduction'. In *Intertextuality: Theories and Practices*. Ed. Michael Worton and Judith Still. Manchester: Manchester University Press, 1990.

Stone, Lawrence. *The Crisis of the Aristocracy*, abridged edn. London: Oxford University Press, 1967.

Road to Divorce: England 1530–1987. Oxford: Oxford University Press, 1990.

Stowe v. Thomas 23 F.Cas. 201 (1853).

Sugarman, David. 'Legal Theory, the Common Law Mind and the Making of the Text-Book Tradition'. In *Legal Theory and the Common Law*. Ed. William Twining. Oxford: Blackwell, 1986, pp. 26–61.

Suggs, Jon-Christian. *Whispered Consolations: Law and Narrative in African American Life*. Ann Arbor: University of Michigan Press, 2000.

Sunstein, Cass. 'Casuistry'. In Post and Rogin (eds.), *Race and Representation*, pp. 309–29.

'Supreme Court Poetry Seminar'. *Mediator* XI/XII (June 1995), 4.

Sutherland, John. *Offensive Literature: Decensorship in Britain 1960–1982*. London: Junction Books, 1982.

Swan, Beth. *Fictions of Law: An Investigation of the Law in Eighteenth-Century English Fiction*. Frankfurt: Peter Lang, 1997.

Swift, Jonathan. *The Complete Poems*. Ed. Pat Rogers. Harmondsworth: Penguin, 1983.

Tavernier-Courbin, Jacqueline. '*The Call of the Wild* and *The Jungle*: Jack London's and Upton Sinclair's Animal and Human Jungles'. In *The Cambridge Companion to American Realism and Naturalism*. Ed. Donald Pizer. Cambridge: Cambridge University Press, 1995, pp. 236–62.

Tennyson, Alfred. *The Poems of Tennyson*. Ed. Christopher Ricks. 3 vols. London: Longman, 1987.

Terdiman, Richard. 'Translator's Introduction'. *Hastings Law Review* 38 (1987), 801–13.

Thackeray, W. M. *The Newcomes*. Ed. George Saintsbury. Oxford: Oxford University Press, n.d.

Thomas, Brook. *Cross-Examinations of Law and Literature*. Cambridge: Cambridge University Press, 1987.

'Reflections on the Law and Literature Revival'. *Critical Inquiry* 17 (1991), 510–39.

'Michael Grossberg's Telling Tale: The Social Drama of an Antebellum Custody Case'. *Law and Social Inquiry* 23 (1998), 431–58.

'*China Men, United States* v. *Wong Kim Ark* and the Question of Citizenship'. *American Quarterly* 50 (1998), 689–717.

Thompson, E. P. *Whigs and Hunters: The Origin of the Black Act*. London: Allen Lane, 1975.

Thompson, Julie Klein. *Interdisciplinarity: History, Theory, Practice*. Detroit: Wayne State University Press, 1990.

Thorne, Samuel E. *Essays in English Legal History*. London: Hambledon Press, 1985.

Threadgold, Terry. 'Performativity, Regulative Fictions, Huge Stabilities: Framing Battered Woman's Syndrome'. *Law/Text/Culture* 3 (1997), 210–31.

Tromp, Marlene. *The Private Rod: Marital Violence, Sensation and the Law in Victorian Fiction*. Charlottesville: University of Virginia Press, 2000.

Tiefenbrun, Susan. 'Semiotics and Martin Luther King's "Letter from Birmingham Jail"'. *Cardozo Studies in Law and Literature* 4 (1992), 255–87.

Tucker, E. F. J. *Intruder into Eden: Representations of the Common Lawyer in English Literature 1350–1750*. Columbia: Camden House, 1984.

Turner, J. Neville and Pamela Williams (eds.). *The Happy Couple: Law and Literature*. Annandale: Federation Press, 1994.

Valdez, Luis. *Zoot Suit and Other Plays*. Houston: Arte Publico Press, 1992.

Valente, Joseph. *James Joyce and the Problem of Justice*. New York: Cambridge University Press, 1995.

Vanden Bossche, Chris R. 'The Value of Literature: Representations of Print Culture in the Copyright Debate of 1837–1842'. *Victorian Studies* 38 (1994), 41–68.

Vanderham, Paul. 'Lifting the Ban on *Ulysses*: The Well-Intentioned Lies of the Wolsey Decision'. *Mosaic* 27/4 (1994), 179–97.

Vickers, Brian. *In Defence of Rhetoric*. Oxford: Clarendon Press, 1988.

Walker, Alice. 'Advancing Luna – and Ida B. Wells'. In *You Can't Keep a Good Woman Down*. New York: Harcourt Brace Jovanovich, 1981, pp. 85–104.

In Search of our Mothers' Gardens. New York: Harcourt Brace Jovanovich, 1983.

Walker, Richard. 'California's Collision of Race and Class'. In Post and Rogin (eds.), *Race and Representation*, pp. 281–308.

Wallace, Edgar. *Sanders of the River*. 1911; repr. London: Greenhill Books, 1986.

Wallace, Jon. 'James Alan McPherson'. *The Oxford Companion to African American Writing*. Ed. William L. Andrews, Frances Smith Foster and Trudier Harris. New York: Oxford University Press, 1997, p. 493.

Ward, Ian. *Law and Literature: Possibilities and Perspectives*. Cambridge: Cambridge University Press, 1995.

Shakespeare and the Legal Imagination. London: Butterworths, 1999.

Warner, Marina. *Monuments and Maidens: The Allegory of the Female Form*. London: Vintage, 1986.

Watson v. City of Memphis 373 US 526 (1963).

Watson, Jay. *Forensic Fictions: The Lawyer Figure in Faulkner*. Athens: University of Georgia Press, 1993.

Waugh, Patricia A. *Revolutions of the Word*. London: Arnold, 1997.

Weatherby, W. J. *Salman Rushdie: Sentenced to Death*. New York: Carroll and Graf, 1990.

Weber, Max. *Max Weber on Law in Economy and Society*. Ed. Max Rheinstein. Cambridge: Harvard University Press, 1954.

Webster, Richard. *A Brief History of Blasphemy: Liberalism, Censorship and The Satanic Verses*. Southwold: The Orwell Press, 1990.

Weis, René. *Criminal Justice: The Story of Edith Thompson*. London: Penguin, 2001.

Weisberg, Richard H. *The Failure of the Word: The Protagonist as Lawyer in Modern Fiction*. New Haven: Yale University Press, 1984.

Poethics and Other Strategies in Law and Literature. New York: Columbia University Press, 1992.

Vichy Law and the Holocaust in France. Amsterdam: Harwood Academic, 1996.

'Literature's Twenty-Year Crossing into the Domain of Law: Continuing Trespass or Right by Adverse Possession?' In Freeman and Lewis (eds.), *Law and Literature*, pp. 47–61.

Weisberg, Richard H. and Jean-Pierre Barricelli. 'Literature and the Law'. In *Interrelations of Literature*. Ed. Joseph Gibaldi and Jean-Pierre Barricelli. New York: MLA, 1982, 150–75.

Welsh, Alexander. *Strong Representations: Narrative and Circumstantial Evidence in England*. Baltimore: Johns Hopkins University Press, 1992.

Wertenbaker, Timberlake. *Our Country's Good*. London: Methuen, 1995.

West, Robin. *Caring for Justice*. New York: New York University Press, 1997.

White, Hayden. *The Content of the Form: Narrative Discourse and Historical Representation*. Baltimore: Johns Hopkins University Press, 1987.

White, James Boyd. *The Legal Imagination: Studies in the Nature of Legal Thought and Expression*. Boston: Little, Brown and Co., 1973.

Heracles' Bow: Essays on the Rhetoric and Poetics of the Law. Madison: University of Wisconsin Press, 1985.

Justice as Translation: An Essay on Legal and Cultural Criticism. Chicago: University of Chicago Press, 1990.

Acts of Hope: Creating Authority in Literature, Law and Politics. Chicago: University of Chicago Press, 1995.

White, R. S. *Natural Law in English Renaissance Literature*. Cambridge: Cambridge University Press, 1996.

Widner, Jennifer A. *Building the Rule of Law: Francis A. Nyalali and the Road to Judicial Independence in Africa*. New York: W. W. Norton, 2001.

Williams, Glanville. *The Proof of Guilt: A Study of the English Criminal Trial*. London: Stevens and Sons, 1955.

Williams, Melanie. *Empty Justice: One Hundred Years of Law, Literature and Philosophy*. London: Cavendish, 2002.

Wilson, Luke. *Theatres of Intention: Drama and the Law in Early Modern England*. Stanford: Stanford University Press, 2000.

Wilson, Thomas. *The Arte of Rhetorique*. Ed. Thomas J. Derrick. 1553; repr. New York: Garland, 1982.

Wittgenstein, Ludwig. *Philosophical Investigations I*. Trans. G. E. M. Anscombe. Oxford: Blackwell, 1974.

Woodmansee, Martha. 'The Cultural Work of Copyright: Legislating Authorship in Britain 1837–1842'. In *Law in the Domains of Culture*. Ed. Austin Sarat and Thomas R. Kearns. Ann Arbor: University of Michigan Press, 1998, pp. 65–96.

Woolmington v. *DPP* [1935] A.C. 481.

Wordsworth, William. *The Prose Works of William Wordsworth*. Ed. W. J. B. Owen and J. W. Smyser. Oxford: Clarendon Press, 1974.

Wynne, Edward. *Eunomus, or Dialogues on the Law and Constitution of England*. London, 1768.

Yeats, W. B. *Essays*. London: Macmillan, 1924.

Young, Alison. 'The Body of Criminality: The Politics of Ordinariness'. In *Law and the Human Sciences: The Fifth Round Table on Law and Semiotics*. New York: Peter Lang, 1992, pp. 545–57.

Young, Edward. *Conjectures on Original Composition*. 1759; repr. Leeds: Scolar Press, 1966.

Young, Filson. *The Trial of Bywaters and Thompson*. Edinburgh: William Hodge, 1936.

Yu, Ning. 'A Strategy against Marginalization: The "High" and "Low" Cultures in Kingston's *China Men*'. *College Literature* 23/3 (1996), 73–87.

Zenger, John Peter. *A Brief Narrative of the Case and Tryal of John Peter Zenger*. In Robbins (ed.), *Law*, pp. 152–63.

Ziolkowski, Theodore. *The Mirror of Justice: Literary Reflections of Legal Crises*. Princeton: Princeton University Press, 1997.

Zomchick, John P. *Family and the Law in Eighteenth-Century Fiction*. Cambridge: Cambridge University Press, 1993.

Index